Praise for *Mohawk Rebel*

"In this book, Claire Raymond dives deep into the history, context, and cultural traditions of the Haudenausonee, whose territory in New York State was stolen, forcing them into exile in Canada. This is an important addition to the understanding of the lens-based work by Mohawk artist Shelley Niro. Niro has created over forty years of practice, a body of work that challenges persistent images of First Nations people while bringing to light Indigenous-centered histories. Niro's photographs and films also denaturalize Western notions of sexuality and gender, shuttling between family and pop culture to create narratives and images that embody Indigenous women's subjectivity. Niro's work is humorous, deeply researched, and intuitively futurist, denying the limiting framework of Indigenous art.

Raymond 'weaves between history and contemporaneity, following Niro's lead,' taking her readers to the land now called New York, the homeland of the Mohawk. Raymond shows how this history so widely unknown in America is a formative and formidable aspect of Niro's oeuvre. You will learn the Haudenasonee as masters of diplomacy, you will find figures like Sky Woman and the Peacemaker reframed in Niro's practice. This book realizes Niro's feminist practice in telling the stories of a contemporary matriarchy still being imagined.

For Niro, New York lies in the way a land exists in memory and imagination born of love and intergenerational storytelling. Readers will never look at contemporary photography, Indigenous art, or the history of America the same way again."

— Wanda Nanibush, curator, writer,
and image-maker from Beausoliel First Nation

"*Mohawk Rebel* is a new and valuable approach to the art of Shelley Niro. Raymond's careful unpacking of Niro's works' meaning involves discussions of the history of the Haudenosaunee settlements in New York State. That we are shown this reality through Niro's eyes, as she reflects on the original homes of her ancestors, is especially moving. Raymond engages effectively with Niro, capturing the intelligence and thoughtfulness of the artist, as well as her sense of humor."

— Dr. Madeline Lennon, Professor Emerita,
Department of Visual Arts, Western University, Canada

Mohawk Rebel

Mohawk Rebel

Shelley Niro's Art and New York State

CLAIRE RAYMOND

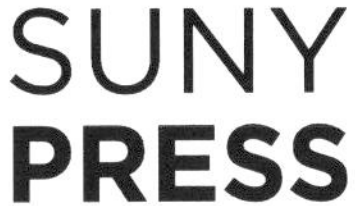

Cover Credit: Frames 1 and 2 from "Abnormally Aboriginal," 2014, color inkjet prints, 54 in. × 34 in. Courtesy of the artist. © Shelley Niro, 2023

Published by State University of New York Press, Albany

For information, contact State University of New York Press, Albany, NY
www.sunypress.edu

Library of Congress Cataloging-in-Publication Data

Name: Raymond, Claire, 1967– author.
Title: Mohawk rebel : Shelley Niro's art and New York State / Claire Raymond.
Description: Albany : Excelsior Editions, an imprint of State University of
  New York Press, [2025]
Identifiers: LCCN 2024019591 | ISBN 9798855800906 (hardcover : alk. paper) |
  ISBN 9798855800913 (ebook) | ISBN 9798855800890 (pbk. : alk. paper)
Subjects: LCSH: Niro, Shelley, 1954—Criticism and interpretation. | New York
  (State)—In art.
Classification: LCC NX512.N57 R39 2025 | DDC 791.43/6257471—dc23/eng/20240919
LC record available at https://lccn.loc.gov/2024019591

Her hand is encased in a gauntlet of steel,
And her thunder but sleeps.

—"Guard of the Eastern Gate,"
Tekahionwake/E. Pauline Johnson[1]

The maternal homeland still waits for the return of her people.

—Shelley Niro, *La Pieta* Artist's Statement

Contents

Illustrations

Acknowledgments

I am immensely grateful to Shelley Niro, who has been a steady support throughout the writing of this book. Admiring her art is a double pleasure because, in addition to being a brilliant and original artist, she is also a good person. I am thankful to Michael Doxtater, the artist's brother, who found time to talk with me and answer so many questions. Thanks are due to Richard Carlin, my editor at SUNY Press, who is always a pleasure to work with. Thank you to Paulina Cossette for dotting the i's and crossing the t's of this book.

I acknowledge that the land where I lived while writing this book, the state of Maine, is Wabanaki land. The Wabanaki people—the Penobscot, the Passamaquoddy, the Maliseet, and the Mi'kmaq—have stewarded the land of Maine for generations, and they have never ceded this land.

My greatest debt is to my spouse, Mark Raymond, for his patience and fortitude far beyond the ordinary.

While this book emerged from many conversations with Shelley Niro, she is not responsible for opinions expressed in the book other than quotes specifically attributed to her. All mistakes are mine.

Introduction

The Past Is Burning

As Mohawk multimedia artist Shelley Niro (Six Nations of the Grand River Reserve, Bay of Quinte Kanien'kehá:ka Mohawk Nation, Turtle Clan) arrived in New York City in early June 2023 to celebrate her career retrospective at the National Museum of the American Indian, forest fires were raging across Canada. The plumes of smoke from these 426 fires rose so high and grew so massive that they blew on wind currents and enveloped New York City, causing an air pollution crisis.[2] As Niro prepared to lead a workshop at the National Museum of the American Indian in New York, the smoke drifted from the Canadian forests deep into New York State, crossing the boundaries that define Mohawk colonial history.

Niro's multimedia art has long acted as a key interlocutor of the meaning of settler-colonial nation-state boundaries. Her work has long performed mourning for the Mohawks' ancestral territory, as most of her people were pushed out of what we now call New York State by colonialist wars, violence, and genocidal political acts during the creation of the United States of America. In June 2023, when New York welcomed her back, as it were, by hosting the retrospective of her life's work, the event was clouded—literally—by smoke that was itself a result of settler-colonialist policies of land management and, above all, settler-colonialist economic policies and ethics. It is this ethos regarding how human beings should care for land that has produced the climate crisis we now face in the twenty-first century: extreme weather patterns that spike, among other disasters, unprecedentedly enormous forest fires. As Niro arrived to celebrate her retrospective, the smolder pushed into the city and lingered. The past was burning, connecting Canada and New York, and articulating in a visceral way how inescapable are the effects of coloniality and how imaginary are the geographic boundaries by which settler nation-states define themselves.

The size and intensity of the June 2023 Canadian wildfires, partially attributable to climate change—to increasingly hot conditions in an ecosystem that once was cool—also resulted from the settler-colonialist urge to control natural systems without taking the long view of understanding them. Indigenous practices of forestry traditionally included periodic controlled burns that served to prevent massive out-of-control blazes. Had Indigenous peoples retained control over this ecosystem, these catastrophic fires would likely not have arisen. As educator and journalist Dina Gilio-Whitaker (Colville Confederated Tribes) makes clear, settler-colonialist, capitalist ways of managing land are very much at odds with Indigenous ethics and traditional Indigenous practices.[3] In contrast to traditional Indigenous land stewardship practices, global warming is an ongoing, extensive event caused by colonialist industrial petro-capitalism.[4]

Niro's retrospective, *Shelley Niro: 500 Year Itch*, hosted in New York City, emphasizes that the past does not vanish but remains around us, shaping the present and the future. As people gathered to celebrate Niro's magnificent work, settler coloniality manifested in every breath of smoke-soaked air. The wildfire-driven air-quality crisis converged with the message that Niro's art has long conveyed: settler coloniality is not a thing of the past. It is our present and, if we do not change, it will be our future. The forest fires that, at the time of Niro's retrospective, were sending plumes of particulate-matter pollution from Canada into New York served as material reminders of this threat.

Ontario, Canada, where the artist and most of the Mohawk people now live, is intimately and historically connected to New York State because this area is the traditional homeland of the Haudenosaunee, meaning "the people of the longhouse" or "people building a house."[5] Niro's art is connected to New York State because she emerges from the Mohawk tradition in which art is not separated from but is intrinsically part of the meaning of place; in the deep history of the Mohawk, their place is the area we now call New York State. As Mohawk artist Sue Ellen Herne notes, "Deeply rooted in our experience of place, our arts shape our 'house' as Haudenosaunee people."[6] Even as her work emerges from Haudenosaunee traditions, in creating her oeuvre, Niro reflects: "I was more interested in work that would not necessarily be seen as Native art, although it was from a Native artist's perspective."[7] This turn in her work is crucial, as it is in her distinctive imbrications with settler-culture tropes that Niro leverages her guerilla tactics of subtle political art that resist and subvert settler colonialism. This visual space she creates might be glossed as a new "middle ground" but one that reflects wryly on the scandalous imbalances of the very contestation.[8] The relative absence of Mohawk people from their homeland is the effect of genocidal campaigns in the eighteenth century and of dishonest settler-speculators in the nineteenth century. Most Mohawk people now live in Canada, although the Akwesasne live across the nation-state border in New York State. As Haudenosaunee historian Richard Hill (Tuscarora) notes, this division is an effect and an evidentiary mark of the continued violence of coloniality: "Even though we say there's no border between our people, there's a border."[9]

Mohawk Rebel: Shelley Niro's Art and New York State honors Niro's achievements in the media of fine art photography, digital media, and film by focusing on those aspects of her work that contend with New York State, the homeland and ancestral territory of the Mohawk.[10] This book explores Niro's artistic returns (and in her oeuvre there are many examples of these) to New York State. Niro has lived in Canada for over sixty years, but she was born in New York. The meaning of New York in Niro's work, however, goes far beyond its being the place of her birth. The artist plumbs the history of the Haudenosaunee—her people—in her works that evoke returns to the area. As art historian Madeline Lennon has eloquently argued, Shelley Niro's art is an art of memory and return.[11] In this return is Niro's refusal to cover up the real history of colonization.[12]

While Niro is often, and accurately, discussed as an artist whose work is humorous and accessible to those who are not Mohawk, in this book I consider the ways her work is somberly and complexly an oeuvre of mourning for the Indigenous genocide that shaped the North American continent.[13] As historian Ned Blackhawk (Te-Moak tribe of the Western Shoshone) notes, "Identifying American history as a site of genocide complicates a fundamental premise of the American story."[14] The same is true also for New York State, the founding of which is inextricably linked to genocidal campaigns perpetrated against the Mohawk.

In Niro's art, one finds a performance of mourning that is subtle, quiet, and woven through the surface content of the work. In this artistic processing of collective grief, her art performs a refusal to accept the terms of settler coloniality's nation-states and their boundaries. In this refusal is the work's vibrancy and claim. Her art performs political resistance by remembering the real history of settler colonialism and the Haudenosaunee. The layers of Niro's work that reach back to New York State, the Mohawk

Valley, the Mohawk River, and the battles and massacres that pushed her people out of the region are not, at their core, humorous—though her work is often characterized by a deadpan wit and a dry, clear-sighted understanding of the real. Rather, Niro's art reaches deep into the pits of our shared knowing of the griefs of settler coloniality.[15] The area we now call New York State is the home of her ancestors and, therefore, the homeland of the artist; Niro notes that when she returns to New York State she feels in her body a shift that is the sense of homecoming.[16]

Much of Niro's work signifies Mohawk history, starkly juxtaposing the tragedies her ancestors endured and survived with the glossy national mythologies of American and Canadian beliefs in patriots and settlers as heroes. Her photography, films, and videos reach a sublime space of refusing to forget. Encoded in her art is the necessary act of return. In early June 2023, celebrating her career retrospective and hosting friends and scholars as part of that event, even as the forest fires raged and sent their plumes of smoke into the city, Niro stayed in this land that is, after all, her own: New York.[17] My book emphasizes the courage of her return and the brilliantly insightful art she creates from these painful visits home. I underscore how, over four decades, her work has revisited, again and again, the Mohawk homeland from which her people have largely been displaced. As I discuss Shelley Niro's artworks, for which a return to New York is central, I return frequently to some key works—*Kissed by Lightning* (2009); the series *Battlefields of My Ancestors* (2015); *1779* (2017); *For Fearless and Other Indians* (1998/2022); *Niagara* (2015); and *It Starts with a Whisper* (1993)—seeking to understand these depictions through different angles of interpretation.[18] Hence, this book is organized primarily by themes. I highlight aspects of Mohawk and Haudenosaunee history together with Niro's artworks that comment on these tragic periods and instate Indigenous resistance in the face of settler aggression.

The forest fires that crossed settler nation-state boundaries, entering New York State from Canada (where the Mohawk were pushed by genocidal settler-colonialist policies that defined the United States at its inception) proved that the boundaries drawn by nation-states are not meaningful in the face of ecological crises. Niro's answer to this reality is to create art that acts as a powerful rejection of settler-colonialist ways of seeing. Inherently limited in my ability to express the full perspective of decoloniality, given that I am a white person mainly descended from settlers in the southeastern United States, I nevertheless strive to illuminate for readers the urgency of the need for reapportioning stolen lands.[19] As a writer and scholar, I honor the brilliance of Niro's art. My goal is to trace the multifarious and intricately allusive layers of this work that, as I will argue, is political art. Her art is perhaps most powerfully political when it references aspects of Mohawk culture that may not be in the purview of white audiences. However, that does not mean that a goal of my book is to lay bare private codes of cultural meaning. Seneca scholar Michelle Raheja notes that while Niro "privileges Haudenosaunee systems, [she] does so by dispensing with fraught notions of authenticity," for Niro does not offer "access to hidden 'authentic,' and mystical epistemologies."[20] As Niro comments, some ways of framing her work can feel "like they're saying, *Go back into your box!*"[21] Contemporary decolonial scholarship needs to be careful not to reinscribe new forms of coloniality. My approach to writing this book is one in which I am aware that Shelley Niro's art emerges from the context of the artist being Shelley Niro, a unique human being who is a citizen of the Six Nations, a Mohawk woman, and a member of the Turtle Clan. This approach coheres with conversations with the artist about her understanding of her work.

Mohawk Time

The Western settler-colonialist tradition of representing Mohawk people is at once masculinist and eliding. Even now it continues to place the Mohawk back in time, locking them in the past as if the Haudenosaunee were not, in addition to being the original people of New York State, also contemporary people, alive and vital in the twenty-first century. As I discuss in chapter 1, a Google search (conducted in June 2023) of the words "Mohawk People" uncannily yields images from the eighteenth and nineteenth centuries at the top of the list of search results. One such image from this era is Benjamin West's painting *Colonel Guy Johnson and Karonghyontye (Captain David Hill)*, created in 1776 (Figure I.1). It shows Karonghyontye as a figure in the shadows who, in his graceful disappearance, seems to usher Colonel Johnson into the light and the foreground. The painting performs the myth that the Mohawk alliance with the British was about the Mohawk supporting the British as such, rather than a strategic, hopeful, and desperate negotiation on the part of the Mohawk for survival in the face of a genocidal invasion by settler colonialists. It also emphasizes male leadership, whereas the Mohawk traditionally privileged female political power.

Figure I.1. Benjamin West, *Colonel Guy Johnson and Karonghyontye (Captain David Hill)*, 1776. Overall: 202 × 138 cm (79½ × 54⁵/₁₆ in.). Framed: 222.6 × 160 × 9.5 cm (87⅝ × 63 × 3¾ in.) Oil on canvas. *Source:* Andrew W. Mellon Collection, National Gallery of Art. Public domain.

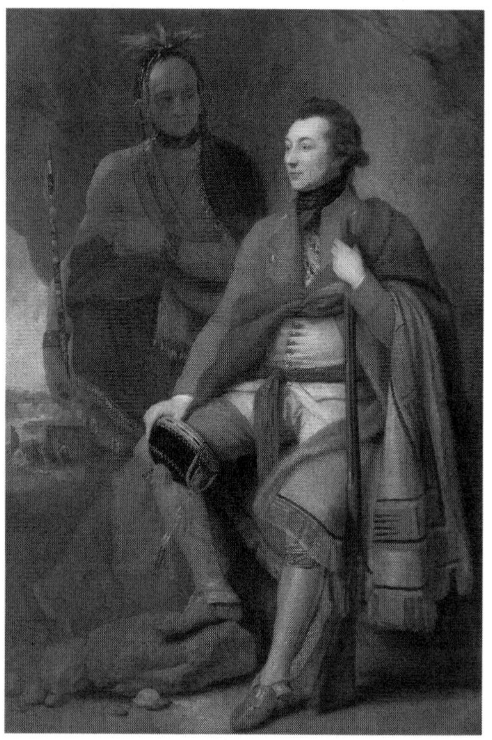

In Benjamin West's painting, the two men are presented disturbingly as doubles, with their clothing similarly structured; yet Karonghyontye is positioned as if he were a vanishing father handing his kingdom to his son, as if it were the pleasure of the Mohawk to give up their land to the invading settlers and then to disappear. Guy Johnson was the nephew of William Johnson, common-law husband of Molly Brant (Mohawk leader Joseph Brant's sister). Although the Johnson family had identified themselves as allies of the Mohawk, they were ultimately concerned only with taking land for themselves.[22] This slant of the inevitability of settler colonialists taking Indigenous land is put forward by West's painting as a given. "The land of the Mohawk *will* become English land" is the message conveyed synecdochally by the logic of his double-figured painting. Niro's work, by contrast, questions and, figurally, undoes this representational inevitability of lost land and of the vanishing Haudenosaunee. Just as West's painting is anchored in New York—where the Mohawk were, among the Five Nations (later Six Nations), the keepers of the Eastern Door—when Niro returns to New York to create art, she is returning as a keeper of this territory. The land stolen, during the formation of the nation, by the nascent United States of America and the early government of the State of New York remains contested land, uneasy in its putatively settled status (see chapter 3).[23] The history of settler-colonialist displacement of the Mohawk is ugly and morally repugnant, as will become clear throughout this book.

Consider Niro's photograph of the Mohawk Valley, *Infinite View* (figure I.2), the second frame in her photographic series *La Pieta* (2007). Framed by protective images of wampum, the picture was taken from above so that it opens a vista down into Mohawk Valley. As the title suggests, the view seems to go on forever, with the distant mountains softly merging into sky. The water and the green valley appear idyllic and untouched by industrialization. The image, placed in *La Pieta*, is a kind of ground zero for mourning the land from which the Mohawk were displaced. It is a

Figure I.2. Shelley Niro, *Infinite View*, *La Pieta*, 2007. 101.6 × 152.4 cm. Giclée Print. *Source:* Courtesy of the artist.

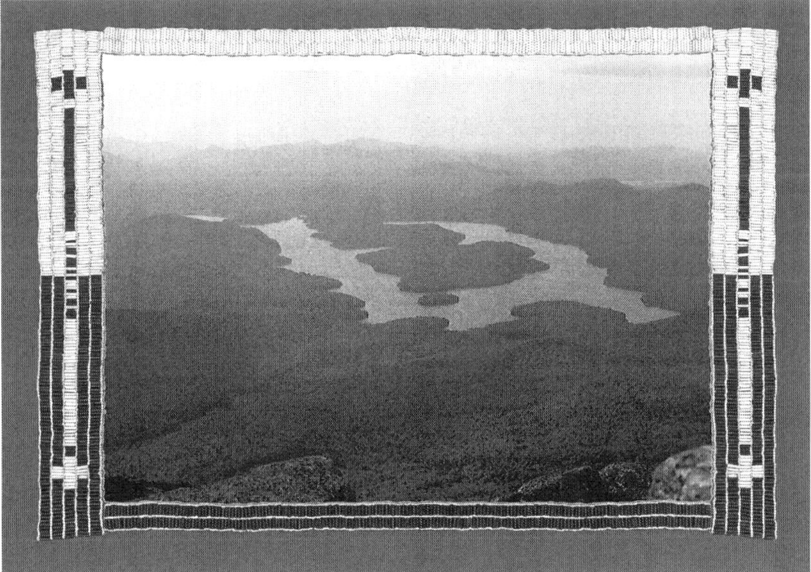

forceful and serene picture that, through its coloring and shading, has the emotional pull of a person who is experiencing homelessness looking through a brilliantly lit window into their former home. The sense of comfort that the image conveys is strong; and yet, because it is placed in *La Pieta*, a series mourning war, Niro's message is very clear: the Haudenosaunee are no longer in New York because of settler-colonialist military violence. The balance of peace and grace that Niro creates in *La Pieta* is counterpoised by the series' clear-sighted revelation of the ongoing harms of settler-colonialist nation-state encroachment. Niro emphasizes that *La Pieta* is a series about war; she states, "I am referring to war and how we have used the bodies of young men like fallen trees."[24] The settler-colonialist military actions that pushed the Mohawk from their homeland resonate in the artwork's mournful critique of colonialist wars. Art historian and curator Wanda Nanibush (Beausoleil First Nation, Ojibwe) writes, "I have always been affected by the way Niro understands the traumatic and anger-filled aspects of continued colonization and [the] dispossession of Indigenous peoples."[25]

Despite the settler-colonialist invasion, for centuries the Haudenosaunee held their ground in what is now called New York State.[26] As nineteenth-century historian Henry Rowe Schoolcraft notes, they "sustained themselves for more than three centuries and a half against the intruding . . . races of Europe."[27] The negotiations and military actions the Mohawk engaged in, from the sixteenth through the eighteenth centuries, to stay on their ancestral land are extraordinary and, as Schoolcraft writes, "gave them a name and a reputation." But the 1779 Sullivan-Clinton scorched-earth campaign (also aptly called the Sullivan-Clinton genocide) forced the Mohawk to leave their homeland and revealed the pressure of settler-colonialist genocidal ideation in relation to the Mohawk. Settler colonialism is the strategy of *erase and replace*—erase the Indigenous people and replace them with settlers—and the pressure, from the beginning of the "settling" of the land that became New York State was to push out the Haudenosaunee to make room for whites.[28] And yet, as historian Laurence Hauptman notes, the Haudenosaunee survived in this generally genocidal context because "they were masters of diplomacy."[29] Hauptman further states that the Haudenosaunee's traditional spiritual practices, including Peacemaker's influence, the Great Law of Peace, and the Condolence Ceremony, gave the original people of New York great strength: "A key to the community is [their traditional] religion; religion keeps the Haudenosaunee together."[30] It is crucial to note here the Great

Law of Peace is the centerpiece of Haudenosaunee survival in challenging circumstances.

Countering the Mohawks' reputation for fierce military strength and strategic negotiation, many of the earliest settler colonialists described the gentleness and kindness of the Mohawk. Writing in 1634, early settler Harmen Meyndertsz van den Bogaert explained that, when he stayed in a Mohawk "castle" (the term he used to describe the Haudenosaunee Long House), "the chief gave us many goods and fed us well, for everything in his house was at our disposal. He told me simply that I was his brother and good friend."[31] At another stop, van den Bogaert recalled: "Six men came from the [Mohawk] council and they presented us with a beaver coat. They gave it to me saying, 'It is for your journey, because you are so tired.'"[32] Of the Mohawk territory itself, Johannes Megapolensis, writing in 1644, recounted the abundance of agricultural riches, "chestnuts, plums, hazelnuts, large walnuts," and "bilberries and strawberries."[33] Megapolensis also writes of the complexity and power of Mohawk society and language, indicating that "the [Mohawks] have laid all the other Indians near us under contribution. . . . This nation has a very difficult language and it cost me great pains to learn it." Describing the Mohawks' skill in war, Megapolensis nonetheless notes that "they spare all the children and all the women."[34] In other words, while settler colonialism, with its genocidal ideation and enactment, did *not* spare Indigenous children and women in warfare, the Mohawk typically *did*, behaving ethically despite the significant pressure brought by settler colonialists, whose arrival decimated Haudenosaunee populations. As historian Daniel K. Richter describes, "Indian populations were reduced by . . . a factor of 90 to 95 percent." Richter draws on the writing of colonialist Adriaen van der Donck (Dutch, 1650s), who stated: "They [the Haudenosaunee] were ten times more numerous before the arrival of the Europeans."[35]

In citing the words of early European settlers, I am already employing biased sources. These European settlers were, at times, sympathetic to the Mohawk, but in the final analysis, they were there to take everything from the Haudenosaunee—including their land, their religion's spiritual traditions, and ultimately their lives. In 1926, Seneca scholar Arthur C. Parker described "The Hollocaust of the Americas," referencing the Sullivan-Clinton campaign and other colonialist acts of violence against the Haudenosaunee, making him arguably the first scholar of genocide studies.[36] In this book on Shelley Niro's art of return, I share the perspective that this land we now call New York is still properly Haudenosaunee land, stolen from the people. Niro's art positions itself as speaking for her people. What does it mean for a woman artist to speak for her people? In using this phrase *speaking for her people* I do not mean that Niro believes she sums up or overrides any other voices. Rather, I express that her motivation as an artist is to articulate the history, sociality, and present-day needs of Mohawk people. Her power as an artist inheres in this deeply collective sense of representational responsibility.

Mohawk matrilineal clans bind together Mohawk culture, as Haudenosaunee curator Deborah Doxtator contends, historically: "Without people in clans to use and connect with the land, the nation would cease to exist. . . . The land, its nature and the kinds of relationships that the people had with it influenced the social organization."[37] The ties between female-headed matrilineal clans as the core organizational structure of Mohawk culture and the land are firm bonds.[38] Niro, as a member of the Turtle Clan, inherits a responsibility to the land. Her work of returning to the Mohawk Valley and to other places in New York State bears out this responsibility as the artist carries it. This role of the artist, as Niro fulfills it, differs from masculinist and racist Western tropes of the artist as an isolated genius who owes nothing to anyone but his own talent. Instead, Niro's practice of art bears responsibility to the collective history and contemporary life of her people and their land. Seeing and conveying these histories through an Indigenous feminist lens, Niro revises the structure of settler colonialism by insisting on the perspective of a Mohawk woman whose ancestral claim to land and place is secure in herself (though unrecognized by settler-colonialist nation-states). As Maile Arvin (Kanaka Maoli), Eve Tuck (Unangax̂), and Angie Morrill (Klamath) argue, "Centering settler colonialism within gender and women's studies and ethnic studies instead exposes the still-existing structure of settler colonization and its powerful effects on Indigenous peoples and others."[39] Feminist resistance in Shelley Niro's work, by contrast, centers perspective within Indigenous feminism: a woman's gaze, Niro's gaze.

A woman is at the origin of Mohawk history and culture. Sky Woman, frequently signified by Niro's art, leaves the Sky World when, pregnant, she falls to Earth where she gives birth to a daughter who in turn bears two sons: Sky Grasper and his difficult twin, Tawiskaron.[40] It is Sky Grasper (Tharonhiawagon) who teaches the Mohawk to grow corn.[41] Of the Sky Woman histories, Shelley Niro notes, "I prefer to frame stories and legends as they have been passed on from generation to generation. I believe these stories would slightly change [in retelling across generations]. I am not committed to one version."[42] Niro clarifies that, in retellings of the story of Sky Woman, we can strengthen ourselves and deepen our wisdom; we can "use the story to our advantage," she notes.[43] In her short video *Sky Woman with Us* (discussed later in this chapter), for example, Niro demonstrates the power of such retellings.

Seneca scholar and historian John Mohawk writes of Sky Woman's story:

> It is a story which begins in the Sky World when the chief of that world convenes a feast and . . . in fulfillment of a vision of renewal the chief casts her through the firmament and into a void where she lands on a turtle. Earth grows on the turtle's back and she gives birth to a daughter who in turn gives birth to twins. The twins create life on the earth. One creates human beings and a set of rules for the people in a story which gives form to the Iroquois ceremonials of thanksgiving . . . [that] Society was structured in a way which protected women and children from physical abuse and especially from sexual abuse.[44]

Mohawk educator Kahente Horn-Miller tells us of Sky Woman:

> The mother of the Iroquois nations is a figure named Sky Woman who brought sacred medicines—tobacco and strawberries—to the earth . . . Sky Woman's . . . daughter, gave the Iroquois fruits and vegetables and birthed the twins Teharonhia:wakon and Sawiskera. These foundational principles of the Iroquois women's tradition are a theory translated in practice to the governance of the Iroquois people under the direction of the mothers. . . . Sky World is a representation of the ideal life in theory, but when Sky Woman came to earth, reality had different outcomes because everything was subject to corruption. It was out of that corruption that Sky Woman learned and . . . taught humanity to continually strive to create Sky World on earth.[45]

Like Niro, historian Michael Doxtater (Thohahoken), who is also Shelley Niro's brother, emphasizes that there are *variants* of Sky Woman's history. Notes Doxtater:

> (1) Skywoman slipped and fell down the hole in the sky caused when Sky Chief dug a hole too deeply, where they were going to plant under the Celestial Tree; (2) The Creator of All Things saw our barbarity and placed Skywoman through the hole dug by Sky Chief to bring gifts and give us happiness and redeem us; (3) Sky Chief dug a hole, and seeing human barbarity, Skywoman was overcome with compassion and jumped through the hole grabbing the strawberries and tobacco medicines they were planting.

Doxtater continues, "The Elders said these three stories show how people can feel about their day: (1) this was all an accident when she fell, (2) Skywoman had no choice and this was all someone else's idea, or (3) we are loved by the Mother of All the Mothers that give our lives purpose."[46] These three interpretations of origin display realism, pragmatism, and optimism. But all variants understand a woman at the center of origins. Through agricultural prowess held by women, Mohawk power and stability emerged. It is through a woman, Sky Woman, that the people connect with their land. It is the traditional role of women to be the keepers of the crops and fields surrounding the village.

Shelley Niro's film *Sky Woman with Us* (2002) enigmatically opens with long, tender shots of Sky Woman in the Sky World tending to her feverish love (played by Chris White). It is night and stars are plentiful.[47] The couple are surrounded by gleaming, well-laid fires and are dressed in rich, warm clothes. In seeking water for him to drink, Sky Woman falls through a hole in the sky around the Celestial Tree and drops down onto contemporary twenty-first-century Earth. Specifically, she falls into the Six Nations Veterans Memorial Park, a space used for the commemoration of Six Nations' veterans of colonialism's proxy wars. The shift from Sky World, which is evoked in warm nighttime colors of deep black and cheering fires, contrasts with the contemporary world of colonized Canada, which is jarring and harsh. Splendid fires are replaced by tinny Christmas lights and automobile headlights and taillights. After her fall, Sky Woman's face transforms from tenderness and care to disorientation and fear. On Earth, Sky Woman, who is pregnant and dressed in a sleeveless gold gown, is shown to be freezing in the snow-laden park. She appears like a woman experiencing homelessness. Mohawk composer ElizaBeth Hill's stunningly affective and rhythmic music that accompanies Sky Woman's fall (in Niro's video) makes us fear that the fate of Sky Woman might be the same as that of too many Indigenous women: unhoused, violated, murdered.[48] But in a move characteristic of the deep hope of resurgence with which Niro imbues her art, after her fall, Sky Woman's beautiful beloved suddenly appears in Six Nations Veterans Memorial Park. Now he is dressed in contemporary clothing suited for Canada's sub-zero winters. It is deep night. He takes a traditionally patterned blanket and wraps Sky Woman safely in it and in his arms. As they walk together from the park, Niro's film juxtaposes the two different nighttime images—of Sky Woman in the Sky World and of Sky Woman *with us*, that is, in the world below—so that the temporal frames are merged and we see the sacredness of Sky Woman below as above.[49]

In this short film, we view an illumination of Niro's previously noted comment, "I prefer to frame stories and legends as they have been passed on from generation to generation. I believe these stories would slightly change [in retelling across generations]. I am not committed to one version."[50] At the film's close, as credits roll, we see Sky Woman walking into a green meadow that could represent the lush Mohawk Valley. Sky Woman, in Niro's 2002 filmic retelling of the story, becomes a pregnant unhoused woman on Earth. And, on Earth, she is sheltered and cared for and becomes whole again. This is the work of the traditional story's retelling in Niro's film: to show that we need to care for each other, care for those experiencing homelessness, care for those who are lost.[51] It becomes a story of human ethics.

Michelle Raheja suggests that Niro's short film *Tree* "features a postapocalyptic world in which Sky Woman appears on Earth again to either heal the wounded environment or enact its final destruction."[52] Niro's fidelity to invoking Sky Woman as a figure who interprets, heals, and also threatens (in the sense of being a warrior of decolonization) is thoroughgoing in the artist's oeuvre. While I do not suggest that Niro herself acts in the role of Sky Woman in her art, it is notable that—like Sky Woman, who is often depicted in Niro's art as a liminal figure, at once with people and beyond them—Niro often returns to the homeland that is now called New York State. In creating art about this place, she cares for this land, even while her people have been pushed off it. It is her art that performs care for the land.

Art as an act of care moves far from masculinist, racist, Western capitalist theories of art.[53] If we locate Niro's expression of art as care in her personal biography, it is important to recall that the Turtle Clan, her clan, are traditionally those who care for the land; as the oldest of the

Mohawk clans, the Turtle Clan's leader, Tekarihoken, was the first to accept the Peacemaker's message of condolence and peace.[54] Niro's care—in her artwork—for the land now called New York State can be understood, then, as an extension of her role as a member of the Turtle Clan. Her work, at times explicitly (and nearly always implicitly) acknowledges and brings forward the Peacemaker's message of condolence and peace. Niro's work eschews Christian typology, instead elevating traditional Mohawk connections to the land and to each other. The efforts of settler colonialists to convert the Mohawk to Christianity were long-standing and, to a significant extent, did alter the culture and religion of the people.[55] But Niro moves beyond this violent imposition of Christianity, leaving behind a history in which missionaries often brought disease and death to the Mohawk. By invoking Mohawk notions of peace and condolence, Niro contests the colonizers' religion by asserting the beauty and power of New York's original spiritual practices, the traditions of the Haudenosaunee.[56]

Historian and critic Rosalyn Deutsche reminds us that "we live in a time of emboldened cruelty and perpetual war," and it is worth noting that this era was ushered in, centuries ago, by the rise of settler colonialism in North America (and in Australia and New Zealand).[57] Deutsche draws on the term "not-forgetting," pulling from the Hague Tribunal, to analyze and discuss artworks that speak to the importance of cultural memory. Indigenous North American artists, however, are not salient in Deutsche's otherwise impressive book, *Not-Forgetting: Contemporary Art and the Interrogation of Mastery*; yet, it is important to point out that Niro's art also is an "act of critical remembrance," as it resists the censoring of memory at the heart of the settler-colonialist nation-state regime, which has created perpetual war.[58]

Concerning linguistic traces of those settler regimes, in this book I use the term "Indigenous North American" as referring collectively to people whose ancestors have been in North America for many thousands of years. About nomenclature, Niro states: "Just say *Indian!* It's what's on my birth certificate," and she explains that this word makes as much sense as any other colonialist name[59]—which is to say that none of them make sense; all these terms reflect coloniality's reach. Writing as a white scholar, there is no comfortable term for me to use, and I understand that Indigenous North American is not a familiar phrase. But with it I am seeking to reflect the collective political action and power of Indigenous peoples, as expressed in the United Nations Declaration of the Rights of Indigenous People.[60] This problematic of naming co-occurs with the crime of land theft. As Niro's self-portrait triptych *Abnormally Aboriginal,* discussed in chapter 1 of this book, makes clear, all terms that reflect political and social structures of coloniality are problematic because the history and present-day reality of settler colonialism is an ongoing injustice.

Niro's artistic returns to New York State are returns that contest settler-colonialist history, returns that ask us to see, clearly and without the scrim of settler-colonialist nation-state ideology, what has been lost in the genocidal violence of the "settling" of the region. Her work also asks us to see what is still there. The land is still there. And the Mohawk persist. Shelley Niro creates art, and she notes that her hope for her people, and for all Indigenous North Americans, stems from the resurgence of Indigenous artists and artworks in the twenty-first century.[61] It is in her returns to her homeland, her persistence in thriving, in making art and beauty from the terrible reality of the North American genocide, that Niro's rebellion takes place, quietly and beautifully, artwork by artwork. Her art does not perform according to settler-colonialist expectations for Indigenous women's art. Instead, she draws on tradition in ways that are meaningful to her privately, and to her people culturally, as she also draws on contemporary idioms with all the freedom one would expect of a great artist.

As critic Laura E. Smith argues, "In the rush to locate truthful and positive images of Native Americans, critics and viewers sometimes lock Indigenous peoples into new frames."[62] Niro's art does not feed settler-colonialist viewers a stable and comforting image of Native American women's art. At times, her work draws from traditional beading and wampum patterns, and virtually every piece references the history and spiritual beliefs of the Haudenosaunee. Her use of these traditional materials and stories is highly innovative and original. Niro's accomplishment, in photography and film, is profoundly contemporary and cosmopolitan. A recipient of the Scotiabank Photography Award (2017), the Hnatyshyn Foundation REVEAL Indigenous Art Award (2017), and the Governor General's Awards in Visual and Media Arts (2017), Niro is a cutting-edge contemporary artist whose work is richly historically allusive. Her 2009 film *Kissed by Lightning* makes contemporary the Hiawatha saga, while her film *It Starts with a Whisper* (1993) highlights Haudenosaunee beliefs regarding the haunted power and the sacredness of the place now called Niagara Falls. My book encounters this historically allusive discourse that is central and crucial to Niro's artistic oeuvre. In this book, I weave between history and contemporaneity, following Niro's lead. Return doesn't always mean return to the past; it can also mean return to the present. Return, above all, in Niro's work is return to the land now called New York, the homeland of the Mohawk.

With the traditional ancestral land of the Mohawk being cultivated land where a culture flourished, it is notable that art was long created by the Mohawk that marked that land. However, not all the forms of artistic practice in which the Mohawk traditionally engaged were transported with the people when they were displaced. Some art remained on their original land. As historian Alan Taylor notes, "Paintings on stones and trees, "pictographs," marked territory as Mohawk . . . One of the most important paintings covered a lofty smooth rock overlooking the Mohawk River. . . . With red ochre the Mohawks depicted a canoe with seven warriors in it. . . . To maintain the painting, the Mohawk continually refreshed the painting even for decades after they had mostly lost their lands in the Mohawk Valley following the Revolution."[63] We can think of Niro's works as the art of return; we can understand Niro as participating in this long-held tradition of maintaining the marks of Mohawk art on their homeland. Her photographs touch the land with their vision and power. Wanda Nanibush notes, "Photography in the hands of Indigenous artists forms a body of philosophical, poetic, and physical knowledge of our relationship to land."[64] Shelley Niro's art invoking, alluding to, and showing what we now call New York State signifies that it is, still, Mohawk land.

Chapter 1

Shelley Niro's Time

Temporality and Indigenous Vision

Across the last four decades, since the 1980s, Shelley Niro (Six Nations of the Grand River Reserve, Bay of Quinte Kanien'kehá:ka Mohawk Nation, Turtle Clan) has built an internationally recognized oeuvre of photography, film, painting, video, and installation that demands to be reckoned with. Her art addresses contemporary Mohawk culture specifically and, more generally, broader issues of colonization in Canadian and US history. As an enrolled member of the Mohawk, Niro's allegiance is to a people who live on both sides of the settler-colonialist border between Canada and the United States. Tuscarora scholar Richard Hill notes, in the formation of colonialist nation-states "The Niagara River became a political border" impacting the Haudenosaunee.[1] Niro is an American-born artist who lives in Canada, and her work forcefully evokes and references the land we now call New York State—the traditional lands of the Haudenosaunee. As Mohawk scholar Douglas M. George-Kanentiio explains, "For the Iroquois, there is no doubt but that their identity as a distinct people took form in the region south of the St. Lawrence River, north of the Susquehanna, and east of the Niagara peninsula."[2] Niro's art does not forget this reality.

Niro uses her camera to create vivid images of Indigenous women that contest oppressive structures of racist and patriarchal gazing, supplanting white notions of indigeneity with a female Indigenous gaze. Scholar Patrick Wolfe argues, in contemplating the "racial regimes" of settler colonialism, Indigenous peoples, despite genocidal violence, are able to "see—and act on—things in other ways."[3] Seeing in other ways is at the core of Niro's art. Key to this different perspective is Niro's refusal of the subjectivity of settler-colonialist time and settler-colonialist definitions of nation-state borders. Her works returning to the heart of New York State reject linear settler time and insist on—and manifest as—the broader gaze of cyclical, Indigenous time. As scholar and educator Margaret Kovach (Nêhiyaw and Saulteaux) emphasizes, Indigenous conceptualizations of time and being are distinct and radically different from a settler-colonialist sense of time in ways that are not codified in mainstream academia: "Eurocentrism within research has yet to be fully unpacked in the academy or in the systems that support it."[4] She contends that, as we attempt to think in our scholarship outside and beyond the confines of "the empire" (i.e., settler colonialism), shifting our understanding to Indigenous conceptions of time, land, and community is essential.[5] In this frame, time is cyclical and returning; land is valuable in itself, not as transfer of capitalist title; and community is the core of ethics and that toward which the benefit of all our work should be directed. To further unpack these issues of temporality and colonization, we can draw from anthropologist Johannes Fabian's work theorizing the violence of settler time to note how temporality, settler political and military power, and the gaze are contested and altered in Niro's photographic and film works.[6] I contend that Niro's artistic returns to New York State pose a visual space of contestation and subtle political revolution: they are activist artworks of profound emotional intimacy. They reject the belief that colonization is a system in which we have no choice but to remain immersed.

Niro's lens-based work in film, video, and photography is the focus of this book. She is a multimedia artist who in addition to film and photography has created numerous paintings and sculptural works, and yet I make the case that her use of the camera posits her most radical subversion of the colonizer's gaze. In photography and film, the gaze is at once mechanized (mediated through a lens) and generalized (presented as if no one had created the images, but had simply captured them). This duality—of vision being at once displaced from the creator of the image and also interpretable as generalized to the viewer (even though, in fact, in viewing lens-based art we are always seeing what the creator of the work shapes and decides to show us)—gives photography and film an inherent political force.[7] Drawing from critical Indigenous theory and Indigenous feminist theory, I explore ways that Niro uses her camera to contest the placement of Indigenous North Americans in a temporality that is subsumed by Western history. As scholar-activist Joyce Green (Ktunaxa Nation) notes, the struggles for Indigenous rights and feminist rights are waged directly against the structures of the nation-state, structures that were created and are sustained precisely *not* for the benefit of Indigenous women: "There remains the paramount problem of colonialism and the difficulty of entertaining the prospect of liberation via the colonial state and its imposed Constitution."[8] Interpreting the overarching ideological enclosure of settler-colonialist beliefs, I extrapolate from Johannes Fabian's influential work *Time and the Other* to note the myriad ways that Niro contests the dominance of Western colonialist time. Niro's deployment of the camera stages an encounter with modernity and colonization, envisioning and claiming her place as a contemporary Indigenous artist while critiquing historical events and political regimes oppressive to Indigenous peoples. Her use of magical realism and temporal dissonance in the films *It Starts with a Whisper* (1993) and *Kissed by Lightning* (2009), and in the sculptural mixed-media work *1779* and *The Essential Sensuality of Ceremony* photographic series, blur the past, present, and future, refusing settler colonialism's imposition of linear Christological apocalyptic time.

Indigenizing feminist theory is crucial to any interpretation of Niro's film and photography. Niro's early work incorporates her sisters and mother in feminist, anticolonialist photographic works. She includes her friend and fellow Indigenous artist Hulleah Tsinhnahjinnie (Seminole/Muskogee/Diné) in the film and photographic series *The Shirt* (figure 1.1). She casts fellow artist Lena Recollet (Anishinaabe) in the short experimental film *Tree*.[9] Heroines are invariably at the heart of Niro's movies. Niro's devotion to the perspectives and perceptions of Indigenous women stages a reckoning with the notions of European time, embodiment, and gender imposed through colonization. In her work, vision and the power of the gaze belong to Indigenous women. Her images not only question but also radically take apart masculinist, white-supremacist beliefs regarding who has the right to define embodied subjectivity in time and, consequently, who has rightful claim to this land of North America.

Even as the stills used in the film *The Shirt* were not photographed in New York, when Niro created the film version of the photographic series, she included intercut video of rivers that cross the Canada–New York border. This emphasizes that the work's wry statements regarding the barbarity and violence of settler capitalism made in *The Shirt* emerge from Niro's specific history as a Mohawk woman whose ancestral land is in New York. In *The Shirt*, artist and scholar Hulleah Tsinhnahjinnie

Figure 1.1. *My Ancestors*, frame from "The Shirt," 2003; color duratrans in lightbox. *Source:* Courtesy of the artist.

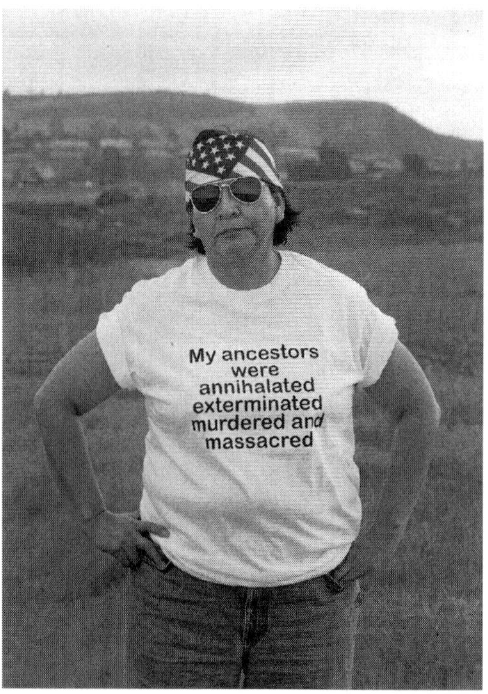

stands in an open field, adorned with a US flag bandana, aviator shades, and a shirt that reads MY ANCESTORS WERE ANNIHILATED EXTERMINATED MURDERED AND MASSACRED. Tsinhnahjinnie, with arms akimbo, faces the camera looking mildly perturbed, very much like a professor staring down a student who didn't do their homework (in fact Tsinhnahjinnie *is* a professor). The humor in the piece is strong, but—as one can tell by reading the words on the shirt—the critique is trenchant. Niro's bright and punchy aesthetic offers viewers a way into the work that seems nonthreatening, yet it is precisely this subtlety that makes her art a kind of guerrilla tactic against colonialism. The work's visual punchline occurs when Tsinhnahjinnie's wife, Veronica Passalacqua, who is not Indigenous and who has very pale skin and red hair, stands alone in the frame wearing the cheap T-shirt of coloniality that has itself been taken off Tsinhnahjinnie's back.

Likewise, in the mixed-media sculpture *1779*, symbolic clothing is used to profound effect. Here, a brightly beaded pair of high-heeled shoes is placed atop an upward-facing digital display that plays a reiterative film of the whirlpool at the bottom of Niagara Falls. The screen and shoes are encircled by a lavish red velvet cloth depicting the number 1779 sewn in white beadwork. This is the year the Mohawk were displaced from their homeland by the brutal Sullivan-Clinton campaign and the year of the Winter of Hunger, when they sought refuge at Fort Niagara and many starved to death. Niro's piece leverages a derealization of time as in the image we are both in 1779 and in the present; this skewing of time is essential to the piece's power. Surreally, the shoes stand atop the whirlpool, emplacing an eerie dissonance of femininity—frightening and uncanny in its surreal scale—as the ultra-femme shoes supervise the specter of genocidal violence that is summed up by that date: 1779. Niro suggests that the shoes represent trashy settler-colonialist culture that has attempted to take over Niagara, while the power of the falls resists this violence and remains animate and sacred no matter what settler-colonialism does.

Niro's art can be read in concert with the work of contemporary Haudenosaunee women artists Jolene Rickard (Tuscarora), Melanie Hope (Tuscarora), Marie Watt (Seneca), and Tracey Deer (Mohawk). In an earlier book, I contrasted her work with Cara Romero's (Chemehuevi) and Matika Wilbur's (Swinomish-Tulalip) photography and online presences.[10] One can also contextualize Niro's work with regard to Confederated Salish, Kootenai, Métis, and Shoshone artist Jaune Quick-to-See Smith's groundbreaking exhibit *Memory Map* (at the National Gallery in Washington, DC, from April 19 to August 23, 2023). But the artists with whom Niro feels close connections are Hulleah Tsinhnahjinnie (Seminole/Muskogee/Diné) and Nadya Kwandibens (Anishinaabe).[11] Notably, Tsinhnahjinnie and Kwandibens, like Niro, create work that unsettles and contests settler temporalities.

Kwandibens's photographic series *Concrete Indians* (2008), *emergence* (2016), and *The Red Chair Sessions* (2022) dramatize and, pointedly, concretize the problematic of settler time, casting Indigenous people as figures of resistance and resurgence. Kwandibens posits her work explicitly in opposition to the temporality of racial capitalism as her inspiration, quoting scholar Howard Adams (Métis): "The racism and colonialism of capitalism will always hold us captive in misery, violence and exploitation. It is time that we recognized our own power and faced the fact that our solutions lie within ourselves."[12]

Tsinhnahjinnie's *Five Minutes Work* (2011) also complicates and contemporizes received settler temporalities and histories of America. This image reclaims a stereoscopic nineteenth-century negative (in cyanotype) of buffalo carcasses and a horse beside which the artist has written in red ink "Excuse me . . . I did not sign up for this," while in white script beneath the image she writes: "the idea that the story of history can be told in one coherent narrative." The digital collage brings together nineteenth-century photographic materiality and twenty-first-century digital technology with a script explicitly contesting the conceit of settler temporality: that is, the erroneous belief that there is one history belonging to one group of people that explains everything about everyone. Tsinhnahjinnie's 1994 *Photographic Memoir of an Aboriginal Savant (Living on Occupied Land)*, a mixed-media work of photography and text, poignantly contests the penchant of settler time for imagining false pasts and falser futures of Indigenous peoples. For Tsinhnahjinnie, as also for Niro, photography is a tool of resistance. Writes Tsinhnahjinnie, "The camera is held with brown hands opening familiar worlds. We document ourselves with a humanizing eye, we create new visions with ease."[13]

Tsinhnahjinnie's *Today I Was Thinking* (2010), a pigment print on fabric, shows "time" as a series of moons, presumably referencing the offensive Hollywood trope of placing into the mouths of faux-Indigenous characters the practice of keeping track of time by "moons." The work's image of buffalo evocatively calls out the near erasure of the American bison by settler predations, while the punched-up pink sky places the work in cutting-edge neo-pop art. The piece elegantly draws a meditation on the problematic of settler temporality while poking fun at settler cliché ideas of indigeneity and mourning the utterly unfunny losses of genocide. This conceptual and sophisticated layered work is part of an important conversation between the two artists—Niro and Tsinhnahjinnie—whose friendship spans decades. I want to emphasize here the importance of this friendship, which informs both Niro's and Tsinhnahjinnie's work and yet is rarely mentioned in scholarship about the artists. As curator Wanda Nanibush (Beausoleil First Nation, Ojibwe) notes, "Today, Indigenous artists are accepted as artists in the mainstream artworld, yet there is still much negotiating of how they are seen by non-Indigenous peoples."[14] The friendship and mutual influence of these two artists transcend clichéd notions of Indigenous artistic inspiration. Articulating agency and active resistance, Tsinhnahjinnie coins the phrase "photographic sovereignty," which illuminates both her own and Niro's practice.[15] A key aspect of this sovereignty emerges in the way the temporal structures of their art sharply disavow settler-coloniality's Christological notions of history.

A core of the cultural structure of coloniality is a belief in linear—and ultimately apocalyptic—time. Christian eschatology instates the cultural belief in time that does not return, an ideological belief in "progress." This credence has far-reaching practical repercussions: apparently, it is easy to destroy this Earth if you believe that you will not need it after the putative end times. This hegemonic notion of civilization is steeped in the problematic of settler temporality. One of the most persistent tropes of Western domination is the implicit belief that Indigenous peoples—the erstwhile colonized—exist somehow earlier than (while also paradoxically being contemporaneous with) so-called advanced European civilization, that Indigenous cultures are literally "primitive," and therefore now defunct, or *out of time*, in the sweep of history.[16] A simple test of the widespread reach of this fallacious belief occurs, as noted in the introduction, if one feeds the words "Mohawk people" into a Google search. Immediately, an image of a 1786 painting of Joseph Brant (Thayendanegea), by settler-colonialist painter Gilbert Stuart, appears on the screen.[17]

And yet, the Mohawk people are alive and thriving now, very much in the twenty-first-century world. This colonialist habit of erasing the living Indigenous perspective, like that of attempting to erase the very lives of Indigenous peoples, stems from the erroneous cultural assumption that Indigenous peoples came before settlers only to pave the way for settlers and then to vanish; this centuries-old habit of thought coloniality finds hard to shake.[18] In the pivotal era of the eighteenth century, European philosophers and natural scientists of the Enlightenment, from Blumen-bach to Kant, contended that Indigenous people—of the Americas, the Caribbean, and Africa—represented the childhood of man, precivilization, falsely arguing that European man was the most intellectually and cul-turally developed—and the only fully civilized—example of humanity.[19] Freud's essays on the uncanny and his discussions of women carried this habit of mind into the twentieth century, during which the Western art world drew from so-called primitive arts of Indigenous peoples to revivify collapsing Western traditions.[20]

Surrealist and modernist art appropriated Indigenous cultures in a sleight of hand, stealing tropes, images, themes, and even artifacts while simultaneously disregarding the capacity of Indigenous people to create art. Even after the offensive nomenclature of primitivism and the egregious anthropological arguments regarding the innate capacities of people of different races were challenged by later twentieth-century Indigenous and non-Indigenous theorists, oppressive habits of thinking about Indigenous peoples through the lens of Western time continue, reflected in contemporary cultural idioms and nation-state laws and policies, not to mention the glaring absence in the United States of a vigorous truth and reconciliation process.

Developing from Fabian's argument that decolonization can only happen when we dismantle the concept of Western time as the overarching frame of history, and drawing from Chickasaw scholar Jodi Byrd's overarching argument in *Transit of Empire* that mnemonic work must be done to decolonize our collective images of culture in time, I approach Shelley Niro's art by noting that time in her work does not conform to settler temporal expectations and visual regimes. As Byrd argues, in the context of museums and the art world, the Indigenous artist and her work function as "a metaphor through which these institutions can confront their complicity in colonialist practices, and is never granted agency beyond its usefulness as sign."[21] Niro's work, despite this oppressive social structure, gathers agency through its subtle and exquisite use of temporal estrangement, creating a dissonant space in which past, present, and future do not adhere to settler time. Her subtle use of temporal estrangement protects the work from assimilation, restructuring the viewer's access to cultural memory. Mohawk belief and knowledge are contiguous with temporality as we move through it, in the perceptions of Niro's art. Her work responds to and refuses the Euro-American practice, in the nineteenth and twentieth centuries, of archiving images of Indigenous Americans and objects they created as a sign of conquest. Along with the erroneous settler belief that Indigenous culture is precursor to settler culture is the settler-colonialist acquisitive drive to possess Indigenous peoples as relics. Historian and philosopher Philip J. Deloria (Standing Rock Sioux) insightfully interprets such acquisition as a mode of trophy taking.[22] In Niro's tropes of return and her refusal of the context of settler time, her work both comments on and resists settler trophy taking. Leveraging irony, pathos, and layered allusion to Mohawk and settler history, her work slips through the gauntlet of settler-colonialist appropriations.

The Art of Return

In Niro's art there is a refusal to inhabit the cultural space of the colonized subject—a refusal to inhabit settler time. When she returns to

New York in her art, she resists settler temporality, which holds that the homeland of the Haudenosaunee now belongs within settler-colonialist, capitalist-temporal structures. Signally, Niro's returns to New York State instate a refusal to stay where coloniality placed her. Every time she goes back to the homeland of her ancestors, every time her art invokes that region, she refuses the terms and time of coloniality.

Niro's work subtly but insistently maps images that refuse this displacement from centrality of Indigenous self, vision, and culture. In her photographs, videos, and films, Niro creates an image-world in which the past haunts the present and the present haunts the past. Her work is not nostalgic. It looks to the past and the future as times that actively cross and imbricate the present. In *Kissed by Lightning* (2009), the heroine is haunted by her husband's sudden death; through this haunting, it becomes clear that her remembered husband is a figure for the Great Peacemaker (Deganawidah). The film concludes with the anticipated birth of a new child who will also be a Peacemaker, moving by turns from the past into the present without forgetting. In this way, the film works as a map for Haudenosaunee survival. Niro's work deploys temporal estrangement to reflect that the temporality of coloniality is violent and its imposition a false front. Haudenosaunee scholar and activist Taiaiake Alfred argues that decolonization and Indigenous resurgence must include reconnecting with the land, reconnecting with each other (members of one's nation and other Indigenous people), and ultimately reconnecting with self.[23]

The frame of surviving and thriving, of how to endure and resurge despite inheriting the massive cultural trauma of genocide that is the reality of Indigenous North Americans, is a thread uniting Niro's works. The feature-length film *The Incredible 25th Year of Mitzi Bearclaw* (2019) engages the question of how a young woman survives when her mother is destroying herself—the mother being a survivor of child abuse inflicted at a government-run residential school, one of several in a system that exacted horrible suffering on Indigenous peoples in the US and Canada deep into the twentieth century. In the United States, Indigenous American parents were forced by law to submit to the state-sanctioned kidnapping of their children through the Browning Ruling, which shamefully contended that Indigenous parents were intellectually incompetent and therefore could not govern how their children were educated. Under the Browning Ruling, "Indians are reduced to children . . . their parental role debased," which gave the fallacious justification for kidnapping Indigenous children and taking them to residential schools.[24] Child abuse (sexual abuse, malnutrition, neglect, and severe beatings) was commonly inflicted on children in the residential schools.[25] Survivors of these abusive facilities often suffered (and still suffer now) from posttraumatic stress disorders, substance abuse, and other mental and physical maladies caused by the residential school experience.

In the film *The Incredible 25th Year of Mitzi Bearclaw*, Mitzi's mother is written by Shelley Niro as a character who embodies the suffering of residential school survivors, her physical and mental health broken, her ability to love torn from her, and an early death.[26] Although Niro does not name Bearclaw's specific residential school, the twenty-first century has seen heart-wrenching discoveries of unmarked graves of Indigenous children buried in the yards of residential schools in Canada. One school in particular, the former Kamloops Indian Residential School, made international news when investigators located the remains of 215 children buried on the grounds of the school.[27]

In facing her mother's suffering and premature death, young Mitzi Bearclaw finds a way toward her own authentic survival. This centering in female power and Indigenous resurgence is typical of Niro's art. In Niro's work, a feminism emerges that is counter to the dominant white-feminist theory of the early twenty-first century that emphasizes the idea that "woman" is a category created by practices of language and other-wise without ontological heft. Niro's emphasis is certainly not biological reductivism; rather, she traces in her photographs, videos, and films the discursive production of Indigenous feminism as a space contested by forceful human beings, Indigenous North American women who do not see themselves reflected in the dominant white culture's views of Indigenous women, nor in settler views of women as such.[28] The consistent visual act of Niro's art is that of calmly interrogating the status quo, revealing its gaps and lacunae through an Indigenous feminist lens. This is achieved in part by depicting Mohawk women not as the dominant white culture sees them, but as Shelley Niro does.

Red Heels

Many of Niro's earlier photographs (from the late 1980s to mid-1990s) are of her mother and sisters. For example, in the six-photograph series *Red Heels Hard* (Figures 1.2–1.7), Niro photographs her sisters together in front of a statue of Joseph Brant, who led the Mohawk to Canada after the United States forced them out of most of New York.[29] Here,

Figure 1.2. Frame 1, *Red Heels Hard,* 1991, hand-tinted photographs, 8 in. × 10 in. each, framed: 12¼ in. × 68¼ in., Collection of the Castellani Art Museum of Niagara University, purchased from the artist., 1994. *Source:* Courtesy of the artist.

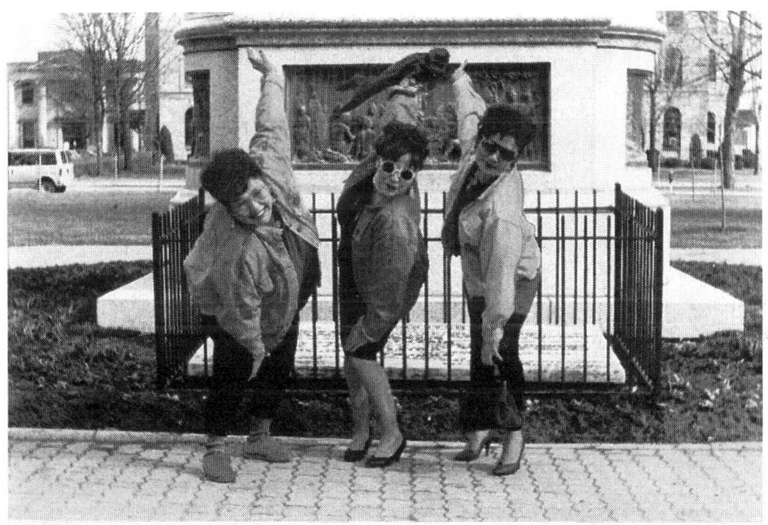

Figure 1.3. Frame 2, *Red Heels Hard,* 1991, hand-tinted photographs, 8 in. × 10 in. each, framed: 12¼ in. × 68¼ in., Collection of the Castellani Art Museum of Niagara University, purchased from the artist., 1994. *Source:* Courtesy of the artist.

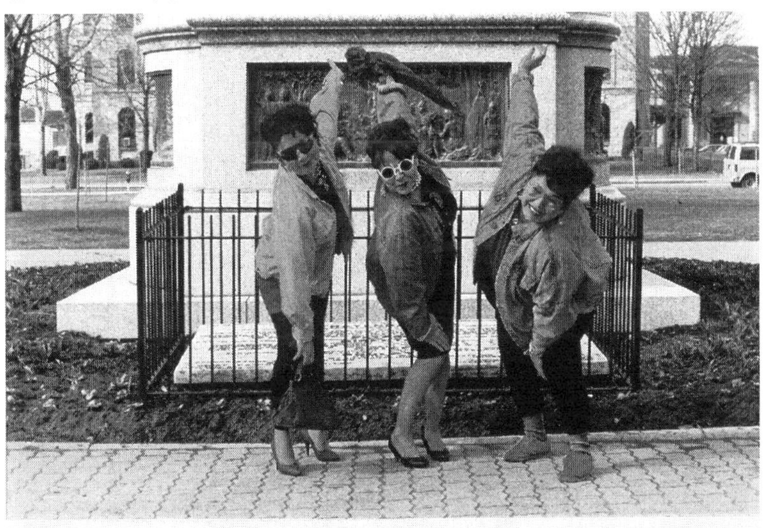

Figure 1.4. Frame 3, *Red Heels Hard*, 1991, hand-tinted photographs, 8 in. × 10 in. each, framed: 12¼ in. × 68¼ in., Collection of the Castellani Art Museum of Niagara University, purchased from the artist., 1994. *Source:* Courtesy of the artist.

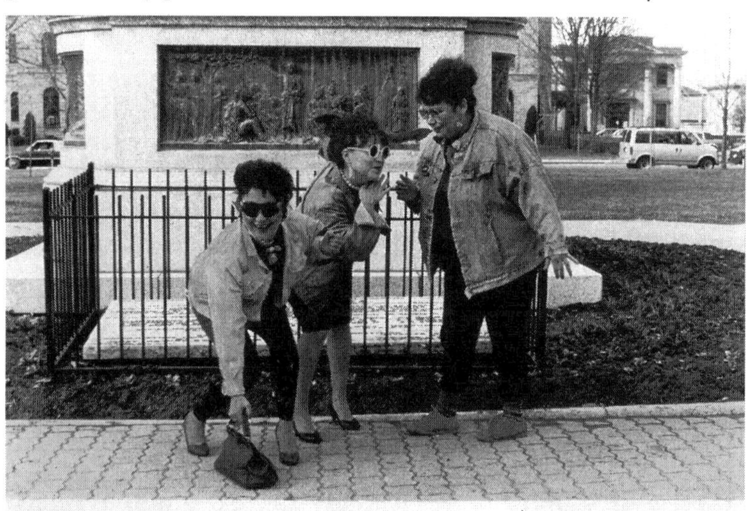

Figure 1.5. Frame 4, *Red Heels Hard*, 1991, hand-tinted photographs, 8 in. × 10 in. each, framed: 12¼ in. × 68¼ in., Collection of the Castellani Art Museum of Niagara University, purchased from the artist., 1994. *Source:* Courtesy of the artist.

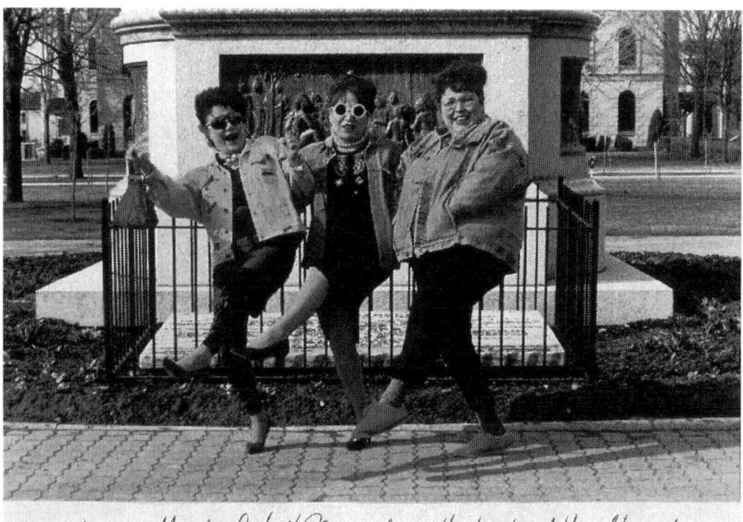

Figure 1.6. Frame 5, *Red Heels Hard,* 1991, hand-tinted photographs, 8 in. × 10 in. each, framed: 12¼ in. × 68¼ in., Collection of the Castellani Art Museum of Niagara University, purchased from the artist., 1994. *Source:* Courtesy of the artist.

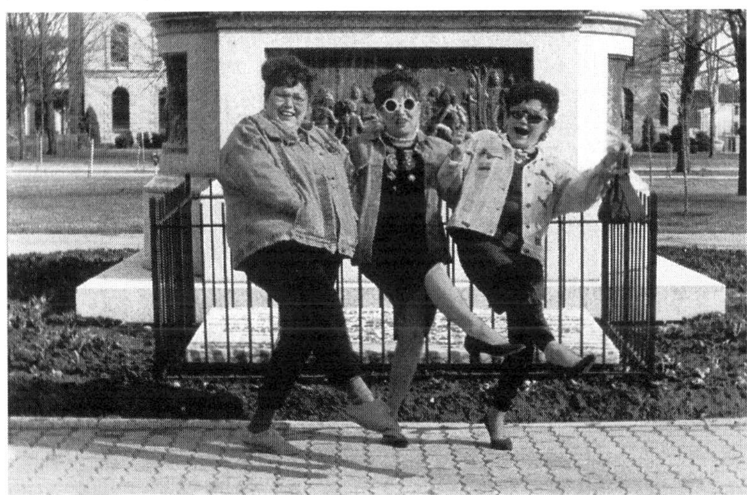

Figure 1.7. Frame 6, Red Heels Hard, 1991, hand-tinted photographs, 8 in. × 10 in. each, framed: 12¼ in. × 68¼ in., Collection of the Castellani Art Museum of Niagara University, purchased from the artist., 1994. *Source:* Courtesy of the artist.

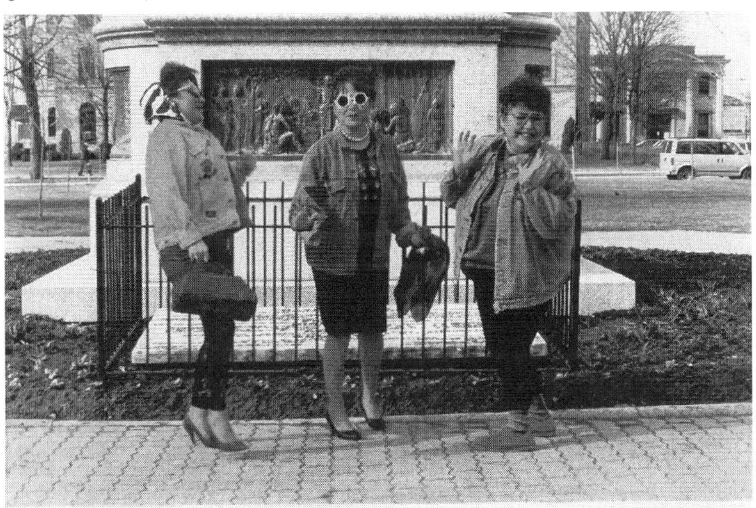

the sisters' contemporaneity plays off Brant's historicity. Niro deepens the allusive discourse of the images by throwing in the curveball reference to Dorothy's red heels in the 1939 movie *The Wizard of Oz*. This film is quintessentially one of settler colonialism, dramatizing the life of Euro-settlers on the plains, a space—until relatively recently—inhabited, stewarded, and controlled by Indigenous North Americans. As Dorothy, the white protagonist, almost loses her life in a tornado that sends her on an internal journey and quest in which she repeatedly wants to go home, the questions of what and where is home are paramount in the 1939 film. While *The Wizard of Oz* resolves with a settler fantasy of completing the task of colonization through the settlers finally feeling that they have "come home" to America, Niro's critique of this settler fantasy spoofs its simplistic and propagandist ideation.

For Indigenous North Americans, *The Wizard of Oz* signifies a different back story. It is not a question of *Tristes Tropiques*, the melancholy of the colonizer, but instead the trauma of the survivor of genocidal displacement that Niro signifies in handwritten script beneath the penultimate frame of the series: "We followed that yellow brick road and clicked our red heels hard."[30] Here, the brutal premise of colonization—that every settler can have a home because every Indigenous person loses their home—is revealed humorously, albeit with a "hard" humor with the kick of a sharp heel (accentuated by the title *Red Heels Hard*). Notably L. Frank Baum, author of the novel *The Wonderful Wizard of Oz*, was a fervent proponent of genocide. In response to the massacre at Wound Knee, Baum (then a newspaper man) wrote: "The Whites, by law of conquest, by justice of civilization, are masters of the American continent, and the best safety of the frontier settlements will be secured by the total annihilation of the few remaining Indians. Why not annihilation? Their glory has fled, their spirit broken, their manhood effaced; better that they die than live the miserable wretches that they are."[31] Niro's decision to allude to the iconic settler fantasy work that Baum went on to create (the film based on his writing) combats, with brilliant metaphoric concision, the brutality and harshness of settler violence and genocide, and presents the spirit of Indigenous resilience and resurgence that characterizes all her work.

Indigenous North Americans cannot "click [their] red heels hard" and go home, back to a continent undistorted by settler colonialism. In Niro's photographic series, the Mohawk sisters cannot go home to sovereign inhabitance of the Mohawk Valley by clicking their heels the way Dorothy did in Oz. Instead, they must find a way to survive and thrive in Canada, as they have for centuries. To create this evocative sense of time, of the present and past merging, and to establish visual sequences of temporal estrangement, Niro delicately hand-colored the black-and-white series of photographs and created border collages that echo traditional Haudenosaunee beadwork to frame the images.

In *Red Heels Hard*, Niro's sisters present Indigenous feminism, Mohawk feminism, through their vitality in the face of genocidal threat.[32] The three women pose as if in the middle of a humorous cancan dance, kicking like Rockettes, while Niro's ironic script, "We followed that yellow brick road and clicked our red heels hard," rolls beneath them in neat handwriting. The critique of colonialism is both of this moment—Niro created these images in the wake of the Oka Crisis (see chapter 4)—and of the deeper past, signified by the Brant statue before which the sisters perform. This juxtaposition exemplifies Niro's implicit use of temporal estrangement. In the series, the Mohawk sisters are not truly at home even though this is where they live, nor do they have immediate hope of going home just by clicking their red heels; in the image, we are neither in the now, nor in the past or future, but in all three at once. It is important to note that, if the sisters could simply click their heels and travel home, they would return to the Mohawk Valley, in what we now call New York State, the creation of which pushed the Mohawk out of their homeland.[33] The text and the sharp coloring of the images indicate the blend of humor, irony, pathos, and temporal estrangement that are characteristic of Niro's oeuvre. The sisters are laughing, but in laughing they are not forgetting or erasing the trauma of displacement. If we follow this yellow brick road created by Mohawk artist Shelley Niro, we will come to a place of reseeing, or seeing anew, the myths of settler colonialism for the violence that they are. The juxtaposition of the background knowledge that Niro created the images in response to the violence of the Oka Crisis by using irony is a quintessential gesture of her work.[34] She approaches situations of raw pain and injustice and fights against them with clear-eyed wit.

Some twenty years later, in *The Incredible 25th Year of Mitzi Bearclaw* (2019), Niro plays forms of time against each other. The film is organized by the conceit of the settler calendar, as images of this calendar separate its scenes; however, the film's internal drama arcs back to the deeper history of the Bearclaw family, and ultimately to all the Indigenous people of the area who are brutally impacted by pollution brought in by settler colonialism's racial capitalism. The impact of environmental degradation is signified by shots of dead fish in the water and by the suffering and youthful death of Charlie B., Mitzi's cousin who is raised like her brother. The emphasis on environmental damage as a form of human suffering is condensed in the dreamscape line when Mitzi, seeing the Earth from space during a vision, exclaims that the planet is dying and that she loves her (Mother Earth) so much. This layering of the film's multiple meanings through temporal play is typical of Niro's approach to filmic art.

Niro's productions vary from short experimental art films, such as *Tree* (2005)—a 35-mm short film that is a meditation on environmental degradation and Sky Woman's response to settler pollution—to feature-length films, including *Kissed by Lightning* (2009), *The Incredible 25th Year of Mitzi Bearclaw*, and *Café Daughter*, released in June 2023.[35] Regardless of length, her films layer temporalities and identities so that the past, present, and future come together in moments of heightened meaning. In *The Incredible 25th Year of Mitzi Bearclaw*, for example, when the heroine experiences traumatic events in the diegetic time of the film, she is cast both backward and forward in time in uncanny scenes with characters named Faith, Hope, and Charity, played by the actors who perform as her parents and Charlie B. These scenes, in the forest and in outer space, illuminate Mitzi's journey not by moving into an entirely personal imaginary space but by connoting a space where Mohawk stories infuse the future as forms of guidance for the present drawn from the deep past.

In her films, videos, and photographs, Niro emphasizes female leads whose worlds are explored with complexity and attention to thriving despite adversity. The works are decolonizing and feminist in that they center Indigenous North American women as the main characters, not supporting characters, and portray them as human beings of brilliance and gifts who face down continuing historical patterns of violence against their community. Given the push of late twentieth and early twenty-first-century feminist theory against what has been called "essentializing," Niro's ability to create a visual and ontological space for Indigenous women is especially notable and commendable.[36] Do we really want—in keeping with poststructuralist, white-feminist theory—to say that the category of Indigenous woman is ontologically hollow? Would that not be exactly the move of colonization, to silence and negate the very ontology of those who are not white men? In contrast to mainstream white feminism, Niro's work emphatically posits an Indigenous feminism that sees Indigenous women as embodied, vivid, twenty-first-century citizens.

There is a wide and undertheorized divergence between poststructuralist feminism that stands with theorist Judith Butler and philosopher

Jacques Lacan in contending that woman is a spurious or invented category, on the one hand, and, on the other, the political situation of Indigenous women who are engaged in an intense political and cultural struggle for visible identity, embodied agency, and audible civic and artistic voice.[37] Judith Butler and the whites who admire her may not like to think of themselves as allied with Lacan, but the idea of the nullity of the meaning of the word "woman" that is at the core of Butler's poststructuralist theory is precisely contiguous with Lacan's idea of the nonexistence of woman. Biological essentialism serves no one well, and yet, as scholar Teresa De Lauretis argues, embodied history accrues in material ways that warrant detailed attention.[38] Scholar and cultural theorist Glen Sean Coulthard (Yellowknives Dene) offers a way through the impasse. Coulthard contends that the imposition of settler nation-state law during colonization "established for the first time a definition of 'Indian' that was tightly associated with patrilineal descent"[39]—in other words, settler culture pushed decisively away from and against Indigenous practices of matrilineal descent. Coulthard continues: "In the years to follow, state-sanctioned gender discrimination within the field of Indian policy would escalate dramatically."[40] And yet, Coulthard makes clear that, even in the face of consistent sexist oppression from settler-colonialist culture and nation-state governance, "First Nations women have always resisted the state's attempt to dispossess them of their rights to land and community membership."[41]

One can extend this theory of Indigenous feminism to interpret Niro's complex approach to representing Indigenous women's experience. Her work is a form of political resistance, stemming from generations of activist Indigenous women, and she refuses poststructuralist erasure. In drawing from Leanne Betasamosake Simpson's anticolonialist work to investigate Niro's oeuvre of photographs and films, we note that beneath the quietness of Niro's images' beautiful surfaces there is a *rebel*—echoing here the title of one of her earliest masterpieces, *The Rebel*, a photograph of her mother (figure 1.8)—who sees that only in refusing colonizing culture can she and other Haudenosaunee thrive.[42]

Along this line, one draws also from anthropologist Marge Bruchac's (Abenaki) work in museum decolonization to encounter the idea of "animacy" in Niro's photographic installations. Niro's works do not fall into the settler category of temporality that dictates art as a sealed, "dead" artifact. Instead, by weaving together photography and textile work, by working between genres, Niro creates living objects. The photograph *The Rebel* shows the artist's mother, Chiquita Doxtater, on a decades-old car, the AMC Rebel, marketed from 1967 to 1970. The photograph contrasts the moribund vehicle with Doxtater's vibrant life force. It may be a reach but perhaps Chiquita Doxtater, the artist's mother, here is positioned on this car somewhat as Sky Woman was held on the turtle's back, as the photograph playfully invokes Niro's clan—the Turtle Clan—while instating Mohawk feminine power in the place of, or rather in place of, derelict and trashy settler capitalist structure (the old car).

As Niro created the image's print, she hand-painted her mother's form in the photograph, imbuing her with a sense of life that emerges beyond and transcends the humorous reflection on poverty (Indigenous economic poverty is a signal effect of colonization), survivance, and resurgence.[43] Niro's mother shines from the print, reaching out beyond her circumstances but also fully aware and critical of the detritus, the trash, that is the main product of settler culture.

In returning to the source of her artistry—her mother—Niro engages the trope of return that governs much of her work. In this sense, return is temporal and spatial, with the latter representing a return to the land now called New York, the Mohawk homeland—even when this is not explicitly signaled. Educator Mark Rifkin argues that Indigenous concepts of time do not acquiesce to dominant Western notions of temporality; this view coheres with my approach to understanding the frequent merging of past and present in Niro's art, a merging of temporalities through which the Mohawk conceptually return to their ancestral homelands.[44] Rifkin's argument focuses more on settler notions of time; he contends that these ideas place Indigenous people in a bind whereby they are "either consigned to the past or inserted into a non-Indigenous present."[45] He notes, in particular, the limited scope of settler ideologies of temporality: settler time is shallow.[46] In the United States in particular, Protestant notions of eschatology, the belief that all time moves toward the final revelation of the saved and damned, frame time as strictly linear and in its linearity moving toward the end times, trashing everything along the way.

This problem of settler time, however, is not only that it ignores Indigenous history, historicity, and presence but also that it encodes the eschatological beliefs of Christianity, a temporal structure in which the end of time is determinative, as if Christianity were the only possible way of understanding and structuring reality. Settler temporality sets the stage for land to be swallowed—as it very much has been and continues to be—by racial-capitalist needs for monetizing the very Earth. In contrast to settler eschatology, Haudenosaunee conceptualizations of time are recuperative and cyclical.[47] Haudenosaunee temporality protects and honors the land, understanding that the land is what must be present and whole and healthy for the people to return to it, as the continuation of Haudenosaunee society necessitates.[48] In this sense, cyclical and ritual time are temporalities that take responsibility for the ways that manifestations and effects of human actions return to impact us.

Niro's art deeply epitomizes this temporality as part of *survivance*, as theorist Gerald Vizenor (Ojibwe, White Earth Reservation) established the concept, articulating vivid Indigenous American life in the haunted condition of Indigenous American culture.[49] Vizenor does not see Indigenous peoples as stuck in "victim" mode; on the contrary, he posits a theory of performing through and beyond the spectrality that is given to them as a role to play by dominant white culture, an overturning of disappearance that becomes the thriving of Indigenous culture in the face of genocidal threat.[50] Niro's work is a form of survivance: her art thrives because it resists the position that the biopolitics of colonialist governments have asserted against the Mohawk, and she resists it by creating images that enliven and revivify Indigenous women. She intends her work especially to be seen by Indigenous North American girls, so that they can reenvision the possibilities for their own lives.[51] Niro's desire to support Indigenous girls and women is deeply personal, drawing from her life experience as a daughter, sister, and mother.

In *The Rebel* (figure 1.8), the artist's mother, Chiquita Doxtater, drapes herself across this car that has seen better days. The car, an AMC Rebel, represents a defunct endpoint of settler consumerism (and what is settler colonialism but a system of consumerism?), but the photograph's critical response to this trash (as used cars ultimately go to the junk heaps that crowd our continent) is humor. It is not that Niro and her mother laugh off the meaning of racial capitalism, but rather that, even in that setting of aggressive coloniality with its cheap material accoutrements, the photographer and her mother find a way to thrive. This thriving is resurgence, their laughter an act of resistance.[52]

The image becomes iconic because it is not only about resistance. It is about life: the life of the mother continuing through the daughter, the mother seen in her daughter's eyes. *The Rebel* becomes iconic because Niro lovingly hand tints her mother's lips, fingernails, and shoes the same red of the brake lights. It becomes iconic because it shows the mother's

Figure 1.8. *The Rebel*, 1982/1989, shot in 1982, shown in 1989; hand-tinted photograph, 28 cm. × 35.6 cm. *Source:* Courtesy of the artist.

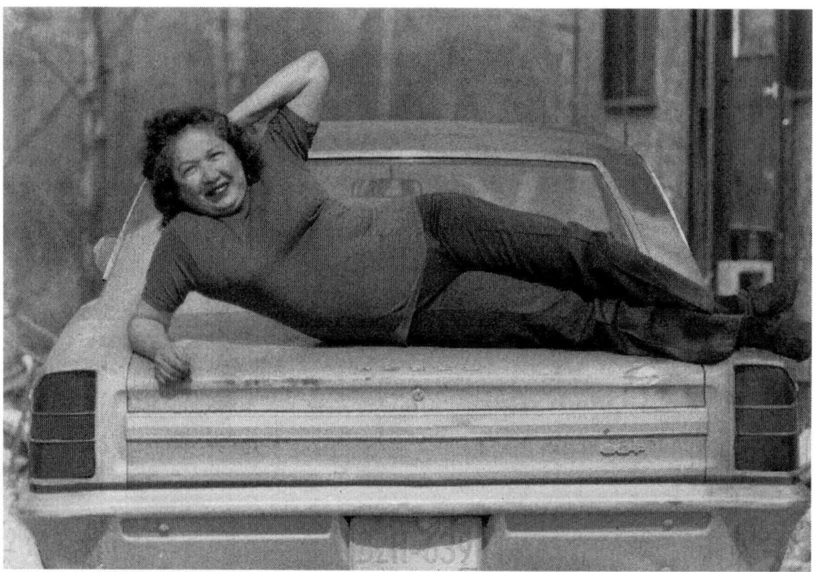

infinite worth in contrast to the car's worthlessness in a subversion of racial-capitalist ideology that promotes the car, the object to be purchased, as the greatest good while simultaneously instigating the erasure of Indigenous peoples (this erasure being the key act of settler colonialism). Niro's *The Rebel* is iconic because it not only resists and refuses but also refutes Indigenous erasure. Here, Chiquita Doxtater embodies the longevity of Indigenous survival. She is not mourning, she is joyful. She is with her daughter and in her daughter's gaze, which becomes the gaze of anyone viewing the image; she is beautiful. The jewel-like reds with which Niro hand tints Chiquita's image suggest the mother's treasured status, a link to ancestors and descendants. In this way, the photograph dramatizes an Indigenous conceptualization of time, one that recognizes and depends on human experience and memory.

Time Travels through Us: Exiles and Returns

Shelley Niro's photograph *Time Travels through Us* (1999, figure 1.9) shows three women with faces bearing a clear family resemblance. The

Figure 1.9. *Time Travels through Us*, 1999, gelatin silver print, cotton and beaded mat work, silver painted wood frame, 94 cm. × 83.8 cm. framed, National Gallery of Canada, purchased from the artist, 2002. *Source:* Used with permission of the artist.

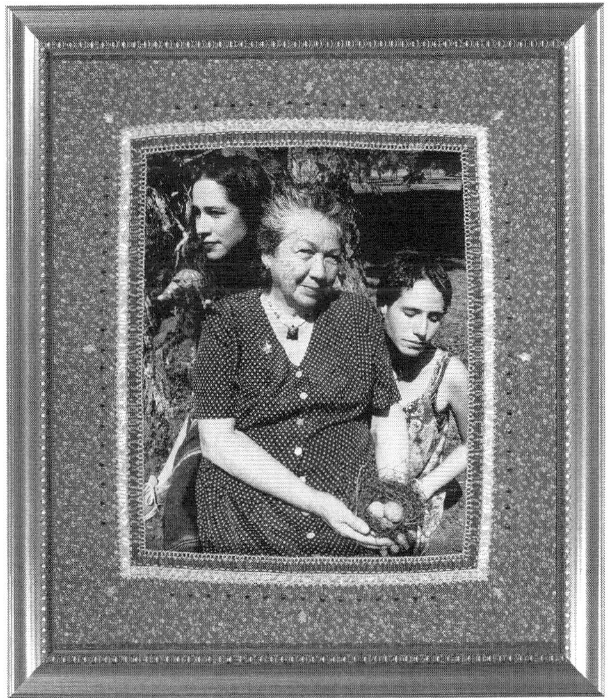

woman seated at the center is elderly and sharp-eyed, with skin creased by exposure to the sun. She looks at the viewer, engaging the artist taking the picture. She wears a turtle pendant and cradles a bird's nest with three eggs, holding them toward the camera, offering them for the photographer to see. To her left, a slender young woman echoes the older woman's facial position, showing a jawline, cheekbones, and mouth nearly identical to that of the older woman. She is also adorned with a small turtle. The younger woman's eyes are closed, and her facial expression is intensely serious, as if she were praying. She is very slight, barely past girlhood. Both women are dressed for summer in breezy cotton garments. The sunlight is very strong across their faces. Finally, behind the older woman, emerging above her right shoulder, is a third woman, perhaps more mature than the woman with closed eyes but significantly younger than the woman who holds the bird's nest. This third woman looks into the distance, her gleaming dark hair shining in the sunlight; she is holding a turtle. The women appear in a wooded area with trees and open space. The photograph is framed with delicate purple cloth and grosgrain ribbons, bringing a tender handmade quality to the piece and expressing an ethos of care that is also visible in the love with which the photograph holds the three women. The haptic element of the framing cloth lends a homey feel to the piece, and yet this coziness also contrasts with the seriousness of the image. The purple of the soft cloth suggests something sacrificial, formal.

The title of the photograph *Time Travels through Us* indeed suggests something heavier than a casual family portrait. The women, in their triune positioning, represent generations of a family: a grandmother and granddaughters. They are the family of the photographer, Shelley Niro, who, invisibly in this image, is the link between the women. She is the daughter of the older woman, Chiquita Doxtater, and mother to the two younger women. The photographer ties the women together through her place as daughter and mother, just as she ties the image of the women together through her role as photographer, standing back from visibility and creating the tender photograph. Her gaze joins them with each other. The signifiers of turtles in the image indicate the women are Turtle Clan.

This photograph stands as a place of extreme tenderness, the emotion of it almost painful as the three women look toward the future with such different expressions and gazes. The older woman looks wise and somewhat wary but also humorous. The young woman with long hair looks gentle and determined, while the youngest, smallest woman looks very serious, as if she is observing another scene: not the one revealed by open eyes of the day but the one shown within closed eyes, of insight. This scene of drawing insight is the anchorage point of *Time Travels through Us*, as the women in the photograph, all in different ways, watch the passage of time. As is characteristic of Niro's art, time itself is at once present, past, and future here; these three temporalities merge and emerge in this photograph.

Time is nested in the women and represented metaphorically by the bird's eggs held by the woman in the center. The image is almost fragile, with the eggs looking vulnerable despite the steadiness with which the woman at the photograph's center holds them. Like so much of Niro's work, the image is at once both painful and beautiful, and it seems to move beyond itself, evoking a sense of something more—something more than "just" three women, grandmother, and granddaughters, in a park in warm sunlight. In Shelley Niro's art and the act of return—returns enacted through mind and memory and image—to the Mohawk homeland of New York State, the question of how the photographer-filmmaker modulates temporality is a guiding thread.

In Niro's film and photographic works, time travel is of the essence. The guiding motif of many of Niro's works is that the past is not over, that history and the places of history continue to matter—making material marks—in the present and into the future. From the short films *The Shirt* (2004) and *Sky Woman with Us* (2002) to the film *It Starts with a Whisper* (1993), and from the feature-length *Kissed by Lightning* (2009) to the photographic series *Battlefields of My Ancestors* (2015), Niro's works dream and articulate the problematic of return. Those who need to return, who remember the place to which they need to return, are omnipresent in Niro's oeuvre. In such returns, her artistic practice connects with her ancestral memories and ties to the Mohawk Valley and to other regions in the area now called New York State, the traditional homeland and the stronghold of the Haudenosaunee. The people's displacement from this region is not over but instead was and remains an act of settler-colonial violence.[53]

Time travels through us, Niro indicates, by cultural ancestry. Through cultural ancestry—through the Mohawk Turtle Clan depicted by the multiple forms of turtles adorning the women in *Time Travels through Us* (and echoed in the intricate frame of the image)—the Mohawk connection to the land that is now called New York State is manifested. Although Niro photographs her mother and daughters for this portrait in Canada, the awareness of their ancestral land of New York State lives in the signifiers of the Turtle Clan that are essential to this photograph. The Mohawk and the clans that are the integument of their culture emerge from the Mohawk Valley, and yet the history of colonization has displaced them from their land. As historian Alan Taylor contends, "In 1783 the British betrayed the Six Nations by abandoning them to the 'care' of the United States, against whom they had been fighting on the side of the British."[54] This betrayal by their ally led to the Six Nations being victimized by the United States' scorched-earth campaign against them, forcing them through brutal and genocidal tactics to flee their traditional homelands.[55]

Time Travels through Us embodies the consistent use of temporal estrangement with which Niro is so brilliant. In her works, time is present, past, and future. With the three women we are in present time in the park and in future time in the unfolding of the family history and also in the past, present, and future in the signifiers of the Turtle Clan. Time traveling through us is the modality of Niro's worldview expressed in her artwork. Niro rejects colonialist ideologies of time as linear and progressive. Instead, she interprets time as circular, familial, and personal. Time circles; the past returns in the present, and the past moves into the future. In this nonlinear understanding of time, the colonialist project of organizing human beings into pejoratively cordoned "primitive peoples" and so-called advanced civilizations is sharply refuted, revealing the ideological falsehoods at the core of settler-colonialist belief and structures of thought.

Niagara

The location of Niagara Falls is especially significant to Niro's oeuvre. Her film *Niagara* (2015, originally titled *Ongniaahra*) was made in memory of her younger daughter who passed away in tragic circumstances.[56] This short film (a little over four minutes running time) does not make explicit the deeply personal subtext of this mourning. Instead, it performs a ceremony of consolation for everyone watching, offering healing to all who pay attention, rather than closing the film within an explicit autobiographical frame. The story returns to the boundary or border of New York State, to the place now called Niagara Falls—Onguiaahra—a place where powerful forces meet. We see the crashing water at Niagara, a boundary between the spirit world and the world of the living. Overlaid on the image of the falls are captions of a conversation between women. They discuss a dream one of them had in which she saw her deceased grandmother, a dream that made the dreamer happy. Against the backdrop of the hypnotically powerful falling water, the narrative seems both otherworldly and deeply human.

The narrative is given entirely visually through words written and superimposed on the filmic images of swirling water. As the film progresses, the captions intimate that this woman, who had the dream of her grandmother, was the grandmother of a woman the film's narrator has lost. The woman who was lost died suddenly and young after spending time in jail. It is she who is most deeply mourned in the film. The woman to whom the dream is recounted is the daughter of the one who tells the dream and the mother of the one who was in jail, but these deep relationships are not made entirely clear during the film; rather, they are suggested, adumbrated. The use of the pronoun "she" in the film conveys intimacy and makes the identities of the grandmother and granddaughter (as they are to each other) hauntingly blurred, as if they had perhaps passed away around the same time. During the film, the filmmaker is the link between the two deceased women, and it is she whose fingers wipe away the drops of water sprayed on the camera in a gesture representing Peacemaker wiping away tears of bereavement in the Condolence Ceremony.[57] The gesture of wiping the water from the lens, and the tears from the eyes of the bereaved, takes place during moments of deepest sorrow in the film and conveys mourning and healing with extreme subtlety and delicacy.

The film proceeds at a steady, slow, solemnly ceremonial pace. It is an elegy to Niro's youngest daughter yet never mentions her name. It becomes, in effect, also an elegy for all Indigenous North American women whom historical trauma has killed young and erased in our era, this contemporary period in which there is an epidemic of murdered and missing Indigenous women.[58] I discuss this film in further detail later in the book, but it is important to note here that Niro's work agitates against the erasure of Indigenous women, with each photograph and film reclaiming their lives and memory. As Mohawk scholar and theorist Taiaiake Alfred notes, the "condolence ritual pacifies the minds and emboldens the hearts of mourners by transforming loss into strength . . . it fends off destruction of the soul and restores hearts and minds."[59]

In touching on such painful histories through art that restores power in the face of sorrow, Niro's films and photographs fill the museum context with intense energy and emotions and life force; the artworks are not static but vibrant conveyances of power. Anthropologist Marge Bruchac argues of museum objects that we must return animacy to the spaces of our understanding of art.[60] In this book, I seek to illuminate the animacy, the life, pulsing through Niro's visual responses to centuries of colonization.

Seeing Niro's film *Niagara* in the context of the Pocahontas Reframed Film Festival in 2017 and again at her career retrospective in 2023, I was struck by the way the film alters the venues where it was shown—the Byrd Theater in Richmond, Virginia, and the National Museum of the American Indian in New York, respectively—bringing an intense life force to these locales. When Niro's photographic and filmic works cross boundaries of time to bring together holistic themes of Indigenous feminism, they present the Indigenous worldview as luminous and vivid, testifying to a continuing genocidal threat in the face of which the Mohawk people, against great odds, survive and flourish on their own terms. When her work crosses from Canada and returns to New York State, her art depicts the vivid, living spirit of survivance: return. Niagara is a place of return because it is a boundary between New York and Canada, and it is sacred to the Haudenosaunee. The Haudenosaunee are those who continually build the longhouse, those structures that early settlers called *castles*, so well built were they.

Abnormally Aboriginal

Niro's film and photography are touchstones in her brand of feminism that decolonizes the gaze. I use the term "decolonize" in this book specifically in connection to the ways that I am arguing Niro's visual work agitates for—in the style of subtle guerrilla warfare—a shift toward the end of the regime of coloniality and a return of land. Māori artist, scholar, and author Rangihīroa Panoho argues that the word "decolonizing" is itself a fabricated term and, when used in art historical contexts, it is hollow and signifies nothing.[61] He makes a good point in noting the facile way that the word can be used in scholarship that yet emanates from and retains all the power structures of Western colonialist sociality. The structure of coloniality, as Panoho notes, continues to place white men and their proxies in the position of gatekeepers, which is why decolonizing as a word can feel so very empty. And yet my suggestion is that Niro's art meaningfully deconstructs those structures and instates and emplaces Mohawk structures of thought, seeing, and survival. That is why I make the case that her art is actively anticolonialist, even as I recognize Panoho's astuteness in perceiving the dangers of the term's use. Whether my own writing, here in this book and in the many other publications where I address Niro's work, is decolonizing is for the reader to judge. But as a member of academia's precariat, my work is *not* supported by the common structures of coloniality, such as well-funded jobs within academia and the plummy grants that co-occur with such jobs.

In artwork that is decolonizing in frame, intent, and effect, Shelley Niro illuminates the history of the Haudenosaunee in contemporaneity with brilliant, subtle, feminist works that deserve greater critical attention. Looking at her sublime self-portrait triptych, *Abnormally Aboriginal* (figures 1.10–1.12 and figure 1.13), one sees that Niro is an original American, a woman whose ancestors lived in upstate New York until, after the Revolutionary War, General Washington drove them into exile. When she brings her art to New York State, when she creates art *of* New York

Figure 1.10. Frame 1, *Abnormally Aboriginal*, 2014, color inkjet print, 54 in. × 34 in. each. *Source:* Courtesy of the artist.

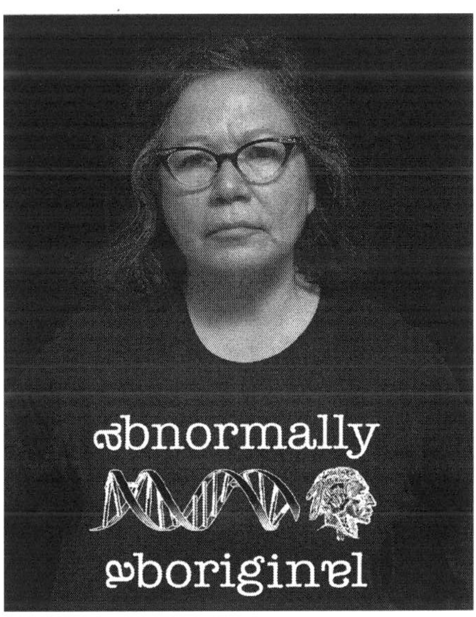

Figure 1.11. Frame 2, *Normal Original*, 2014, color inkjet print, 54 in. × 34 in. each. *Source:* Courtesy of the artist.

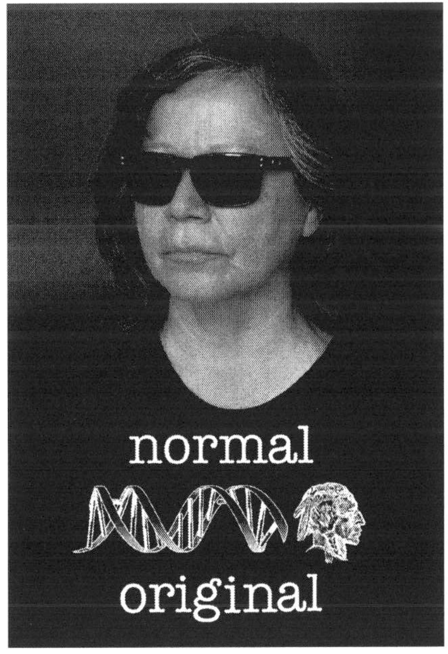

Figure 1.12 Frame 3, *DNA Helix,* 2014, color inkjet print, 54 in. × 34 in. each. *Source:* Courtesy of the artist.

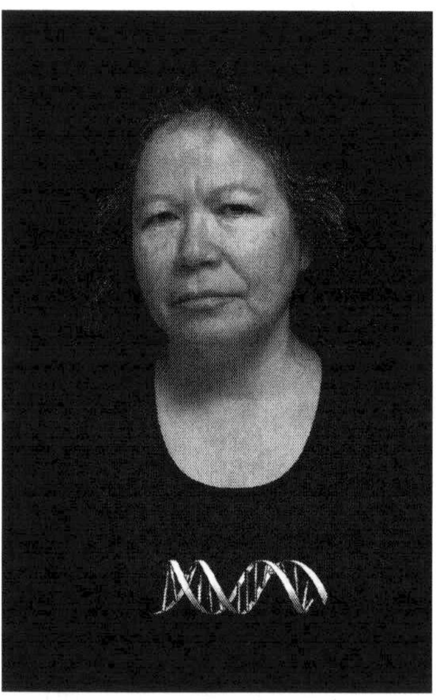

Figure 1.13, *Abnormally Aboriginal*, triptych, 2014, color inkjet prints, 54 in. × 34 in. each. *Source:* Courtesy of the artist.

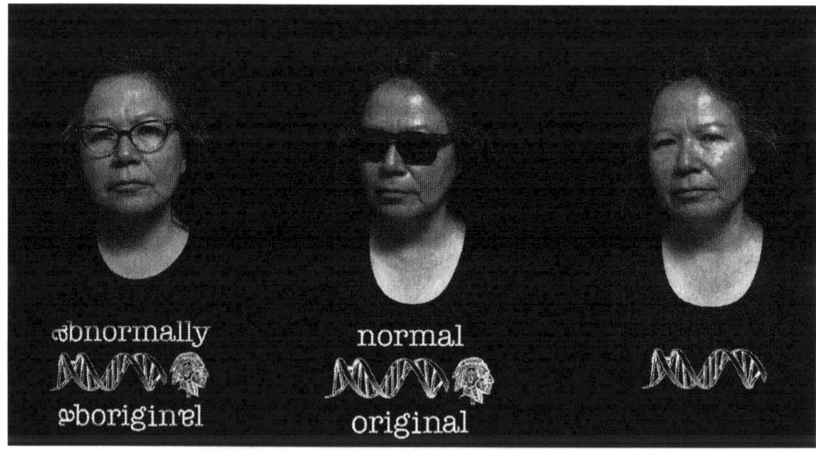

State, Niro shows the power of the homeland even in exile. She reverses the "transit" that settler colonialism makes through not only Indigenous land but also, as scholar Jodi Byrd (Chickasaw) argues, through the very symbolic work of socially conceptualizing indigeneity.[62] Niro's triptych self-portrait (figures 1.10–1.12 and figure 1.13) is itself a return because it shows the face of the artist who—being Mohawk—is of the land we call New York State; she is ancestrally of that land, and the land belongs to her in a way unlike any of the settler descendants who live there now.

In the initial frame, we see the artist wearing cat-eye glasses and watching the viewer inquisitorially. Her middle-aged face is shown without makeup and without coyness. Her gaze is penetrating. Before an entirely black background, she wears a T-shirt with skewed letters stating ABNOR-MALLY ABORIGINAL. This wry and ironic commentary on the artist's identity estranges the idea of being an Indigenous woman because Niro does not see herself as "Aboriginal" or for that matter, "Indigenous," a settler term (and the one that I use in this book), but rather as a member of the Mohawk and the Turtle Clan. The image spoofs and critiques settler-colonialist patterns of taking power by naming others. In the next frame, the artist returns wearing dark glasses. Here, she looks, in the words of Joan Didion (not writing about Niro's art) like a *cool customer*. Her gaze is angled slightly away from the viewer and, still against the black backdrop, she wears a black T-shirt that now says "Normal Original." Here, the false trappings of settler-colonialist naming have been stripped away and we see the artist as she is to herself: normal, the norm, and original, or of the origin. Not only is she original to this land (and by "this land" I mean the area now called New York), but she is also original to herself, as we all are. She makes the point that rubrics that group us by race/ethnicity are merely manifestations of settler-colonialist nation-state governmentality, of herding people to control them. Resisting this control, Niro is her own normal, original self and appears in the image both powerful and in control of the act of being seen. As noted, this triptych, expanded to wall size, faced the visitor at the entrance point to Niro's retrospective, at the National Museum of the American Indian in New York, confronting each person entering the exhibit with the artist's originality, as she defines it.

Chapter 2

Battlefields of Shelley Niro's Ancestors

New York's Mohawk Valley is the traditional stronghold of the Mohawk people pushed north by colonization and scorched-earth campaigns during the eighteenth century. In Shelley Niro's (Six Nations of the Grand River Reserve, Bay of Quinte Kanien'kehá:ka Mohawk Nation, Turtle Clan) activist series of photographs *Battlefields of My Ancestors* and her films *It Starts with a Whisper* (1993) and *Kissed by Lightning* (2009), the act of returning to New York State to lands traditionally central to Mohawk identity and culture is dramatized as metaphysical confrontation. She deploys art to agitate broadly for Indigenous North American access to ancestral lands in what are now called the United States and Canada.

Images from Niro's series of photographs *Battlefields of My Ancestors* (figures 2.1–2.10) retrace the paths of the Mohawk as they were pushed out of New York State into Canada in the eighteenth century, under violent pressure of erasure by the emerging settler-colonialist United States. George Washington's ordering of the genocidal Sullivan-Clinton campaign in 1779 is only the most egregious instance of settler-colonialist displacement and an attempt to erase the Haudenosaunee. In the *Battlefields of My Ancestors* series, Niro returns to what we call New York State to photograph—to document—the places where her ancestors were slaughtered.[1] The series is an exercise in reasserting power and a formal instatement of familial melancholy. The photographs of sites of ancestral loss and erasure—the revivification of ancestral presence through photography—are a subversion of the enforced invisibility of Indigenous peoples in the American cultural imaginary. *Battlefields of My Ancestors* exposes the revelation of the true story of colonization rather than the myths told by the colonizer. It is

Figure 2.1. *Mohawk River*, from *Battlefields of My Ancestors*, 2015, 17 in × 22 in. each, Color duratrans for lightbox. *Source:* Courtesy of the artist.

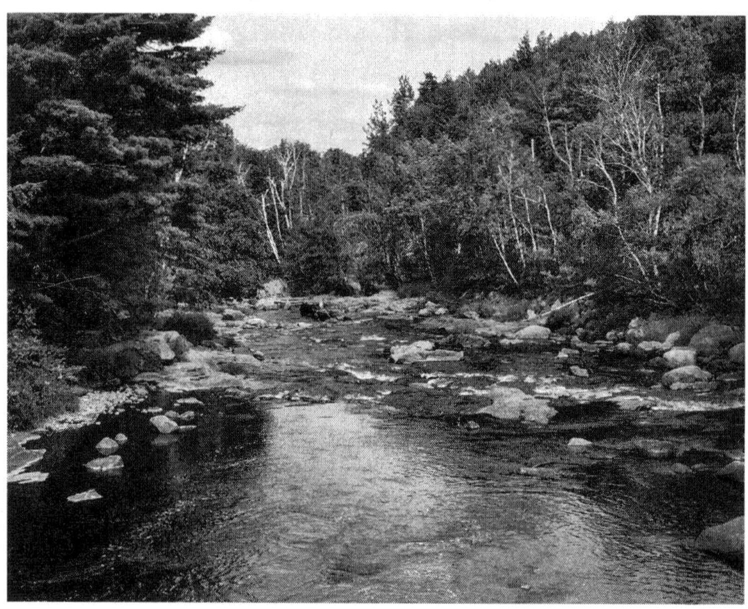

Figure 2.2. *Gar-Non-De-Yo*, from *Battlefields of My Ancestors*, 2015, 17 in × 22 in. each, Color duratrans for lightbox. *Source:* Courtesy of the artist.

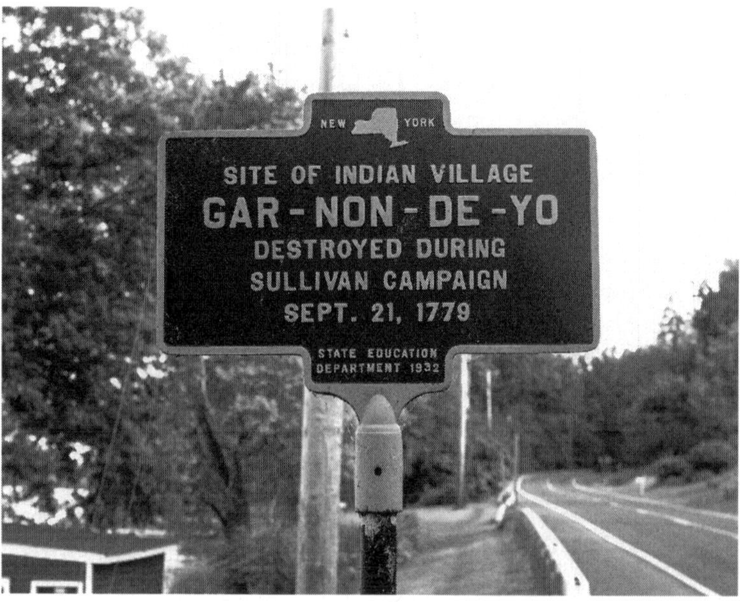

Figure 2.3. *Ten Pretty Indian Houses*, from *Battlefields of My Ancestors*, 2015, 17 in × 22 in. each, Color duratrans for lightbox. *Source:* Courtesy of the artist.

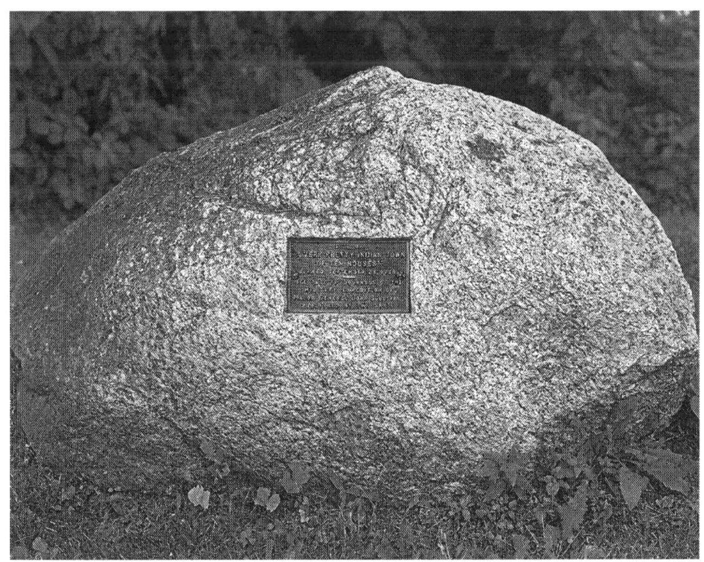

Figure 2.4. *Niagara Falls*, from *Battlefields of My Ancestors*, 2017, 17 in × 22 in. each, Color duratrans for lightbox. *Source:* Courtesy of the artist.

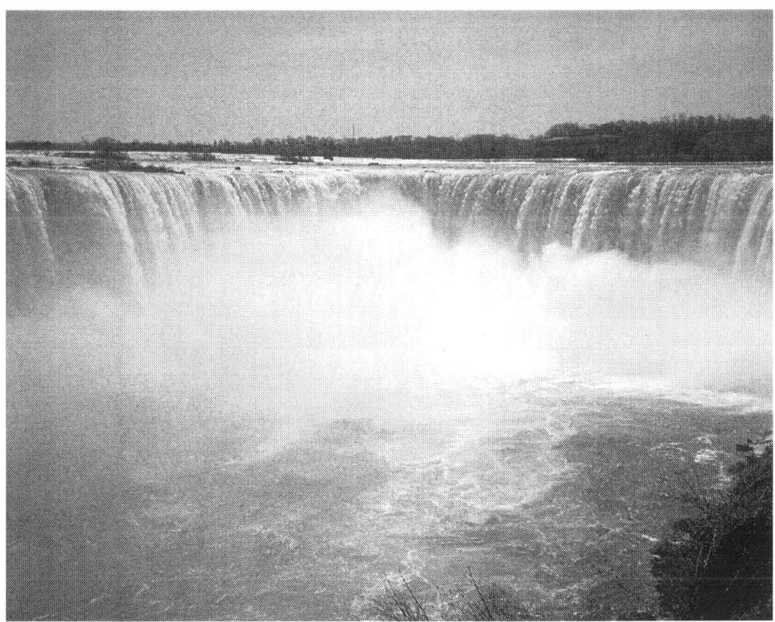

Figure 2.5. *Sullivan-Clinton Campaign*, from *Battlefields of My Ancestors*, 2015, 17 in × 22 in. each, Color duratrans for lightbox. *Source:* Courtesy of the artist.

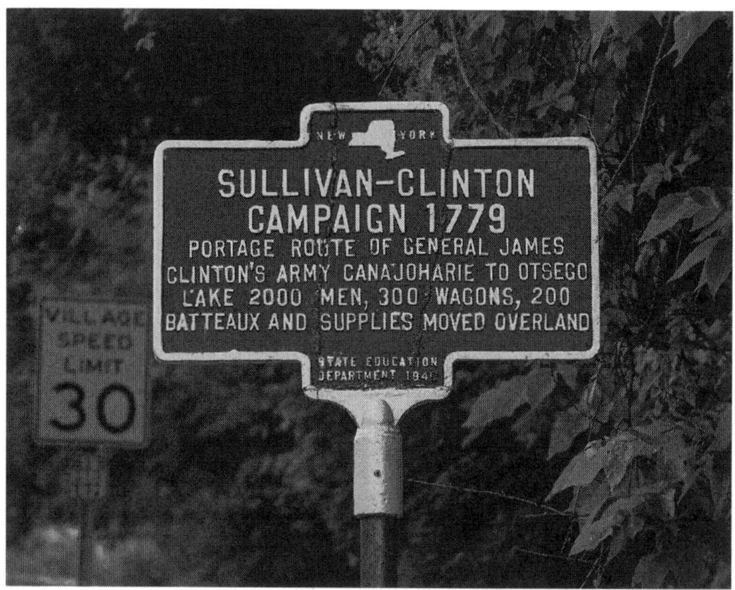

Figure 2.6. *Site of Indian Village*, from *Battlefields of My Ancestors*, 2015, 17 in × 22 in. each, Color duratrans for lightbox. *Source:* Courtesy of the artist.

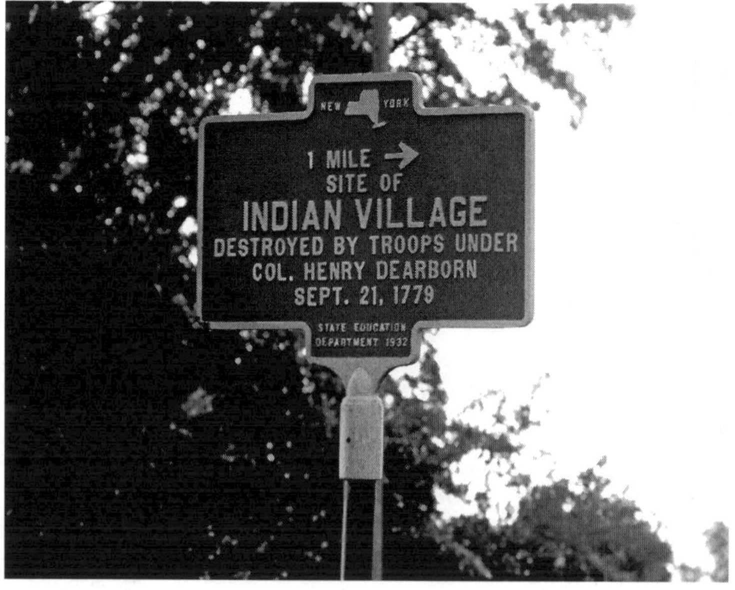

Figure 2.7. *Burrough's Point*, from *Battlefields of My Ancestors*, 2015, 17 in × 22 in. each, Color duratrans for lightbox. *Source:* Courtesy of the artist.

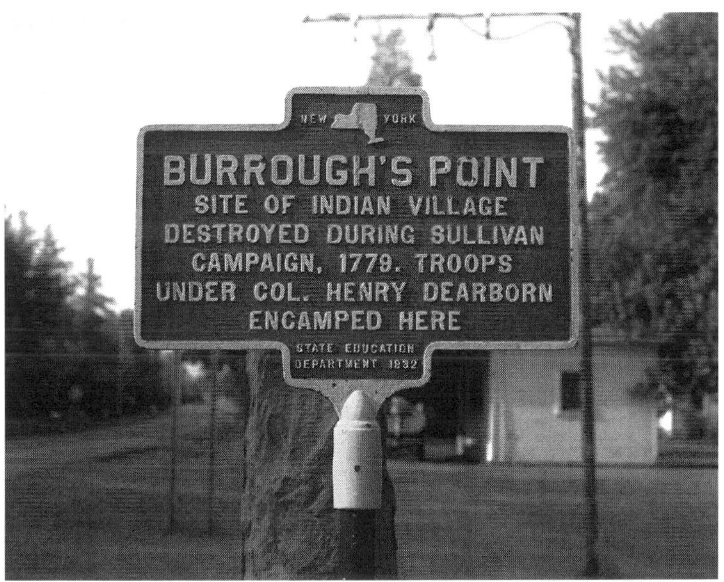

Figure 2.8. *Where the Mohawk Meets the Hudson*, from *Battlefields of My Ancestors*, 2015, 17 in. × 22 in. each, Color duratrans for lightbox. *Source:* Courtesy of the artist.

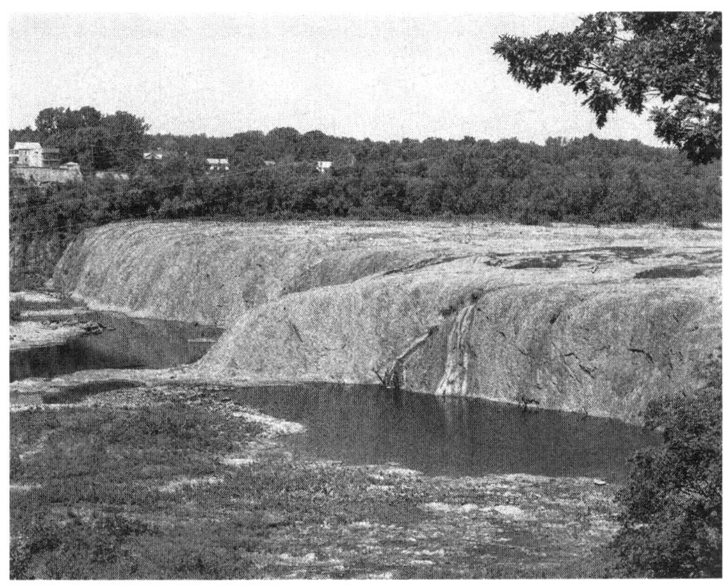

Figure 2.9. *Adirondacks*, from *Battlefields of My Ancestors*, 2015, 17 in. × 22 in. each, Color duratrans for lightbox. *Source:* Courtesy of the artist.

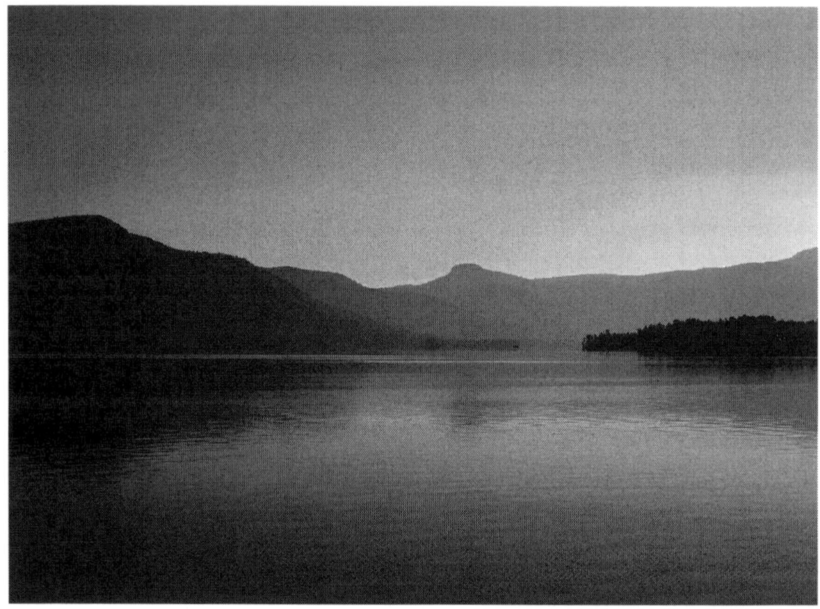

Figure 2.10. *Dean's Cove* from *Battlefields of My Ancestors* 2015, 17 in. × 22 in. each. Color duratrans for lightbox. *Source:* Courtesy of the artist.

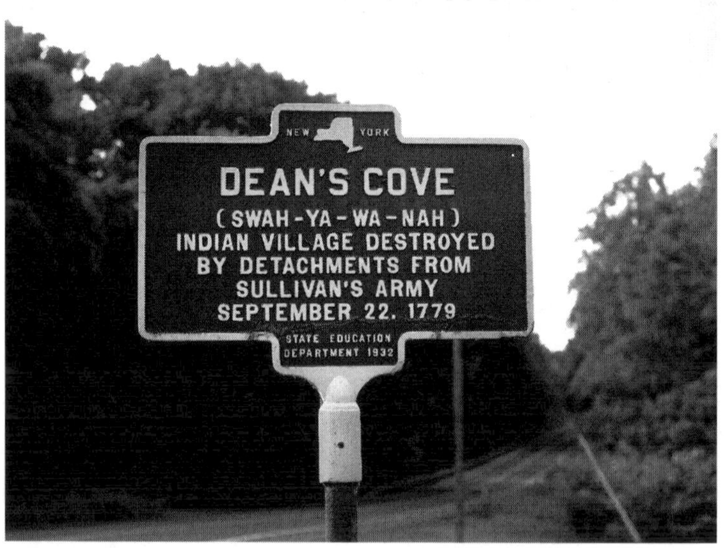

important to emphasize that this photographic series is of a reiterative journey: successive returns to the Mohawk homelands that Niro and her sister and other family members made together over forty years. Slowly, Niro created the painfully made images that are *Battlefields of My Ancestors*; she continues to expand the series, so it is not a closed work but rather one that is ongoing.[2]

Battlefields Across Time

Beginning with a soft and sorrowful image of the Adirondacks and moving to individual images of the Hudson River, the Mohawk River, and Niagara Falls, Niro's *Battlefields of My Ancestors* includes several photographs that focus on New York State plaques commemorating the murder and displacement of Mohawk peoples during the Sullivan-Clinton campaign of 1779. The blue and yellow plaques are quotidian in the settler-colonialist nation-state landscape. They denote "triumphs" of settler-colonialist violence (that is, genocidal violence) that pushed the Mohawk out of their homelands, razed their crops, burned their homes, and killed the people. That the plaques celebrate genocide is a quiet fact of American national history. Niro's subtle photographs show the everyday, "normal" world of New York State—the backroads and nondescript houses, the deep-green summer trees—framing the plaques that celebrate Sullivan's and Clinton's total war (i.e., war that spares no one and nothing) against the Mohawk. The scorched-earth war against the Mohawk was essential to creating the United States as we know it now; genocide is the spine of our nation. Niro's photographs sharply critique this total war, demonstrating how banal the evil of settler colonialism really is. The photographs chillingly reveal how settler-colonialist culture commemorates and celebrates its own acts of violence.

Settler-colonialist nation-states were created with the express purpose of stripping what our own legal system calls Aboriginal title (i.e., the inherent Aboriginal right to land; see chapter 3) from Indigenous North Americans.[3] Indigenous North American nations could look for no benefit from participating in this settler culture because its very existence strove to erase theirs. This is the ideology of "erase and replace" that defines settler colonialism. To create the nation-state entity of New York State depended on erasing and displacing the Six Nations who had long stewarded that land, which served as their traditional homelands.

Audra Simpson (Kahnawà:ke Mohawk) connects juridical epistemology with land theft, noting that an imprimatur of settler-colonialist ways of knowing and legal structures enables the taking of lands "wrested from those that belong to it, and those to whom it rightfully belongs."[4] Such settler-colonialist ways of knowing include Western visual tropes of seeing land and claiming land through such visualization. Landscape photography is a paradigm of such seeing. Niro's *Battlefields of My Ancestors* deftly takes apart the acquisitive settler gaze (of traditional landscape photography) across American lands and replaces this gaze with her Mohawk gaze, expressing not only critique of genocide but also love for the land, devotion to it, and tender mourning for its theft.

Formally, the images in Niro's *Battlefields of My Ancestors* are estrangements of the traditional (Western and colonialist) landscape device of framing land as colonized space. Her *Battlefields* photographs contest and refuse settler-colonialist representational claiming of Indigenous land. In decolonizing the landscape, Niro foregrounds signage that shocks, with its dispassionate evidence of genocidal displacement, while the background shows the land retreating. Pointedly contrasting with foregrounded offensive signage, the land, as Niro evokes it in the images of *Battlefields of My Ancestors,* is tender and perspectivally infinite. It is Indigenous land as seen by an Indigenous artist's camera. As I have suggested in an earlier publication on this important and magisterial series, the formal effect of the series is that of uncanniness.[5] By this I mean that Niro's activist use of foreground and depth of field makes the viewer vividly aware that the normative colonized American landscape of New York State is not gentle. If the settler gaze coverts the suppressed history of genocidal violence against the Six Nations, Niro's photography deploys uncanniness to show us to whom the land rightly belongs. It is not Niro's point of view that is uncanny; rather, her art reveals the uncanniness of the American condition as a space of settler coloniality that does not acknowledge itself as founded on violence.[6] The formal work of the images in *Battlefields of My Ancestors* is to create a visual contestation of American genocide, broadly, and particularly the failure of Aboriginal title to meaningfully protect Indigenous lands for Indigenous peoples.

The photographs of the *Battlefields of My Ancestors* series (figures 2.1–2.10) are melancholy and deeply haunting, emphasizing perspectival force so that the roads seem always too distant and the landmarks too close. The signage that populates many of the images presents an achingly mournful view of history. Placed by the government of New York, the structures appear to celebrate—even commemorate—the killing and displacement of the Haudenosaunee, Niro's ancestors. As Niro photographs these signs, she employs a technique that I find similar to the temporal dissonance in her movies. Where, in her films, Niro estranges time, bringing the past and the present and the future into contiguous and overlapping spaces and moments, in the photographs of *Battlefields of My Ancestors*, Niro employs spatial estrangement, creating haunting vistas where the closeness of the offensive signs plays off the eerie perspectival reaches of the surroundings. Niro's use of roads is spectacular here. In the backgrounds of the signage, the streets always seem to be leading toward hollowness, emptiness, nothingness. The highway system that the nation-state, the United States, has built across Haudenosaunee land is revealed in Niro's photographs as a form of violence. This revelation is historically and aesthetically accurate, for the Haudenosaunee were pushed by military campaigns out of the state and cheated by treaties and dishonest speculators who worked hand-in-glove with state government, specifically to make the land of New York State a place for transport: a place through which settlers could cross westward.[7]

In *Gar-Non-De-Yo* (figure 2.2), a standard "educational" plaque hung by the State of New York in the 1930s (and still maintained today) marks the site of a Haudenosaunee village destroyed during the Sullivan-Clinton campaign; the sign indicates the date of this genocidal act was September 21, 1779. Niro's photograph quietly takes apart the comfortable feel of a rural New York State roadway, asking the viewer to reconsider the terms of celebrating the so-called triumph of progress as settler-colonialist forces destroyed Indigenous property and people. She asks us to imagine that day, September 21, 1779, and the grotesque violence of American troops destroying a Haudenosaunee village. The annihilatory force of settler colonialism is emphasized in this photograph, which centers the plaque, while the roadside on which it is located retreats into melancholic distance.

Niro's photographs extend the uncanny vistas of the nation-state, showing us the ways that Indigenous erasure is at the heart of the settler nation-state project. The image depicting where the Hudson meets the tributary Mohawk (*Where the Mohawk Meets the Hudson*; figure 2.8) is in black and white, taken with analog film. In Niro's characteristic deadpan approach, what we see is at once obvious and mysterious. The photograph, in pale and dark grays, shows a semi-industrial space of a river's confluence. The impact of the image is its placement in Niro's *Battlefields* series. Here the Haudenosaunee participated in one of the bloodiest battles of the Revolutionary War. Strategizing to maintain their presence on their ancestral homeland, the Mohawk allied with the British against the so-called American patriots. During this battle, large numbers of Mohawk men were killed, and it was here that some Haudenosaunee (not Mohawk) decided to side with the American forces, instigating a painful and damaging breach within the Six Nations.[8] The Haudenosaunee's ancestral homeland was a warzone throughout colonization, as settlers fought to push the original people off their land. But during this Revolutionary War period, New York State was particularly bloody. The British strategy of attempting to isolate New England regiments from other parts of the fledgling United States meant that the Haudenosaunee territory was used as a barrier. The Mohawk and other Haudenosaunee, desperately attempting to navigate survival in their ancestral land, strategically fought along with the British. Joseph Brant (Thayendanegea) and his sister, Molly, with her husband, were loyal to the British. The bloodshed of Molly's people—Niro's people—at this battle brought them nothing good. The British did not return the Mohawks' fidelity and loyalty, and despite fighting and dying in alliance with the British, the Mohawk ultimately lost their land.

With this meaning behind her serene photograph of the river, the full message of Niro's *Battlefields of My Ancestors* depends on knowledge that many non-Indigenous Americans do not have in the present day. The battles that ultimately pushed the Mohawk out of the Mohawk Valley are not taught from the Mohawk perspective in mainstream American or Canadian schools. Niro's series turns the lens and asks that we contemplate those losses not as triumphant "progress" toward the settler-colonialist vision of racial-capitalist totality but instead, conversely, as tragic betrayals and genocide of her people. In this way, Niro plies a duality in her work wherein it is legible on a surface level to all viewers—and on a deeper level to some viewers. She is conscious of this duality and purposely structures her work this way.[9] The emotional force of the photographs is accessible to any viewer who takes the time to look.

Niro's love for the land is eloquently expressed in this series. When she photographs the Mohawk River (figure 2.1) and the place where the Mohawk and Hudson Rivers meet (figure 2.8), using analog photography, the tenderness of the images is almost overwhelming. Against the backdrop of the region's violent history, the river is a space of loss and mourning. As the Mohawk are separated from their rivers, the rivers also suffer from the lack of Mohawk stewardship. This site where Peacemaker once stood is now a polluted confluence, abused by settler patterns of industrial-capitalist practices: "For thirty years ending in the late 1970s, the General Electric Company (GE) discharged as much as 1.3 million pounds of polychlorinated biphenyls (PCBs) into the Hudson River from its capacitor manufacturing plants in Hudson Falls and Fort Edward, New York. The PCBs remain in the river sediment."[10] Although some efforts have been made to clean the rivers, they still regularly fill with fecal matter through sewage overflow, and elevated levels of phosphorous lead to toxic algae blooms.[11] The Mohawk River flows through the Mohawk Valley, the very place whose well-managed abundance—the result of Indigenous American stewardship, as Dina Gilio-Whitaker (Colville Confederated Tribes) explains—drew such idyllic descriptions from the earliest settlers.[12] Niro's lens here looks at once through the present and the past. Her view is always deep, through history to the present day, making the connection.

Niro's photographs record not only where Mohawk people were violently treated and displaced but also (interconnected with this displacement) places where the land itself is suffering because of how settler capitalism uses it. The photograph *Niagara Falls* (figure 2.4) reveals the dirtiness of settler-colonialist buildings at the edge of the stunning rapids. Taken from a perspective that shows both the power of the falls and the encroachment of settler colonialism on the land, the photograph is textual documentation of a rigorous melancholy, a clear-sighted vision of the harms of colonization that is not bathetic but plain and real. It reveals that the power of the falls is a force beyond settler pollution even as the polluted water is part of the bitter subtext of the image. And yet, when the artist reaches the Adirondacks, her camera records a scene so peaceful (see figure 2.9) that it exudes the feeling that returning to New York, even in its reopening of painful inherited and personal memory, is also healing for her. When Niro photographs the Adirondacks here in late afternoon, she softens the vista so that we have a deep feeling of homecoming in looking at the image. The Adirondacks, in her photograph, appear as a place of solace and peace but also a place that is unreachable. The sorrow of the scene is heavy. The image seems at once to present a place where one is beckoned to stay and be at home and at peace, yet it is also estranged from the viewer, placed at a distance. The image conveys infinity and grace, showing that the land could never be entirely taken from the Mohawk, whose historical ties to the land reach back millennia. Niro's view, her gaze, becomes the homecoming she shares with us through this photograph.

Return to Battlefields

The quietness of *Battlefields of My Ancestors* belies the forcefulness of its message and its method. Niro, in creating the series, spent years revisiting the sites where her ancestors were killed and displaced. Each visit was a personal submersion in the pain of remembering. The photos titled *Sullivan-Clinton Campaign* (figure 2.5), *Site of Indian Village* (figure 2.6), *Burrough's Point* (figure 2.7), and *Dean's Cove* (figure 2.10) all trace the artist's painful return to New York State. In these images, the light often looks liminal, as if it were evening, as if we'd come to the end of a long day: the weary traveling artist, seeking a way back to her people's homelands, is confronted with settler colonialism's uncanny celebration of its own violence. Finding the sites of Haudenosaunee villages, Niro uncovers the cold markers of their desecration and destruction.

Niro's memories of her birth state (she was born in Niagara Falls, New York), which she left in early childhood to move with her family to Canada, are familial and cultural memories, stories handed down through her father's family for generations so that the memory of the Mohawks' ancestral homeland is potent and well known to her. She grew up hearing her father describe the area of the Mohawk Valley like the promised land, even though he had never been there and was retelling memories shared by his grandmother.[13] The geography of New York State stays with the Mohawk people many generations after they were largely forced out of their homeland. Returning through art is a political act, a form of activism.

Because the pain and intensity of feeling while being back in her homeland can become overwhelming, Niro notes that she creates this series very slowly, pacing herself.[14] This comment yields insight into her art: the practice of looking at painful history is coupled in her work with restraint. There is a sense of abiding grace that permeates the photographs and films, even as they encounter the pain of genocide. Yet, survival, thriving, and resurgence are at the core of her practice, as she locates the ability to create art, poetry, films, and knowledge as the way to survive and thrive. This essential quality to her work is voiced through Charlie B.'s lyric poetry in *The Incredible 25th Year of Mitzi Bearclaw* (2019), and it is spoken by Niro herself, as she explains that what gives her hope for her people's future is the flourishing of art—film, television, theater, photography, poetry, fiction, scholarship—being created by Indigenous North Americans.[15]

Art is deeply connected to land in Shelley Niro's work. The act of returning to New York to create art, and to show her art, is—as her brother, the historian Michael Doxtater (Thohahoken), puts it—a small war, *petite guerre*, or art as guerrilla warfare against colonialist land theft. Each time she returns to reclaim New York as her ancestral land, a skirmish is won for the Mohawk. As geographer and theorist Natchee Blu Barnd notes,

> The American colonial project was effectively centered on encouraging particular kinds of Native mobility (relocation, land session, assimilation) while discouraging other kinds (use rights, internal trade routes, counter-colonial alliances, revitalization movements, sovereignty) all the while using this complex of interventions to subsidize and facilitate broader European American capacities for and possibilities of mobility. In short, Native people were moved away or out of the way so White people could move around and settle down. Indeed, settler space is secured and defined only when Indigenous mobility is denied, and only through this denial.[16]

By going back to New York State, her ancestors' homeland, Niro denies settler-colonialist regimes that control Indigenous movement. She moves; she goes home. When Mavis Dogblood, in *Kissed by Lightning*, drives out of Canada and into New York, she is a figure for Shelley Niro, pushing back into the territory that is still, by ethical rights, Haudenosaunee. Likewise, each image that Niro creates of New York State for *Battlefields of My Ancestors* performs a refutation of settler geographies.

Niro's series *Battlefields of My Ancestors* is the visualization of an ongoing double journey. The road signs not only mark hideous moments of Mohawk displacement but also connote Niro's own embodied return to the homeland along the roads that are now conscripted by the settler nation-state. This double journey of returning to the place from which the ancestors were displaced is critical to the subtle aesthetic of the works. The vanishing points of roads are strategically emphasized in her photographs so that we feel in our bones the sense of an incomplete journey, a journey that painfully goes on because the resolution, the stable homecoming, cannot occur in the settler-colonialist nation-state status quo.

Battlefields of My Ancestors makes visible the obscene terms of settler colonialism's attempted erasure of Indigenous presence. At her 2023 retrospective, the images of this series were shown sequentially on a plasma screen so that, as the viewer stood still in front of the display, the places where the Mohawk fought for the land appeared before their eyes and then passed on. This transient display brought home the depth of loss the Mohawk have endured. The trope of settler nation-states is to create the illusion that the land of the nation-state is properly and aptly in the possession of settler colonialists. This is reflected in the normalizing of the haunting plaques that signify the settler state's celebration of the geno-cidal acts committed on its land, now home to New York State's touristed backways. Niro's return is quietly observant. The act of returning to New York, returning to the land, returning to the place of her ancestors with her camera witnessing, disturbs settler colonialism's seamless fake—the false belief that America's land is always already settler land.

Resurgence and Indigenous Stewardship

Where the Mohawk Meets the Hudson (figure 2.8) maps territory that Niro reencounters in her short film *Peacemaker's Test* (2020). It is here, where the Mohawk and Hudson Rivers meet, that Peacemaker proved himself as a prophet of peace. In her work *Peacemaker's Test*, Niro explores the historical and cultural meanings, for the Haudenosaunee, of this place of union. Niro explains, "*Peacemaker's Test* is the sacred place on the edge of a city called the Cohoes." Of the place where the rivers join, she tells us: "This is where the Peacemaker was challenged to prove he was the prophet the territories had been waiting for. After centuries of violence among the tribes, he appears, promising peace. He survives after being thrown into the waterfalls where the Mohawk River meets the Hudson. This is the beginning of the Iroquois/Haudenosaunee Confederacy."[17] The color video, which returns to the same site as Niro's earlier black-and-white analog photograph, allows us to imagine Peacemaker's survival. It allows us to envision the survival of peace in the place now called New York State. As author Alicia Elliott (Haudenosaunee) eloquently notes, "Shelley Niro's work reminds us that beauty is always apparent, if we remember to look for it. It's just as evident in the sublime terror and awe of the thundering waterfall of *Peacemaker's Test* as it is in the smallest fossils of prehistoric life in *Resting Place of Our Ancestors*," a four-photograph series painted by Niro in 2019.[18] As noted earlier, the place of the rivers' confluence, like the rivers themselves, bears the scars of heavy industrial pollution; however,

Niro's view of the rivers echoes eloquently on many levels. Retaining a vision of this location as the place graced by Peacemaker, she symbolically reclaims it from the violence and contamination.

The British betrayal of the Haudenosaunee, and the United States' stripping the people of their traditional land in what is now called New York State, is especially sharp given the history of agreements that the federal government and New York State backed out of. Historian Louis Knafla reminds us that "the Iroquois Confederacy [the Six Nations] was promised statehood in the late eighteenth century," and yet, "from the 1780s onward [after the Sullivan-Clinton campaign] Six Nations lands were taken indiscriminately by settlers."[19] Stealing land from the Six Nations was integral—not tangential—to creating New York State[20]; land stolen from the Six Nations *became* New York State.

Still, the Haudenosaunee were able, in previous centuries, to resist colonialist absorption.[21] Historian John Demos indicates the length and depth of the Mohawk resistance: "The 1660s [we]re a time of particular crisis—war ha[d] become a way of life for the Mohawk" because their land and their lives had been invaded by European forces who burned their houses and settlements to the ground.[22] In other words, war was *not* always a traditional way of life but became so out of necessity during colonization. This is a significant point. Guy Johnson, William Johnson's nephew, wrote that the Mohawks' "natural genius" was for warfare, apparently without reflecting on the obvious fact that the Mohawk had been under invasion for centuries (by the time Guy arrived in the late eighteenth century) and had risen to the challenge of becoming genius at surviving.[23] Legal scholar Rebecca Tsosie (Yaqui) notes that what is needed now is for Indigenous people to assert their own stories.[24] Niro's work is part of this effort. Her photography shows us what these colonialist wars were all about.

As Niro indicates in *It Starts with a Whisper* (1993) and the photograph *500 Year Itch* (1992), the Mohawk have been navigating and surviving colonization and genocide for over five hundred years. Following Haudenosaunee law means adhering to ethics communicated to the people by the Creator or Life-Giver with ethics that are shared and communal.[25] By contrast, settler law is, by definition, adversarial. As Knafla points out, during colonization, settler laws and notions of property were used to "extinguish Indigenous title in a discriminatory manner."[26] Professor Haijo Westra draws on the work of sixteenth-century Mexican theologian Alonso de la Vera Cruz to argue that land stolen from Indigenous North Americans resulted from wars that lacked just causes and therefore were not legal, according to Grotius's "just war" theory of land theft.[27] Similarly, Westra notes that, during the seventeenth century, theologian Francis Sylvius held that there was no ethical or legal right for settlers to take lands that clearly had long belonged to the Indigenous peoples of North America.[28]

Westra emphasizes that settler law was deployed to strip Indigenous peoples of their land without their consent, and therefore is, even by settler definitions, extralegal. The difference in the meaning of the land, between settler and Indigenous cultures, is starkly connected to capitalist structures of commodification. As environmental ethicist Brian Ballantyne explains, Indigenous land is "not a commodity but the heritage of the community, the dwelling place of generations."[29] The traditional Haudenosaunee concept of land not as commodity but as *the dwelling place of generations* repeatedly calls Shelley Niro back to New York State. Stories passed down through the generations of her family after they were forced out of New York filled the artist's mind when she was a child. As she grew up, she had a notion of what the Mohawk Valley was like, the image of it in her mind, even though she never visited it until she was older.[30] These ideas and this influence shape *Battlefields of My Ancestors*.

Mohawk historian Michael Doxtater explains that the traditional peace that the tribes maintained through the structure of the clans—the Bear, the Wolf, the Turtle—prevented the kind of annihilating wars that settler colonialists brought to the American continent.[31] Deeply ingrained and long-practiced traditions of ensuring safety and survival for everyone in the Six Nations (as opposed to only for those "on top" of the social order) mean that Mohawk sociality is structured on the practice of mutual decision-making. The people of the flint's brutal treatment at the hands of the US settler-colonialist military drove them north, out of the Mohawk Valley, but the land of New York State remains valuable to the people, and it remains *of* the original people. This is because, for thousands of years, the Haudenosaunee practiced the traditions that ensured peace. Scholar Richard Hill (Tuscarora), paraphrasing the words of an unnamed Mohawk elder whose voice was recorded by anthropologist J. N. B. Hewitt a century ago, notes that "the concept of duality in Haudenosaunee philosophy [is] a reciprocity that exists in all things."[32]

Of Haudenosaunee traditional belief, Richard Hill notes, "The idea was that this beautiful earth was given to us . . . Everybody gets their equal share . . . so it's about sharing the resources of this land. But in order to share it there are some simple rules. One is you only take what you need."[33] The purpose of gathering information about Indigenous people's beliefs, continues Hill, is "to pass it on to people like myself" (to knowledge-keepers who are members of the tribal nation); "otherwise, they [non-Indigenous researchers] come to our communities, harvest all the knowledge, get all of the objects, and off it goes, and you never see them again."[34] Shelley Niro concurs with this understanding and registers deep frustration with interpretations of her work that put it in a box so as to "diminish its power."[35]

In his presentation "The Four Worlds of Onkwehonwe Life, Prophecy and Memory," Michael Doxtater makes clear that the Great Law of the Haudenosaunee concerns planting the Celestial Tree (the Sky World tree) on Earth.[36] In the connection between peace and place, land is not incidental but vital to the Great Law of Peace. The settler-colonialist, capitalist notion of land as a consumable resource does not tally with the traditional Six Nations' belief that comprehends land as part of the moral and ethical way that the people—including the Mohawk, as the people who strike a spark—live. To the Mohawk, then, the land of what is now called New York State is not just a piece of real estate worth however much in a market economy (this would be the point of view of settler-colonialist, racial capitalism); instead, the land is intrinsically part of the moral and ethical way of living for the Six Nations. Civilization, as the Mohawk have developed it over millennia, is entwined with the land.[37]

Historian Daniel K. Richter explains that the reach of the Mohawk homeland had to be vast to accommodate traditional practices of agriculture and periodic rebuilding of longhouses.[38] The landscape was infused with spiritual meaning, with the understanding that the land and animals were direct descendants of their original role in the Sky World prototypes, which the Good Twin (De'hae'hiyawa'k 'hon/Sky Grasper) had created on Earth; with the aid of his father, Turtle Man, Sky Grasper created the nourishing world in which human beings can live, and he also created humans.[39] In the cultural memory of this creation, the role of place is essential; hence, belonging to the area now called New York State is not incidental and random but purposeful and sustaining.[40] In creating peace, abundance, and "Good Mind," the Mohawk took trade and peace to be one thing.[41] Doxtater explains that the ethics of reciprocity and exchange were and are essential to Mohawk views of what it means to be human on this Earth, with peace and spiritual power shaping human relationships.[42] From Mohawk cosmology and ethics, suggests Doxtater, emerge ethics of alliance, the Great League of Peace and Power.[43] Power is what emerges from alliance, reciprocity, and spirit. Peace and power are thus entwined—not opposite but flowing together. Scholar and educator Ned Blackhawk (Te-Moak tribe of the Western Shoshone) emphasizes that the Great League of Peace long precedes contact.[44]

Deganawidah/Tekanawite, the Peacemaker, offered words of condolence to the bereaved Hiawatha,[45] who became the Peacemaker's aid in sharing the news of peace with the people.[46] These ceremonial words of condolence and the accompanying exchange of gifts signify the values of the Haudenosaunee, which Richter glosses as "imperturbable; patient; good will; selfless."[47] Notably, in this traditional Haudenosaunee social structure, male elders and leaders were not the sole locus of power; instead, women—Clan Mothers—were equally socially powerful. In traditional Haudenosaunee decision-making, coercion was never used. Instead, consensus and mutual agreement were the goal.[48] But the political power of Haudenosaunee women (within their communities) was sharply diminished by settler-colonialist policies, a theme that Mohawk theorist and educator Audra Simpson unpacks in *Mohawk Interruptus*.[49] In her photographic series *La Pieta*, Shelley Niro mourns the losses imposed by colonialist wars from a decisive Indigenous feminist perspective, fusing her understanding of colonialist wars, traditional Haudenosaunee ethics of peace, and the maternal gaze.

La Pieta

In the haunting conceptual series *La Pieta* (figures 2.11–2.16), Niro returns to New York State to create the second photograph of the seven-image series (see figure I.2). This area is deeply connected with Mohawk history and, in particular, with a memory of a time of peace and balance. As Mohawk historian Michael Doxtater explains: "Before 1492 Indigenous people had developed a civilization that produced a cornucopia, infrastructure, and a social structure as sophisticated as any in the world. As an advanced civilization, Indigenous people possessed a conception of the good life that was communicated in signs and symbols that still exist. Everyone gets to eat. Everyone gets to be healed. Everyone gets to be happy."[50] Doxtater refers to the moral imperative to restore balance to the world and notes four foundational principles of Mohawk belief: peace (*skennen*), sovereignty (*tentewatoweiehake*), freedom (*enkatatariwasnie*), and democracy (*ensewennasohnhake*).[51] He states that the signs and symbols of these fundamental principles are encoded into the pattern of building the traditional longhouse and into patterns of wampum, "Tekeni Tiiohate Onekehnrha

Figure 2.11. *Passage #1, La Pieta*, 2007, giclée printed canvas, five panels: 101.6 cm × 152.4 cm; two panels: 71.12 cm × 152.4 cm. *Source:* National Museum of the American Indian purchase from the artist. through the You Me Gallery (Hamilton, Ontario), 2009. Used with permission of the artist.

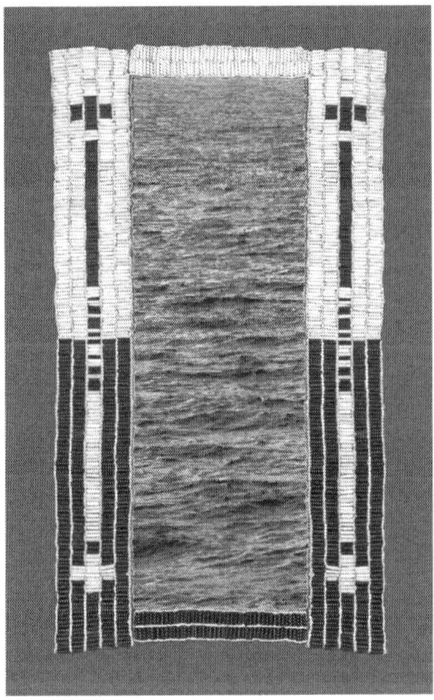

Figure 2.12. Sorrow, *La Pieta*, 2007, giclée printed canvas, five panels: 101.6 cm × 152.4 cm; two panels: 71.12 cm × 152.4 cm. *Source:* National Museum of the American Indian purchase from the artist through the You Me Gallery (Hamilton, Ontario), 2009. Used with permission of the artist.

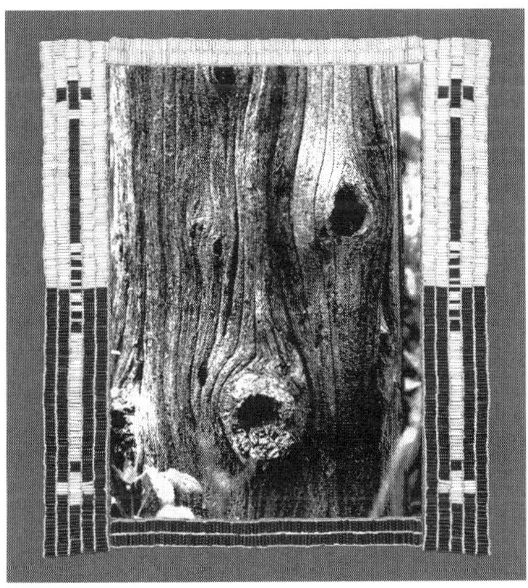

Figure 2.13. Hearing Trees Fall, *La Pieta*, 2007, giclée printed canvas, five panels: 101.6 cm × 152.4 cm; two panels: 71.12 cm × 152.4 cm. *Source:* National Museum of the American Indian purchase from the artist through the You Me Gallery (Hamilton, Ontario), 2009. Used with permission of the artist.

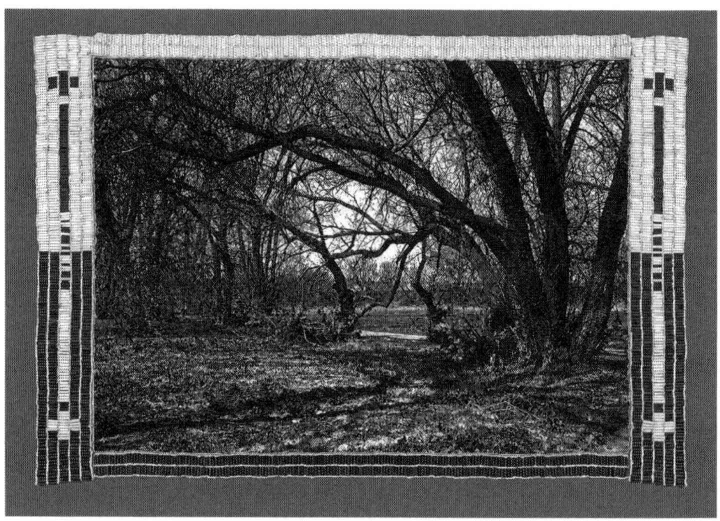

Figure 2.14. Tomorrow, *La Pieta*, 2007, giclée printed canvas, five panels: 101.6 cm × 152.4 cm; two panels: 71.12 cm × 152.4 cm. *Source:* National Museum of the American Indian purchase from the artist through the You Me Gallery (Hamilton, Ontario), 2009. Used with permission of the artist.

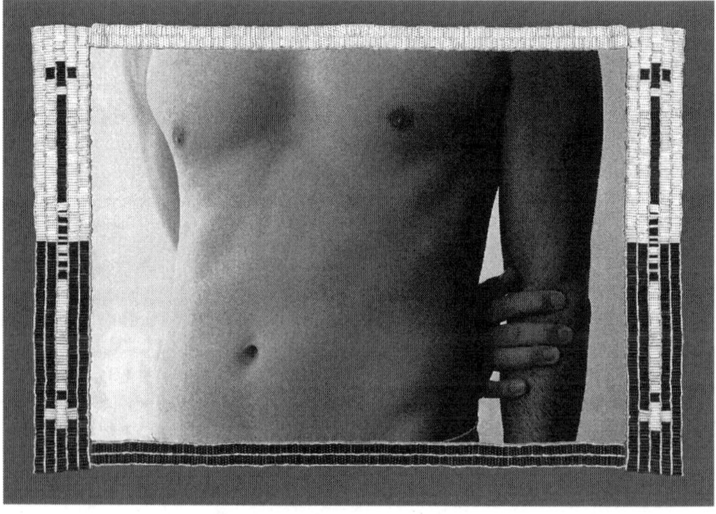

Figure 2.15. On the Edge of Awakening, *La Pieta*, 2007, giclée printed canvas, five panels: 101.6 cm × 152.4 cm; two panels: 71.12 cm × 152.4 cm. *Source:* National Museum of the American Indian purchase from the artist through the You Me Gallery (Hamilton, Ontario), 2009. Used with permission of the artist.

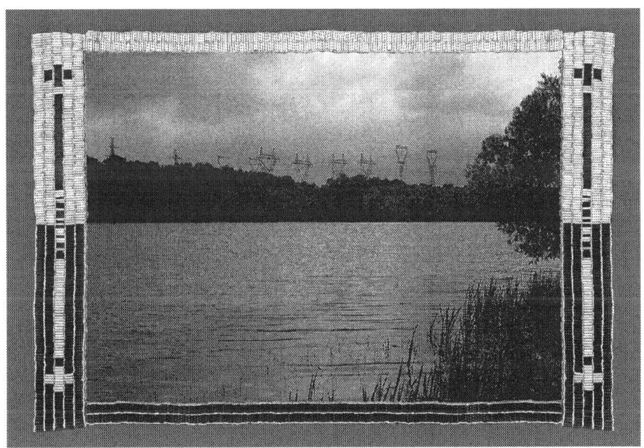

Figure 2.16. Passage #2, *La Pieta*, 2007, giclée printed canvas, five panels: 101.6 cm × 152.4 cm; two panels: 71.12 cm × 152.4 cm. *Source:* National Museum of the American Indian purchase from the artist through the You Me Gallery (Hamilton, Ontario), 2009. Used with permission of the artist.

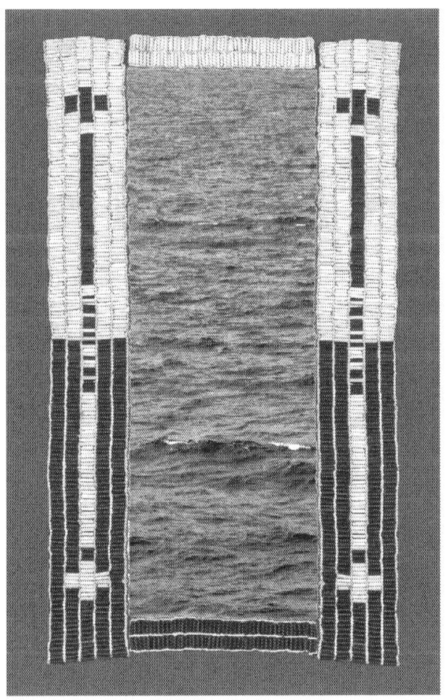

Ontatirihwa' atashera."[52] The longhouse, then, and the Haudenosaunee as the people who build the longhouse, is not simply an architectural practice but a spiritual and ethical one. As Doxtater explains, a "civilization based on peace, and the power of reasonable thinking by the United people," is the Haudenosaunee tradition, a tradition disturbed (to put it mildly) by colonization. In this tradition, "no one is healed until we're all healed."[53] It is the communal ethics of Indigenous tradition that Doxtater emphasizes. Siblings Doxtater and Niro are Turtle Clan. The traits and responsibilities of the Turtle Clan—to keep balance and to understand the other side—recur in Niro's work that manifests returns to New York State.

In her photographic series *La Pieta*, the water that opens and closes the series references birth and death. "Water brings us into and out of this world," states Niro in her artist's notes to this series.[54] The image of shining blue Pacific water (which Niro understands as a sign of birth) prepares us for a return to New York State, as the following image is a calm and haunting photograph of the Mohawk Valley. Niro captured the photo while standing opposite on a mountain in late afternoon, so it has the feeling of a gaze coming from above, and the image seems to reach into the eternal, reconnecting Niro, a Mohawk woman, with the Mohawk Valley that is the place of her ancestors. Doxtater, writing on the effect of the Sullivan-Clinton campaign on the Haudenosaunee, argues that the people's population before this devastation was well over a million, whereas afterward it dwindled to fewer than forty thousand. He notes that George Washington, "village burner," was a key source of this genocidal violence against the Indigenous people of New York.[55] As Niro's photographic series *La Pieta* is a meditation on the harms of war, in particular the harms of settler-colonialist total war, it is apt and appropriate that Niro returns to New York, her homeland, for parts of the series because this area is the key scene of the worst military pillaging to impact the artist's ancestors. The land theft did not begin nor end with the Sullivan-Clinton campaign.

In the second treaty of Buffalo Creek (1838), the Mohawk and other Six Nations members signed an agreement to "cede and relinquish to the United States all their right, title, and interest to the lands secured to them at Green Bay by the Menominee Treaty of 1831, excepting the following tract, on which a part of the New York Indians now reside."[56] This forced and unjust stripping of Haudenosaunee lands created a territory to which return is necessary and essential. Doxtater contends that the Haudenosaunee ultimately need to rekindle the sacred fire that was lost through the treaties of Buffalo Creek.[57]

Niro returns to New York, in the second image of the series, as the place of peace. In Niro's photograph *Infinite View* (see figure I.2), which shows the Mohawk Valley, waterways appear as life-giving. Viewing the series, the power of the water is preeminent, framed by wampum in the pattern that signifies the connection between earth and sky, the living and the dead, and red that signifies blood, death, and life.[58] As *La Pieta* develops, it is a poignant argument against all colonialist wars that cause so much suffering not only for Indigenous peoples but also for all the mothers, including settler-colonialist mothers, who lose their sons to this needless warfare. The artwork is committed to protesting total war, the kind of war that typifies racial-capitalist, settler-colonialist societies. This protest must be couched in a return to origins, a return to the original place of the Mohawk because it is the stripping of land from the people, and the expulsion of the people from the land, that is fundamental to the template of total war that guides settler-colonialist society. *La Pieta* combines the photograph of the Mohawk Valley with images from Canada, juxtaposing the beauty and serenity of the people's ancestral homeland with the roughness of what has happened to them and where they are now. This return to ancestral land, of deploying art to reclaim stolen land and to mourn lost lives, is subtle and enigmatic. Looking at the series of images, we see water, ravaged earth, a young man's torso, power lines, and again blue water. The images take effect cumulatively through slow contemplation; or, as Niro has described the effect of her art: "The more you have something, the more you look at it, the more you think about it, you can develop layers of your own knowledge and put it into the work. . . . It's very multilayered and sometimes I don't understand what I'm doing until it gets done."[59]

By contemplating the photographs of *La Pieta*, we sink through layers of meaning. We can approach the work through awareness of Michelangelo's *La Pieta* (1498–99), the sculpture of the Virgin holding the dead body of the crucified Christ. Through this poignance and pain of the mother's loss of her son, Niro connects the suffering of Indigenous North Americans as victims of genocidal campaigns, including the Haudenosaunee who were forced out of New York, with the suffering of all mothers whose sons are fodder for settler-colonialist wars. In this way, she can be understood to not only critique settler colonialism but also to offer and extend empathy to those *within* settler colonialism who also suffer the violence of this regime, in particular, most women. Michelangelo's *La Pieta*, created at a time when settler colonization was new and when the genocide of Indigenous North Americans was not yet enacted, makes Niro's reference to the Italian *Pieta* all the more moving. When Michelangelo created his work articulating tragic maternal suffering, the great genocide of Indigenous North Americans was just about to occur. This, the largest known holocaust, was set in motion during the first contact of 1492. The suffering of the land when Indigenous stewards are forced off it is parallel, in Niro's work, to the suffering of the people who were made to leave their ancestral territory. She speaks of the land of New York as the "maternal homeland" of the Haudenosaunee.[60]

As the series progresses, we move from water (figure 2.11, *Passage #1*) to the beauty and calm of the Mohawk Valley (figure I.2, *Infinite View*) to the ravaged tree (figure 2.12, *Sorrow*) and vulnerable torso of a young man (figure 2.13, *Hearing Trees Fall*), returning to the scene of the Earth in desolate winter (figure 2.14, *Tomorrow*) and monstrous power lines above the Grand River (figure 2.15, *On the Edge of Awakening*), before finally returning to the water (figure 2.16, *Passage #2*). This sense of cyclical suffering and hard-won survival pervades Niro's work generally, as a deep awareness of history, not only as loss but also as return and healing. The ravaged tree photographed at close range becomes an emblem of suffering and also survival. The winter forest, photographed from a slight distance, suggests a time of liminality where, from death, Earth can find a way back, ultimately to healing and to life. The young man's torso, tenderly evoked at close range, parallels the ravaged tree, and the title of the image, *Hearing Trees Fall*, emphasizes this connection. The artist notes that, in war, young men's bodies are like "fallen trees," used up and destroyed. The power lines above the river look like monsters, yet *On the Edge of Awakening* suggests that it is the river, and the Mohawk people themselves, who are on the edge of resurgence, of reclaiming sovereignty and ultimately land.

Niro does not offer easy resolutions but strives for truthful recognitions. Her *La Pieta* quietly but surely questions the centrality of settler-colonialist art as the foundation of valuable aesthetics. It is not that Niro critiques or dislikes Michelangelo—she has spoken of her admiration for his art—but rather that, by naming her work "La Pieta," she critiques the position of settler art as defining and effectively supervising Indigenous artworks.[61] She parallels the intense sorrow experienced by believers just after Christ's lifeless body comes down from the cross with the grief and mourning following the genocide of Indigenous North Americans.

Moreover, Niro's *La Pieta* invokes through its photographic journey the genocidal campaigns that pushed the Haudenosaunee out of New York. The work, as she makes clear in her artist's statement, is both an articulation of Haudenosaunee history as victims of US treachery, betrayal, and genocidal violence, and a broad reflection on war and mortality as such.[62] As Niro comments in her artist's statement, "Mothers will cry forever." The sorrow of the mother is expressed only in figural terms in settler-colonialist myths of Christ's sacrifice, but Niro's Mohawk rendition of the theme widens and deepens the meaning of this loss because her work includes the ways that being human connect deeply with the land, the Earth. In Niro's *La Pieta*, the Haudenosaunee loss of their homeland is mourned, and the land's suffering in losing the Haudenosaunee manifests in searingly poignant and mysterious images framed by wampum. She writes, "The maternal homeland still waits for the return of her people."[63] In this sense of potency, conveyed by the poetic images of the series, inheres the resurgence of Niro's work: the ability to move beyond resistance to return to the land.

La Pieta deploys photography as a mode of witness with Niro's characteristic subtlety. To understand precisely how this is a work of return requires background knowledge of Mohawk dispossession. Without that history, the mysterious pull of the images allows you to experience a general sense of return and of mourning. As Niro states, in her art it is always the goal to offer viewers experience on multiple levels: the surface level that most everyone can ascertain and the deeper level that requires historical knowledge to access.[64] Niro's work is often called accessible, and yet this surface accessibility is only the entryway to its meaning. Her art unfolds and rejoins through deeper layers of historical and cultural allusion.

The use of wampum in *La Pieta* is highly original. When I presented a short paper on Niro's *La Pieta* at the College Art Association annual conference, an audience member questioned whether it was appropriate for me to call the design framing Niro's La Pieta "wampum," given the history of wampum as a means of recording Mohawk history and formalizing treaties.[65] After that conference, I spoke with Niro about her use of wampum, and she vigorously argued that precisely because of wampum's history as a tool of inscribing memory and codifying treaty agreements (wampum as a form of inscribed language, a tangible notation system for making agreements and making permanent the memory of them), it belongs as the frame of *La Pieta*.[66] For *La Pieta* itself is a kind of treaty—an inscription of memory and a signifier of the Mohawk relationship to the land. It is a work of quiet and great suffering, mapping the Mohawk expulsion from the homelands, laying the foundation for return.

Scholar Audra Simpson argues that geography is crucial to resistance. Simpson eloquently shows how the nation-state practice of ignoring the Jay Treaty (1794) creates continuing dispossession in Mohawk lives.[67] Reflecting on the tragedy of Mohawk displacement and dispossession of their land, a tragedy that is the result of settler-colonialist violence, Niro's *La Pieta* expansively mourns the loss of New York State as the place where the Mohawk have lost access to and control of their ancestral territory. Comprehending this loss in its connection to mortality as such, Niro deploys the wampum pattern. In her words:

> I began by thinking of poppies and how they have become the symbol of past wars. We immediately know what their place is. I was going to put a representation of what a poppy might look like in wampum beads. I was also thinking about what Tom Porter had said as he explained a wampum belt he was holding at a gathering many years ago. The belt he held was held up and down, not sideways. There was something that looked like a cross. He said anthropologists say this design was influenced by the church. He said this symbol is confused with the Christian cross. But he went on to explain it is a traditional symbol showing the spirit world and the Earth. There was a line representing the earth and a shorter line continuing showing the Sky World and the direction your spirit leaves once you pass on. Remembering that story, I started to make a wampum belt representing war and keeping in mind a poppy. I wanted this belt to also have a balance of black and white. Good and bad. . . . I wanted the red cloth behind the belt to be obvious about representing bloodshed. Together with the beads and the red broadcloth, I wanted to contain the photos, to be seen as [a] Haudenosaunee comment of how we are aware of the outside world and we are affected by the activity of outside forces.[68]

Wampum expands the reach of the photographic series *La Pieta*, formalizing it as a Haudenosaunee response to genocidal practices that have pushed the people off their lands. This artwork is a treaty working toward peace, reconciliation, and return. Haudenosaunee historian Richard Hill notes, "Wampum beads aren't just beads . . . they are devices by which the memory of our ancestors is passed on to the future . . . I could hold a set of beads that were maybe 500 years old and the memory of my ancestors are locked in those beads."[69]

Wampum in *La Pieta* is a signifier of the Haudenosaunee connection to and memory of the traditional homelands, in what is now called New York State. Haudenosaunee culture emphasizes peace and power; power is what emerges from alliance, reciprocity, and spirit. Moreover, awareness of the loss of ancestral homelands is central to the grievous work of return that Niro's *La Pieta* performs. As Richter reminds us, for the Haudenosaunee, "the landscape was infused with spiritual meaning . . . with the understanding that the land and animals were direct descendants of their original role in the Sky World prototypes of which the Good Twin (Sky Grasper) had created those on Earth; with the aid of his father, the turtle."[70] For the Mohawk, to be expelled, in genocidal displacement, from the ancestral territory was not only to lose the ability to nourish themselves—as their expertise in agriculture and land and game management was superior—but also to be stripped of the landscape that held, and still holds, spiritual meaning, a landscape inscribed with meaning. To represent mourning for such a landscape, of which her people have been deprived because of genocidal settler-colonialist wars, Niro deploys a unique multimedia approach of photography, textile, and wampum in *La Pieta*, inscribing a new treaty: one that centers mourning, survival, and resurgence.

Chapter 3

Aboriginal Title and Racial Capitalism

Shelley Niro's (Six Nations of the Grand River Reserve, Bay of Quinte Kanien'kehá:ka Mohawk Nation, Turtle Clan) activist art, created by returning imaginatively and literally to lands from which her people were violently dispossessed, is a political act. We can further illuminate these works—including the *Battlefields of My Ancestors* series, *1779*, *Niagara*, *Kissed by Lightning*, *It Starts with a Whisper*, the *La Pieta* series, and others—by reading their scenes of return through the lens of US laws of Aboriginal title. This common-law doctrine states that there is an inherent Aboriginal right to traditional land or territory, but in practice that right is treated as a weak right in settler law, and it is disregarded by settler nations regularly and with impunity. The falseness and speciousness of settler-colonialist language regarding the legitimacy of invaders occupying Indigenous lands is addressed by Niro's art. Through art-as-act-of-return to land, Niro demonstrates the weakness of Aboriginal title as a legal statute and vigorously illuminates the lack of ethical structure at the heart of the settler-colonialist project of displacing Indigenous peoples. In Niro's work, imaginative and real returns to Mohawk territory now claimed by New York State are identified as essential to the survival of contemporary Mohawk. Weaving together the creation and circulation of art as a ceremonial practice for healing, and the function of art as political activism, Niro's artistic acts of return to her people's homeland expose the multiple pathologies of false statements that have been integral to the formation of the United States and Canada as nation-states, as settler discourse wrote and writes its fantasy of legitimacy.

In this chapter, I take a deeper look into the legal structure and history of Aboriginal title. It may not be immediately evident why this matters for understanding Shelley Niro's art and its relationship to New York State, but I contend that to read her art's relationship to New York State as anything other than a subtle political statement arguing for land rights is to miss the heart of the art. Niro's art addresses Aboriginal title and other methods of taking land from Indigenous people—the very acts of theft that have "built" our nation—with elliptical gestures that reclaim the land by memory, knowledge, care, and understanding.

Re-Storying

Niro accurately locates violence, not triumphant progress, at the core of the settler-colonialist genocide that dispossessed the Mohawk of their land, and she reflects this in her series of photographs *Battlefields of My Ancestors* and *La Pieta*, as well as her photographic series *Resting Place of Our Ancestors* and *Ghost Wall*, as will be discussed in this chapter. Niro reveals the pain caused by settler-colonialist violence—to the people and to their land. The battles, massacres, and scorched-earth campaigns against the Mohawk preceded the capitalist nation-state's formation. Genocide was the condition of our nation's formation. Early accumulation, for settlers and speculators, meant strategically taking the Mohawk lands, making those lands capital in the possession of settlers and speculators. The unjust wars against the Mohawk in what is now called New York State produced the original people's position as impoverished actors in this capitalist play. Niro's return to the region in *Battlefields of My Ancestors* signifies her keen awareness that the settler-colonialist so-called *creation* of land as capital was actually a process of violent theft and genocide. In doing so, she sets straight our awareness of the real history of New York.

At the core of creating capital by recodifying land are the concepts of who is Indigenous and who is settler, argues Rebecca Tsosie (Yaqui); in this implicit structure of capitalism, "race" is a social construct intended to facilitate and make permanent the violence of settler-colonialist theft of Indigenous land.[1] Economist David Harvey, interpreting Marx's theory of early accumulation, concurs that the use of violence and force to strip the preproletariat of land and thereby create a landless workforce subsequently compelled to work for the bourgeoisie instigated the genocidal pressure of settler colonialism.[2] The need for endless new markets, with capitalism's voracity to expand, Marx noted, led to the near extirpation of Indigenous North Americans, an extension of how it had quelched efforts of European peasants to achieve equity.[3] Scholar and philosopher Brian Burkhart (Cherokee) argues that, in Western modernity, "becoming a fully human subject requires the domination of an 'other,'" because the social structure of coloniality (which is coterminous with the social structure of Western modernity) only defines a human being as that which dominates a less than fully human being."[4] This construct is distinctly at odds with the Haudenosaunee Great Law of Peace and other Indigenous ethical systems. Burkhart notes that in Indigenous ontology, "Human beings have intrinsic value."[5]

Within the settler nation-state, however, the category of "Indigenous" is always already framed as a category of displacement. Tsosie notes that the supposedly racialized categories "white" and "Indigenous" are structured by the undergirding premise of racial capitalism that encodes the state of being "white" as a form of property in capitalist exchange.[6] Citing the work of Ian F. Haney López, Tsosie contends that the law specifies "the relative privilege or disadvantage in U.S. society" of each racial category, bearing in mind—as Tsosie rightly does—that race is itself a social construct.[7] Indeed, her point is that the law is one of the most formidable tools for creating the social construct of race in settler-colonialist capitalism. Tsosie contends that

> from the country's inception, America's social, legal, and economic institutions utilized conceptions of race and property to establish and maintain the racial and economic subordination of non-White peoples. In the earliest years, this was done primarily using racial hierarchies and stereotypes that "justified" the enslavement of Africans and the dispossession of Native people from their lands and resources. Jurists posited that both were uncivilized groups of people who could not qualify for citizenship or rights commensurate with those of civilized persons.[8]

The ideological construction of race, Tsosie argues, is essential to the process by which settler-colonialist capitalism stripped, and continues to strip, Indigenous peoples of their lands. Argues Tsosie: "Therefore, the Doctrine of Discovery that was used to claim 'title' by the first European sovereign to discover 'vacant lands' was extended to lands occupied by 'uncivilized' peoples."[9]

Niro's photographic series *Resting Place of Our Ancestors* dives into this question of the ties of the Mohawk (and all Indigenous North American people), to this American continent. *Resting Place of Our Ancestors* (2019), a four-image black-and-white series, reveals fossils embedded in craggy stones. The intensely close-up and tightly framed views of the series bring home the reality that the ancestry of Indigenous North Americans is tied to this continent in ways totally unlike the ancestors of settlers. Niro's camera declares an understanding of the earth itself as sacred. Aboriginal title is given scant weight in settler law; by contrast, Niro's *Resting Place of Our Ancestors* shows the weight of ancestry, of what it means to be from a place—this place—where one's ancestors have been for some thirty thousand years.[10] The series compels us to unsee the settler perspective on land (land as property) and to see the land as the place of ancestors, specifically the ancestors of Indigenous North Americans. The hypnotically engaging photographs of *Resting Place of Our Ancestors* were taken near Cayuga, New York.[11] Here, the photographer returns to New York State and creates art that fiercely shows how deep the meaning of ancestral land goes. This land, in Niro's images, is the opposite of capital to be sold for profit. Instead, in the haunting close-range images of *Resting Place of Our Ancestors*, Niro shows us the sacredness of the land. Quietly, her battle against settler colonialism is fought with the strength of a profound connection to her ancestors.

Tsosie persuasively argues that now, in the twenty-first century, we must "expand the discussion about 'whiteness' to include the international dialogue about 'human rights' and its implications for Native peoples' substantive rights to land, ancestral remains, and genetic resources at the domestic level."[12] She contends that discussion of race, in coloniality, is really discussion of "property in the sense of ownership claims to valuable and scarce resources."[13] In this chapter, we consider how Niro's art that returns to New York State exposes the problematic of Aboriginal title as radically insufficient protection of Indigenous rights to land. The machinations deployed by colonizing settlers and speculators to strip the Mohawk of their land extend across centuries and include deceit as well as genocidal violence.

The Mohawk Valley

In the last decades of the eighteenth century, Mohawk politician and translator Molly Brant; her brother, leader Joseph Brant (Thayendanegea);

and her common-law husband, William Johnson, enlisted Mohawks living in what is now New York against the French. By making strategic alliances, the Mohawk of this area sought to retain control of their traditional lands. Their goal was to act as landlords, allowing the settlers to stay on Mohawk land in exchange for payments through a lease.[14] But settler-colonialist capitalism works by entirely displacing, not paying rent to, Indigenous peoples. The settler colonialists used physical and verbal violence to establish illegitimate juridical control of the land that is now called New York. This system of racial capitalism creates capital through the imaginary category of race and renames land as capital. Legal scholar Katharina Pistor argues in *The Code of Capital* that land in the capitalist regime (which is contiguous and coterminous with settler colonialism) is an object to be sold, and its objecthood, as a salable entity, is supported by the nation-state.[15] Yet Aboriginal title ostensibly protects Indigenous rights. Aboriginal title persists in settler law as a kind of haunting, a space where the system of law that was created to instate and maintain capitalist dominion over Indigenous spaces admits to a problem in its own core: the problem of capitalism's lack of ethics. The laws that create capital—Pistor explains that these laws do not so much govern as actually *create* capital—are a code that establishes and sustains the circulation and accumulation of capital. They are not an ethical code. But many legal systems—in traditional Haudenosaunee culture, for example—*are* ethical codes. They are codes geared toward fostering goodwill and a thriving culture among a group of people. And so the law of Aboriginal title lingers in settler discourse as a spectral space recognizing the idea of law as an ethical structure—as honor—rather than as a structure constitutive of land possession in settler states.

Dina Gilio-Whitaker (Colville Confederated Tribes) writes that the myth of America as a wilderness is a crucial ideological underpinning of settler-colonialist land theft.[16] From this, we can interpret that, when seventeenth-century settlers discussed the "natural" plenitude of Mohawk lands, they were actually describing the effects of centuries of skilled Mohawk land management.[17] But the notion of wilderness and wildness and indigeneity entwined runs long, wide, and deep in the settler-colonialist psyche and is a companion of the false belief that Indigenous peoples did not cultivate the land.[18] The idea that Guy Johnson expressed of the Mohawks' so-called natural genius for war is nothing more than a reflection of the Mohawks' skill, intelligence, and determination to survive genocidal invasion.[19] The Mohawk sought a path to enduring on their land, always looking for alliances that would enable them to stay on their traditional lands, always developing modes of being that strategically protected their survival, even as they were the targets of genocidal invasion. Taylor contends that the Haudenosaunee "defended an alternative vision of political space where natives persisted in autonomy between settler regimes, rather than divided and absorbed by them"; he goes on to note that Jeremy Adleman and Stephen Aron distinguish between borderlands and borders: Natives defended borderlands while settlers created bordered states, the state of New York and the boundary with Canada.[20]

Land theft and the legal frame of Aboriginal title are painfully entwined in the history of settler displacements of Indigenous people. Of Aboriginal title, legal scholar Brian Slattery asks, "Is it a customary right rooted in Indigenous law, a right under English common law, or a *sui generis* right?"[21] Aboriginal title, notes Slattery, extends from ambiguous legal principles. The ambiguity of these settler-colonialist principles stems from the conflict between the capitalist view of land and what one might call basic ethics of human being, ethics that honor the land of ancestors, the burial places of ancestors, the social, religious, and ethical meaning of land. The capitalist view of land, by contrast, is coterminous with the settler-colonialist view of land, and it holds that land is for sale, for money, and belongs, through some version of manifest destiny, to settlers, not to Indigenous peoples. The structure of racial capitalism is the structure of settler colonialism, theorist Charisse Burden-Stelly suggests.[22] The conflict between two opposing views—settler/capitalist versus Indigenous/sacred—of what land means hovers around Aboriginal title, which Tsosie describes as a "weak" right.[23] By this, Tsosie means that, in the US and Canadian legal systems, the right of Indigenous peoples to their land is contingent on the whims and desires of the settler nation-state. Niro's 2015 series of black-and-white photographs, *Ghost Wall*, imbricates the superficial skein of laws that reach across land, making it into property; she counterposes settler views of land with her photographs of the haunting depth of fossils. The close-range series of fossil images asks us to encounter the granular tactile materiality of the land, to understand and see the land not as an extension of human ideas of it but as its own beautiful, haunting entity. In Niro's *Ghost Wall* the land has its own story, not dependent on human beings. Taken at the edge of Lake Erie, these images hold time, allowing us to look through strata at former lives, the lives of all that materially built the land. Niro's 2019 series *Resting Place of Our Ancestors*, taken outside Cayuga, similarly extends from this deep gaze, using the camera to witness the encounter of the present with the past in and on (and of) the land. The unsparing gaze of these images brings us face to face with the knowledge that the earth of New York State is the ancestral place of the Haudenosaunee and, literally, holds the ancestors of the Haudenosaunee: not just a few generations, as is the case with settlers, but thousands of years of ancestry hold this land, their land.

Slattery, with a slant toward speaking well of the settler-colonialist state, emphasizes hollowed notions of settler privilege: "The fundamental principle of the 'honour of the Crown' obliges the Crown to respect Aboriginal rights, which in turn requires it to negotiate with Indigenous peoples with a view to identifying those rights."[24] Slattery notes that Beverley McLachlin, chief justice of Canada, clarifies the matter by stating that "Canada's Aboriginal peoples were here when Europeans came, and were never conquered."[25] Slattery argues that Aboriginal title is a sui generis law, one that does not fit with other types of settler-colonialist law, but what is the effect of this liminal status?[26]

It is important to clarify that the reason Aboriginal title does not fit easily within settler legal systems is because Aboriginal title contains in its essence the unsolved and unresolved conflict of the project of settler colonialism. The overt surface myth of settler-colonialist capitalism is that it represents itself as *progress*, a necessary destiny for all humankind by which the monoculture of worldwide capitalism erases all other cultures.[27] The connotated meaning of this denoted myth is that conquest must be allowed to take everything: every natural resource, every stretch of land, and—if necessary to obtain the resources and the lands—*every Indigenous life*. But beneath this overt myth of progress festers the subterranean understanding that the Indigenous people of North America *never* ceded their land to the project of settler-colonialist capitalism. Moreover, this unceded land constitutes not part but the *entirety* of North American land. There is no place in North America that is, strictly speaking, free of the problem of Aboriginal title, just many (perhaps most) places where it is ignored. As Mohawk leader Joseph Brant commented in 1793, "It seems natural to Whites to look on lands in the possession of Indians with an aching heart, and never to rest 'til they have planned them out of them."[28]

Taylor notes that Brant "recognized the power of borders and boundaries in settlement and . . . advised Natives to lease rather than sell land . . . stay in the role of 'landlords' to the invaders."[29] By contrast, settler colonialism was conducted—and is predicated—on the baseless assumption that colonizers have a God-given right to Aboriginal land, creating a system founded, at times obliquely and at times obviously, on the practice of denuding Indigenous peoples of their land on the irrational and illogical premise that such land is destined for settler possession. There is no rational basis for this justification of land theft, but in all the ways that it has flowed toward the ideological notion of manifest destiny, the theft of Indigenous land by settler colonialists and speculators has become its own rationale. Curator Wanda Nanibush (Beausoleil First Nation, Ojibwe), writing of Niro's photographic series *History of the World*, notes that "it is the Earth that reigns over us and we are her children, all humans and all living beings—everyone. We are part of her, our first Mother, and always will be."[30] This view of land stands in stark contrast to settler-capitalist appropriation of land as a form of capital.

In settler nation-state mythologies, settlers *should* have the land because settlers *can* have it; this is tautological logic. As Taylor notes, this approach works by "diminishing Aboriginal title to a temporary possession," even as the "doctrine of preemption" ensured Indigenous North American poverty and landlessness in the regime of coloniality. The supposed "sovereign right of preemption has (over time) been naturalized as if it were real"; the "dual process" of dispossessing Indigenous people and creating land as private property holdings "constructed the state of New York, the United States, and the British Empire in Canada."[31] The "success" of the settler-colonial invasion of Haudenosaunee land depended on stripping the Haudenosaunee not only of their own physical presence on the land but also of the legal ability to rent or lease the land to settlers, thereby maintaining the powerful position of landlords.[32]

Aboriginal title for the Mohawk Valley was effectively "expropriated and extinguished" when the majority of the Mohawk were forced, by the Sullivan-Clinton campaign, out of New York State.[33] Discussing the layers of national, international, and common law that entwine in Aboriginal title, Mohawk historian Michael Doxtater (Thohahoken) argues that even by the terms of settler-colonialist law, most of the land of New York State still belongs to the Haudenosaunee. He contends that the push, a century ago, by the United States and Canada to destroy traditional Haudenosaunee governance and forcibly replace it under threat of violence—with tribal councils handpicked by the nation-states—reflects the latter's awareness that the land is still Haudenosaunee land.[34] Historian Louis Knafla notes that conflicts arising around Aboriginal title reflect overall patterns of colonization as "settler states sought to turn communal and collective rights into individual ones."[35] Niro's *Resting Place of Our Ancestors* tenderly gestures toward the ultimate ineradicable communality of her people's homeland. One could even say that *Resting Place of Our Ancestors* shows us that communal and collective land rights are all we really have when the veneer of settler capitalism—with its illusion of individual exceptionalism—is stripped away. Her series *Resting Place of Our Ancestors* figurally strips away precisely this veneer. The ancestors are fossils metaphorically, as pictured in the stone wall photographs, and literally, as all human beings descend from earlier living beings, and the Haudenosaunee's history is the living history of this land that we now call New York (human remains are not pictured in Niro's photographic series). Niro's point in this elegant and subtle series is wide ranging and profound; she asks us to learn anew our connection to North American earth and to see it not as a resource for profit but as sacred.

In the struggle over Aboriginal title, the difference between settler ethics—emphasizing individual drive for personal aggregation of wealth—versus Haudenosaunee ethics—centering on responsibilities to the collective whole—is laid bare. Capitalism as a system in which land is commodified inherently privileges the notion and practice of individual accumulation of wealth, while Haudenosaunee economics prioritize the idea of shared abundance.[36] Capitalism interprets land as commodity, while Haudenosaunee sociality and custom understands land as part of the reciprocal relationship between the people and their ancestral home.[37] As Richter contends, the goal of traditional Haudenosaunee ethics is "not to accumulate goods but to be in the position to provide them to others."[38] Haudenosaunee ethics "obliged those with abundance to share with those in need."[39] The meaning of land that provides sustenance, then, is antithetical in settler versus Haudenosaunee ethos. For settler states, private land that generates personal wealth is the goal, whereas for the Haudenosaunee, communally fertile land that provides abundance to all is the ethical standard.

Given these radically different ethical frames, Knafla (writing of Canadian law) is correct in pointing out the problematic way that "the onus of proof on Natives who never assented to the view that the underlying title to their land resides in the crown" structures an unjust system wherein "the proof of Aboriginal title" must be made in terms of settler-state law.[40] Forcibly converting the Haudenosaunee to participate fully and exclusively in the system of capitalism was one of the main goals of earlier eighteenth-century colonizers.[41] Presuming a supposed preemption right to Aboriginal land, "state and colonial leaders declared imminent and inevitable their acquisition of Indian land . . . diminishing Aboriginal title to a temporary possession."[42] Settler legal policy did not respond to but rather *created* Indigenous poverty and landlessness in the regime of coloniality.[43]

Shelley Niro's art is part of this movement of Indigenous self-assertion for the return of stolen land. Her art implicitly declares a claim on the land of New York State that works on a level deeper than the law. Her photographic and filmic works reach to a core of truth that subverts naturalized settler paradigms of land claim. Repeatedly, settler-state law—whimsically, at its pleasure, and for its sense of need—extinguishes or fails to recognize Aboriginal title. As Mohawk scholar Douglas M. George-Kanentiio explains, settler legal practices simply change the laws whenever it looks as if Indigenous people might be able to use settler law to gain control over, or return of, their land.[44] While early European settlers were in fact aware that North America was inhabited by civilizations comparable to their own, the influence of Hugo Grotius and Emmerich de Vattel—and their theories of just war and the need for wars to reshape land holding—meant that the rights of Indigenous peoples to their traditional lands were considered either nonexistent or secondary to the desires of settlers for that same territory.[45] Thus, even as Enlightenment philosopher Jean Jacques Rousseau's well-known argument that wars did *not* confer settlers' rights to expropriate title (i.e., right to traditional land) from Indigenous people held some philosophical sway in the eighteenth century, practically speaking, the doctrine of Aboriginal title offered no protection to the Haudenosaunee, for both the British and the United States betrayed the people of the longhouse. Niro's subtle and poignant returns to the tragedy of war—in *Battlefields of My Ancestors* and in *La Pieta*—visually invoke the history of violence that provided the context in which settler law became the window dressing for land theft.

The problematic of Aboriginal title has not been resolved. Indeed, a struggle for water rights in Indigenous communities has been ongoing for decades. The US Supreme Court ruled in 1908 that Indigenous American nations have as much right to clean water as they do to their land, but in practice this right—interpreted to fall under the rubric of Aboriginal title—has scarcely been honored. In June 2023, the Court ruled that the Navajo nation does not have rights to clean water, in direct reversal of the notion and practice of honoring Aboriginal title.[46] As Knafla and Westra make clear in *Aboriginal Title and Indigenous Peoples*, Aboriginal title draws from Rousseau's theory of rights and is expressed as a form of natural law—moral and ethical propriety—but is not honored in Canadian and US practice.[47] Instead, the whims and perceived needs of the settler nation take precedence over the moral obligation of respecting Aboriginal rights. Consider the Akwesasne Mohawk on the Saint Lawrence River. As noted in chapter 2, beginning in the 1950s, General Electric and Reynolds Metals began using the river to discharge their industrial effluent, inundating the river, the fish, and the Mohawk who fish in the river with industrial chemicals known as PCBs. This assault by the racial-capitalist, settler-colonialist use of the land—and ethics of land—took place at the behest of the US government, which had widened the river to establish it as a space for industry.[48] Mohawk artist Alan Michelson focuses on these rivers, and I interpret Niro's more conceptual and elliptically symbolic work as equally invested in providing care for sacred Mohawk waterways.

When Niro photographs the Mohawk and Hudson Rivers in the series *Battlefields of My Ancestors* (see chapter 2), she reflects not only spaces from which her ancestors were pushed by genocidal policies and military actions but also spaces that in a secondary, ongoing act of colonization are damaged by ongoing settler-colonialist, racial-capitalist industry. Pollutants in these rivers, which are traditional sources of power and sustenance for the Haudenosaunee, change the land. The settler state's approach to rivers, fish, land, and human beings is that of racial capitalism. Rivers, land, fish, game, and humans are all valued according to what profits they and/or their actions may bring. Niro's *Battlefields of My Ancestors* contests this vision of land and humanity.

In Niro's series, connection to ancestral land is visualized as the right, the obligation, the duty, the capacity, the reciprocal exchange in which the people—the Haudenosaunee—have a relationship of care with the land. Niro expresses this care in *Battlefields of My Ancestors*, particularly in the earlier images of the series that reflect and signify returns to New York. As anthropologist Darren Ranco (Penobscot) points out, Indigenous notions of knowledge differ markedly from settler-colonialist epistemology.[49] Ranco notes that, in eastern woodland Wabanaki epistemologies, to know about a natural system is to have the responsibility to care for it. By contrast, he contends, the settler-colonialist view is that to know about a natural system is to have the capacity to take something from it. Niro's view of care and ethical responsibility to the land emerges from Indigenous epistemologies and encodes ethics in their substance. To know is to *take care*. The photographs in *Battlefields of My Ancestors* that return to New York are created as a way of taking care of the homeland of the Mohawk.

Returning to Niagara

The artist's return to New York State is an essential lodestone in her work. This is particularly true in her film *Niagara* (2015, originally titled *Ongniaahra*), which is also discussed in this book's first chapter. Niro comes back to this border, back to the place of Haudenosaunee power, Niagara Falls. The Haudenosaunee filmmaker returning to the ancestral land is the essence of this short film. The nation-state border may resist her, but she gazes across it. In creating this poetic film that mourns her daughter (see chapter 1), the border resists her, but she moves across it.

The intensity of loss is a layered experience in *Niagara*. In the short film, the loss of the daughter is elliptically and emblematically connected to the loss of the ancestral land; Niro seeks condolence by going to the border, the place where she can see New York State. The history of losing the land is traumatic and disturbing, as I discuss throughout this book. After the Revolutionary War the British, to whom the Mohawk had allied, betrayed them. In a deeply sadistic turn, this betrayal was couched by the British prime minister Lord Shelburne as benevolent, suggesting he was leaving the Mohawk in the power of settlers to help the Mohawk: "Left to the care of their neighbours [the United States] to soften and humanize their [the Mohawks'] hearts" even as the Mohawk had been fighting on the side of the British against the fledgling United States. Historian Alan Taylor makes the point that "the campaign to depict the Six Nations as 'bloodthirsty savages' and 'primitives' needing 'care' greased the way for this betrayal to become acceptable to the national psyche."[50] Being left to the "care" of the new nation actually meant that the Mohawk became the victims of clear genocide, a genocide foundational to New York State and to the United States.[51]

In the "care" of the United States, the Mohawk were pushed out of the Mohawk Valley by the brutal and genocidal Sullivan-Clinton campaign (also called the Sullivan-Clinton genocide) to become refugees at the border of the new nation-state (called the Niagara frontier), where many died of exposure and starvation in the winter of 1779. Of this genocidal campaign, it is important to note its instigator as George Washington, America's first president. He wrote to his generals:

> The expedition you are appointed to command is directed against the hostile tribes of the Six Nations of Indians, with their associates and adherents. The immediate objects are *the*

total destruction and devastation of their settlements and the capture of as many prisoners of every age and sex as possible. It will be essential to ruin their crops now in the ground and prevent their planting more. . . . Should Niagara fall into your hands in the manner I have mentioned you will do everything in your power for preserving and maintaining it by establishing a chain of posts. (emphasis added)[52]

Here, the ruining of crops directly led to the starvation of the Mohawk, who were skilled farmers. Likewise, the so-called preservation of Niagara referred to by George Washington means stealing the place for the settler nation, the United States, while committing genocide against the Mohawk. General Washington's goal to destroy the Haudenosaunee is clear. He urged his armies to "carry the war into the heart of the country of the Six Nations . . . cut off their settlements, destroy their next year's crops, and do them every mischief of which time and circumstance will permit."[53]

Like the film *Niagara*, Niro's sculptural mixed-media work *1779* (2017)—which depicts a pair of high-heeled shoes standing atop a digital display playing a recording of Niagara Falls (see chapter 1)—returns to this crucial area, this border, Niagara, where powerful natural and sacred forces emerge. It meditates on the Winter of Hunger (1779–80) when, following the Sullivan-Clinton campaign, the Mohawk sought refuge at the boundary of Fort Niagara and starved.

Niro's artist statement written to accompany the work, first shown at the Art Gallery of Hamilton in 2017, eloquently and forcefully notes that:

Six Nations history is one of the most documented communities with accounts involving the creation of the United States of America and Canada. The history is blood-soaked and rife with political propaganda. The Iroquois have often been seen as the vilest and blood-thirstiest people to have erupted from the Earth's surface. After the signing of the Declaration of Independence in 1776, Haudenausaunee communities were destined to be stamped out. It was God's will and this had to be obeyed. Besides, they had all of this great land now known as the state of New York . . . George Washington was the most terrifying person to the Haudenausaunee. Washington carried the name "Town Destroyer." This was whispered amongst Iroquois communities. He commissioned the Sullivan-Clinton campaign against the Oghwehowe. They burned crops, long-houses and livestock. He wanted to eliminate their existence. His words to Sullivan and Clinton were "defeat the Iroquois."

In the winter of 1779, after the Sullivan-Clinton campaign, the survivors of this scourge tried to make their way to Fort Niagara. They were convinced the British would be in better circumstances where they would be able to provide food and shelter, until they could once again return to their traditional homeland and start anew. Five thousand made it to Fort Niagara. Most starved to death along the way. The survivors hardly had any clothing on their backs, empty bellies, near death, they reached Fort Niagara disappointed by the reception they received from their British allies. This [work] serves as a memoriam to the people who didn't make it. And it serves as a memoriam to those who did. There are no photographs showing the destruction of the land and livelihood. There is no photographic documentation of physical brutality giving evidence of Iroquois people being erased from their homeland. With *1779* I want to show an aggressive procession within the confines of North America and how the land was taken.

Niro states:

As repayment to the Six Nations for the land they lost and for their loyalty to the British during the American Revolution, six miles of land on both sides of the Grand River was purchased from the Mississauga First Nations from its source to its mouth and was given to the Iroquois. The Haldimand Tract is approximately 950,000 acres. This land continues to be a debacle and a convenient modern-day land grab. When the Six Nations arrived on the shores of the Grand River in 1784, I can only speculate their reaction to the land that lay before their eyes. They were tired, war worn and hopeful. They must have been anxious to start plowing fields, building houses and again making their society safe and sound, functioning for their families.

Around the year 2000 I found a pair of stiletto high heels at a Value Village store. The spikes and goldenness of the heel caught my attention and gave way to thoughts of chances of fortune. I immediately thought of Niagara Falls and how it represents cheap thrills and the "get rich quick" schemes it conjures. Niagara Falls to the Haudenausaunee represents all that is sacred. The natural power of the falls as it cascades over the escarpment and the sound of roaring thunder as it does make the visitor aware of their own spark-like destiny against nature. As I make my way past the neon lights [of Niagara Falls], the Ferris wheel, the man's voice urging you to take a chance and all of the other cheap attractions, I remind myself of what this place used to represent and to whom.

Niro notes:

[The year] 2017 marks the one hundred fiftieth birthday of Canada. There will be many celebrations and festivities across the country. I remember 1967. The year commemorated one hundred years of Canada as a country. I was thirteen at the time. I was a member of a marching band from the Six Nations Reserve. On that hot, sticky day we marched in a parade in Brantford. Our uniforms were made of felt and mine had fringes cut into the bottom of the skirt because I was a girl. We wore headbands with a feather . . . We wore our band uniforms with pride, happy to participate in that historic day. I don't remember how long we had to march or the music we played. I just remember I played the alto saxophone, sweat pouring down my face. Since then things have changed drastically. Today we would never put our children in costumes that showcased stereotypes of our Native culture . . . What were our parents thinking? In their time this was the best they could do with no financial backing. They wanted their children to take part in an event that most Canadians saw as joyful and hopefully leading to better things to come.

As I contemplate the years that have culminated until now, I feel the Indigenous world has increased in knowledge, awareness, justice and in imagination. We no longer have to process our whereabouts, or get permission to move forward from the local Indian agent. Education is the key element here, in every category. We are learning our history and how it has affected us, rarely in a positive light. History books had to be reinterpreted and written from our perspective . . .

> The intergenerational trauma in Indigenous people is still evident today. We, however, are learning how those past events have made an impact on our souls and minds. With this knowledge we are working towards making society purposeful and enriching. We work in the direction of ending the trauma and letting our children be children.[54]

In her eloquent artist statement, from which I have quoted extensively, Niro makes clear that the stripping of land from the Haudenosaunee, concurrent with the creation of the United States, was an act of intentional genocidal violence. Her awareness of the history is well informed and insightful. She elaborates on the connection between settler-colonialist land theft and capitalism, noting the "get rich quick" schemes that abounded and persist in settler-colonialist capitalism. Her art's response to this loss is, on the surface, lovely and even glittery. Focusing my discussion on the filmic and sculptural elements of this work displayed as part of Niro's career retrospective, *500 Year Itch*, I note that this installation *1779* mourns that winter of 1779–80 when so many Haudenosaunee starved to death, and those who survived lost their homes and homeland. Niro's mixed-media sculpture stands as testimony to Haudenosaunee values and spirit: those aspects of the people and their culture that enabled (and enable) them to survive. The work performs condolence and renewal.

In the filmic (video) element of *1779*, the force of the moving water of Niagara is paramount. The video moves beneath a clear half-globe. The import of this structure is to allow us to see how Niagara is the world; it offers an homage to the power and force of Niagara while also creating a sort of snow-globe effect through which we look back in time, through which—in characteristic Niro fashion—the past and the present merge. The bright feminine shoes stand above the scene of starvation and devastation—as if they are otherworldly, or suggest a kind of subversive female force; that is my reaction looking at the piece in the context of her retrospective. Niro's artist's statement and personal communications indicate that the shoes stand as signifiers of cheap tourist kitsch and settler violence. I see a possible connection between these brightly adorned heels and the allusion to Dorothy's ruby slippers in Niro's earlier work *Red Heels Hard* (see chapter 1). In both cases, signifiers of violent settler femininity are captured and repurposed for Mohawk feminist resistance. In Niro's sculptural *1779*, the rich burgundy cloth draped before the assemblage, with "1779" grandly stitched into it, creates an ironic formality where the destruction of the Haudenosaunee world is translated into settler-colonialist rhetoric of faux high class and wealth (get rich quick!). The people's forced march, on which so many died, and the Winter of Hunger, during which so many more perished, were entirely the effect of General Washington's decision to destroy the Mohawk so that the United States could take the land of what is now New York State. Niro's art allows us to know about and focus on the genocide at the heart of New York history.

In this shift in perspective, from the triumphalism and self-congratulatory narrative of settler-colonialist culture—for example, the celebration of the Fourth of July and the myopic rhetoric of patriotism in the United States—to a deep awareness of the foundations of New York State, Niro's art is, paradoxically, quintessential New York art. Her work fights for the return of land because its eloquence, depths, and breadth in connection to the land and the people's history with the land show us that to preempt Haudenosaunee "rights" to their land is to disturb the actual foundation of this land. Her layered art is a guerrilla tactic of the highest form. The multimedia work *1779* offers an almost frothy, exuberant semisphere enclosing sparkling shoes that evoke feminine power, Dorothy's magical red slippers (that bring her home) critique settler gaudiness and "get rich quick" use of land, as the work counterpoises the power of Niagara, a place of spiritual and metaphysical force with the tragedy and trashiness of settler violence.

In its beauty, Niro's work draws us to contemplate what 1779 meant and means to the Haudenosaunee. It was the year when, after centuries of resisting settler-colonialist violence and violation, the Haudenosaunee were violently pushed from their ancestral homelands. It was the year when explicitly genocidal campaigns were waged against the Haudenosaunee at the behest of the future father of the United States, the first president, George Washington. It was the year when the people fleeing for their lives sought refuge at Fort Niagara and many starved and froze, so that the Winter of Hunger is singed into the collective consciousness of the Haudenosaunee. As a year, 1779 is a signifier of a profound collective trauma for the Haudenosaunee. In this process of genocide perpetrated against the people, we can see a mockery of Aboriginal title, a mockery of the idea that settler-speculator landgrabs ever respect Aboriginal title. The United States and New York State in their formation depended on—even required—the destruction of the Haudenosaunee and the rupture of the people from their homeland. Haudenosaunee ancestral right to the land was in no way protected as the United States and New York State were created out of speculation—get-rich schemes—for which genocide was a necessary precursor and handmaid.

Collective Trauma and the American Genocide

The cascade of trauma caused by the Sullivan-Clinton genocide can be understood as collective trauma. Psychologist Gilad Hirschberger defines collective trauma as

> psychological reactions to a traumatic event that affects an entire society . . . the recollection of a terrible event that happened to a group of people. It suggests that the tragedy is represented in the collective memory of the group. . . . Collective memory of trauma is different from individual memory because collective memory persists beyond the lives of the direct survivors of the events and is remembered by group members that may be far removed from the traumatic events in time and space.[55]

Niro's *1779* project, as do all her works that return to New York State, gives haunting and gorgeous aesthetic form to a collective trauma that her people survived. And yet, one must be careful not to allow the language of psychology to sanitize what settler-colonialist barbarity did to the Haudenosaunee. Because settler colonialism uses psychological theory to separate violence from the effect of violence, to hermetically seal off violent acts and instead discuss the difficulties of the violated, psychological theory can be duplicitous. What Niro's work illuminates, in returning to New York State, is the violence of settler colonialism, the barbarity of this system that tried to justify theft of land and genocide through the mythology of a Christianity unrecognizable in the teachings of Christ.

For the Haudenosaunee, the collective cultural memory commemorated in Niro's *1779* is traumatic, but it goes far beyond that psychological term. The collective cultural memory is a knowledge of the viciousness and lack of ethics of a system, settler-colonialist capitalism, that is still very much in place and the guiding force of the United States now. In creating a mixed-media sculptural work that returns us to that bitter year, Niro refuses to sweep the past under the rug and refuses to submit to the settler-colonialist program of forgetting. In Niro's brilliant visual cosmology, the real history is never disavowed or buried. The globe of *1779* returns us to Niagara, the roiling waters; it returns us despite the fake velvet of decorum that settler-colonialist rhetoric attempts to place across the violence it commits. In the false mythology of contemporary settler colonialism, Indigenous North Americans are presented as a buried past. But the reality Niro shows us through her art is that the Haudenosaunee are not simply New York State's past. On the contrary, the Haudenosaunee are still deeply and intensely connected to the state, not only the diminished number who live there still but all of the people building a long house are still the people of this land we now call New York.

Mourning in Place

Niro notes that, in connecting with such painful cultural memories, when her work returns to New York State, she has to give herself space not to work for too long at one stretch, so that the horror of what it means for her people to have endured genocidal efforts to destroy them does not overwhelm the present-day task of creating art.[56] Pain and resilience are twin forces in Niro's work.

In *Niagara*, a short film (discussed previously) about familial loss and healing, the evocation of family is suggestive rather than direct. The film connotes intense intimacy but also some degree of anonymity. It is in anonymity that a certain kind of history moves: the history of people as a family, as a group. The history of human beings keeping land sacred. Aboriginal title—the unfulfilled promise that the invading settler-colonialist government would respect millennia-long Indigenous land possession—pulls at the edges of all the stolen land in North America. The weakness of Aboriginal title, as a source of protecting Indigenous rights, is that its force only relies on the "honor" of the invading settler-colonialist government, and that honor is scarce inasmuch as the very act of settler-colonialist land appropriation is without honor.

Niro's *Niagara* looks hauntingly at the place of the falls from the view of doubled losses and resilience in the face of grief. In this video, the person filming the falls and whirlpool, as a person with knowledge of Indigenous North American history, language, and beliefs, is positioned as an Indigenous North American. We know this because during the film they enact the Condolence Ceremony gesture of wiping away tears (droplets of Niagara on the camera lens). The film is a visitation to this loss of Indigenous presence in Niagara. But it is also a work of mourning for the person whom the narrator of the film has lost, and a work of healing and condolence, invoking the Condolence Ceremony.[57] It is a visual elegy. But it is more than an elegy; rather, it is different from the Western, settler-colonialist view of an elegy. For, by staging the work of mourning in Niagara, the Haudenosaunee place of sacred power, Niro shifts the notion of time at the heart of Western views of elegy. *Niagara*, the film, is a work of art that encodes and stages a ritual of condolence in the context of return. This code of return emerges from, engages, and manifests as a Haudenosaunee conceptualization of time. Rather than the narrowly linear, ultimately apocalyptic temporality of Western settler-colonialist time, Haudenosaunee time allows for the vivid presence of the past in the mind of the present. Haudenosaunee temporality structures the meaning of return differently.

When Niro stages artistic returns to New York, she does not do so in a vengeful way, but as a corrective to genocide, a beautiful and forceful act of reinstating Mohawk time, the time of return, and Mohawk presence in the people's traditional homelands. In the film *Niagara*, she "accepts"—to use the psychological nomenclature—and is consoled regarding the grievous loss of her younger daughter. But she also comes to a place—the place of her own birth and a border, as the film states—where above and below, past and present, spirits and the embodied living all entwine and where loss is not forever. The border, the liminal place, Niagara, is the place for mourning a loss that is not spoken in the film but is intimated, not because the loss becomes final in that place, but because the liminal place holds the vivid presence of the past in its power, the power of Niagara. It is not that Niro's film denies the meaning of loss—the lost daughter, the lost land, so many losses—but in creating condolence for unbearable loss, the film creates, manifests as, and reflects a differential Haudenosaunee epistemology, an understanding of temporality that enfolds continuation. Mourning continues, but so does surviving; the power of the place of the falls gives power to the work of art that returns to this place. The vividness, the livingness, of Niro's art is strong here. The Condolence Ceremony of her film *Niagara* occurs in this place, at this border because it is sacred.

Lineage

Niro's emphasis on survival and renewal runs throughout her photographic and filmic works. In the feature film *The Incredible 25th Year of Mitzi*

Bearclaw (2019), when poet and playwright Charlie B.'s poetry is read aloud, the story is that of survival—the descendants of Indigenous North Americans *surviving*, feeling the sun on their skin. The act of return is the act of survival. Creating art that invokes and represents New York State, the Mohawk ancestral land, is an invocation and act of survival. Whereas settler-colonialist notions of time and land merge in the linear temporal frame of racial capitalism, Niro's art that returns to New York rebuts these strictures. Settler-colonialist, racial capitalism encodes land through the temporal structure of ownership: only one person or entity owns the land at a time. Over time, though land changes ownership in settler-colonialist, racial capitalism, the aggregation of land owned by white men is the bulwark and spine of this system. In taking her art back to New York, Niro subtly but unmistakably refuses the properness of settler-speculator land theft. In her art she invokes land that is Haudenosaunee, and she invokes land that is women's province.[58] It is the Haudenosaunee tradition of women's stewardship of land that Niro's art honors and that in turn sustains her art. The temporality of Haudenosaunee culture is the temporality of return, cyclical and deep in remembrance. Niro's art refutes and refuses settler time with force when her work commands its place as part of New York State.

Similarly, in *Battlefields of My Ancestors*, Niro's staging of scenes of return to homelands expresses Indigenous feminism (discussed further in chapter 4), a trait that carries across all her work. Her strong emphasis on the co-participation of sisters, aunts, grandmothers, in scenes of reclaiming traditional lands, adumbrates a feminist praxis that refutes patriarchal structure and the history of US law regarding land. As theorist and educator Verna St. Denis (Cree and Métis) lays bare, feminism and indigeneity are deeply entwined. She notes, quoting Alan Johnson, that in settler-colonialist capitalist patriarchy, "Women's place is to help contain men's resentment over being controlled by other men. . . . Men are allowed to dominate women as a kind of compensation for being subordinated to other men because of class, race, or other forms of social inequality."[59] The subordinate place of women in settler-colonialist society is inherently and inextricably tied to racial capitalism, as is the genocide of Indigenous North Americans. In Niro's feminist Indigenous work, we experience the double strength of an Indigenous woman refuting and refusing racial patriarchy. Niro's returns to New York State are, in the best sense of the phrase, *women's work*. These returns are a woman's job because they symbolically reinstate not only Indigenous presence in lands from which the Haudenosaunee were displaced by genocidal military campaigns of the fledgling United States but also because Niro's art that returns to New York State insists on the traditional Haudenosaunee sociality in which women are the land-keepers, the ones who keep farms, orchards, villages.

In *Niagara, Battlefields of My Ancestors*, and *1779*, Niro returns to a site of terrible communal pain, the collective trauma of the Haudenosaunee pushed out of New York after the Revolutionary War, seeking refuge and instead finding starvation. In *1779*, the video of the whirlpool is suggestive of both turmoil and power—the power of the Mohawk to overcome adversity and the sacred power of Niagara. Despite the people's hardship in suffering through the genocidal campaign against them, survival and beauty hold in this work. The lush beadwork of *1779* is a mordant piece of visual wit, a memorialization of a year so painful that it is stitched forever into the people's minds. In bringing that stitching to graphic realization, Niro opens a potent space for resistance and return: resistance to coloniality and return to and of ancestral land. *1779, Niagara,* and *Battlefields of My Ancestors* deploy evocative visual poetry to reclaim Haudenosaunee homelands.

Chapter 4

Guerrilla Wars

Indigenous Feminist Resistance

In fighting the ongoing violence of settler colonialism, Shelley Niro (Six Nations of the Grand River Reserve, Bay of Quinte Kanien'kehá:ka Mohawk Nation, Turtle Clan) joins her women activist ancestors, fighting *petite guerres*, or guerrilla wars, using art as her weapon, suggests Niro's brother, Mohawk historian and educator Michael Doxtater (Thohahoken). Doxtater interprets Niro's art as political activism inheriting and extending the work of a long line of activist Mohawk women. The tradition of women as those who keep the land and culture is at variance from settler culture in which women are encouraged to be passive, docile, and voiceless. Even now, as I complete the edits of this book in March 2024, US Senator Katie Britt (Republican, Alabama) delivered the response to the State of the Union speech in a voice carefully modulated to mimic the tonal range of a child, demonstrating that even now in settler culture, a woman who is an elected lawmaker must strive to appear childlike and powerless.[1]

Mohawk culture instates a very different structure of gendering. Traditional Mohawk social structure, Doxtater explains, contrasts sharply with settler-colonialist sociality. Traditional Mohawk society, he notes, was balanced in three parts—the Chiefs/male leaders, the Clan Mothers, and the people's fires—each with power and voice. The Clan Mothers were the decision-makers who chose who would lead. Doxtater vigorously argues that the US and Canadian governments' action of dismantling the traditional structure of self-governance and replacing it with tribal councils was an act driven by settler-colonialist desire to retain the land stolen from the Mohawk, which the settler nation-states' governments, contends Doxtater, knew was still legally Mohawk land.[2] Colonialist structures of governance also dismantled women's traditional power in Mohawk culture. According to Doxtater, it was the knowledge that the Haudenosaunee still had the title to most of the land in New York that spurred drastic action on the part of the US and Canadian governments, in attempts to silence and disempower the Haudenosaunee. The Canadian government sent the Royal Canadian Mounted Police to the Six Nations to perform a coup, where they forcibly dismantled the people's traditional governance structure, described above, and installed in its stead a tribal council that was friendlier to, and to a significant extent controlled by, the settler-colonialist nation-state, states Doxtater. These and other violent efforts to control the Haudenosaunee, so as to keep the stolen land, have present-day manifestations and implications. As Doxtater makes clear, settler colonialism isn't over. It is ongoing.[3]

He clarifies that the usual translation for the Mohawk, people of the flint, should instead be "where the flint strikes" or "where lightning strikes the ground and sparks the flash," and explains that the name is connected to the mines around Canajoharie in what is now called New York State.[4] Doxtater characterizes the Mohawks' forced removal from this area and other aspects of settler colonialism in New York, and in North America generally, as genocide, an understanding of the United States' history that is becoming increasingly prevalent among scholars.[5] An activist with Six Nations Against Pollution, Doxtater explains that the Haudenosaunee's access to potable water is still in crisis. The Nestlé corporation draws clean water from sources that, by the 1701 Nanfan Treaty and the 1784 Haldimand Tract, belong to the Six Nations. Because these treaties are not respected, the people are stripped of their own clean water and given no choice but to drink contaminated water, which leads to high cancer rates in the community. Doxtater notes that, in fundraising efforts for clean water for the Six Nations, Niro has donated her work to be auctioned.[6]

As a member of one of the oldest families of the Turtle Clan, the *Satekariwate* ("they weigh matters"), Shelley Niro reflects in her art her family's trait of hearing both sides of a conflict and processing thesis and antithesis to reach a synthesis.[7] One can see in Niro's work the effort that is always made toward balance and inclusion. While her work is—as Doxtater rightly states—a form of guerrilla defense of her people and traditions, it also holds space for everyone who comes to the work with an honest heart and clear mind to be included in its peace. Niro's art, in

Turtle Clan tradition, "hears both sides" in the sense that the work not only is capacious and healing for the Indigenous people for whom the work is made but also is capable of changing the ways of thinking carried by settler colonialists' descendants. Niro is "living our history," says Doxtater, who argues that getting back the land is imperative. He also makes the larger point that it is less meaningful to regain the ancestral land if the Earth itself is destroyed by settler-colonialist, industrialist capitalism.[8] In placing Niro in a lineage of politically powerful Mohawk women, Doxtater frames a compelling interpretation of Niro's art in which activism is the dominant component of the work. In this context, Niro's art expresses connection with the land by manifesting continuation with her ancestors. In this chapter, I consider her artworks' potent, subversive, and often understated political activism. I emphasize the force of Indigenous feminism in Niro's art.

It Starts with a Whisper

Visual and cultural studies scholar Michelle Raheja (Seneca) interprets Niro's film *It Starts with a Whisper* (1993) as a "Matriarchal Time/Space Machine," noting that the film's staging of temporal and geographic returns offers a path for the young heroine Shanna "through communal memory, to negotiate her way towards a new status as a healthy Haudenosaunee woman."[9] Time in Niro's work is intricately and deeply connected to Haudenosaunee history that occurs in New York State. Her art's invocations of her people's history are also invocations of the land of New York, before the Haudenosaunee were pushed out. Feminist Elizabeth Weatherford argues, "Niro's awareness of history is sharply represented by her confronting bitterness over the constraints placed upon Indigenous people and turning it into a vision of having power over the present."[10] Niro's early film *It Starts with a Whisper*, created with Anna Gronau, charts its young Mohawk protagonist, Shanna's, return to Niagara Falls. As the film begins, we are in Canada, in Tutela Heights. Shanna, wearing traditionally beaded garments featuring the Celestial Tree, walks where the memory of the vanished Tutelo people—the few survivors absorbed into Haudenosaunee populations—haunts the young woman.[11] As she walks, Shanna hears the voices of her loving ancestors telling her that she is young and that her sorrow is too heavy.[12] The film introduces at its outset the reality that the young Indigenous protagonist needs to know and connect with her ancestors if she is to thrive. Vivid ghosts speak in *It Starts with a Whisper*; their whispers begin the film, and these ancestors continue to speak to the young woman, directing her in how to survive in the aftermath of the Indigenous genocide that is the real North American history and culture, however else settler mythologies might wish to define it.[13] Raheja notes, "The film offers a counternarrative for exploring the thematics of history, loss, and the spiritual by overturning nostalgic discourses of the vanishing Indian. . . . [Niro] links the present and future to the traumatic past of the Tutelo."[14]

As the narrative of *It Starts with A Whisper* unfolds, Shanna is invited on a vacation with her three aunties, who are traveling to Niagara Falls, having won the trip playing bingo. As the women travel across Canada to New York, the scene beyond them is old-fashioned black-and-white reel footage. This background depicts the sense of place that being in exile—the Mohawk pushed into Canada—creates. The places they pass through on their way back to their homeland, New York, are unreal, depicted like newsreels and disconnected from the vivid family of the three sisters (played by Niro's sisters, Deborah Doxtater, Beverly Miller, and Elisabeth Doxtater) and Shanna in the car.[15] Inside the car, the aunties are full of humor and spirit, eating and joking, while young Shanna is downbeat. When they arrive in Niagara, the tacky tourist hotel signs stun Shanna; they flicker, disorienting her.

But even as Niagara initially presents as a garish tourist trap, it is here at the border, at Niagara—a place of traditional Haudenosaunee power—that Shanna finds the voices of the ancestors, not just of her nation but of other Indigenous North American nations: the names of those that have survived and those that have vanished but whose names are still known and the spirits of those whose languages are lost and unknown. Raheja argues that these voices open "the possibility for a visual sovereignty that imaginatively performs epistemes that do not easily conform to linear plottings of time and Western juridical notions of property, [staging] creative virtual spaces of community."[16] Scholar Penelope Myrtle Kelsey interprets the entire film *It Starts with a Whisper* as a contemporarizing performance of the Condolence Ceremony, noting that the film begins with the stirring of ashes (part of the Midwinter Ceremony) and verbally invokes the experience of the Sullivan-Clinton genocide. Kelsey contends that "Niro's use of Condolence tropes and imagery in contemporary contexts successfully remakes, re-envisions, and innovates Haudenosaunee tradition keeping to evolving, dynamic effect."[17] The ancestors' voices rising to comfort Shanna in the context of the sacred place, Niagara, transform the young woman. During the course of the film she becomes able to "see through" trashy settler culture to Haudenosaunee history and the sacred presence that is always there in Niagara and also to see, across the border, the land now called New York.

The aunties and Shanna take a hotel room (their bingo prize) in a honeymoon suite in Niagara, where they dress in colorful gowns and perform a humorous and biting burlesque song and dance, mocking settler colonialism as a failed romance:

> You made me speak gibberish instead of my language
> But you can't control my mind.[18]

The punchy scene sharply critiques what colonization has done to Niagara and emphatically places the ability to reject colonization in the mouths of Mohawk women, whose song lyrics spoof and refute the substructure of coloniality, cleverly turning the trope of white femininity's enforcement of girlish sexiness to a direct expression of sanctified anger, "I'm pretty . . . mad at you," with "you" being all representatives and enactors of colonization. Raheja identifies the aunties as "tricksteresque," noting that they appear in the credits as "Matriarchal Aunts/Clowns."[19] Niro describes the scene's trenchant critique of settler culture: "For a number of years the Hollywood medium has used the Indian, so now the Indian is using the Hollywood medium."[20]

Set at the boundary zone, the sacred liminal space that is Niagara, the film gathers the borders between past and present, Canada and the United States, the living and the dead. The film ends on midnight, January 31, 1992, marking the five hundredth year of genocidal colonization. As fireworks fill the sky, the aunties and Shanna share an elegant cake shaped like the Earth. As Raheja indicates, they read a "poem by nineteenth-century Mohawk writer Pauline Johnson as Shanna cuts an Earth-shaped cake (symbolizing the destruction of this 'world' . . . and prophesizing . . . transformations). As the cake is cleaved in half, fireworks in the background constellate to form an image of a tree sitting atop a turtle—the Haudenosaunee visual icon for the female-centered origin of the world."[21] The land is still theirs, and they can still regain sovereignty despite the horrors of five hundred years of settler colonialism.

Bringing the young protagonist to Niagara for this temporal dividing line, crossing the boundary into the 501st year of colonization, Niro's film articulates the importance of Niagara, the importance of the return to face New York State, the homeland of the Mohawk. It is in facing New York that the Mohawk women, the three aunties and young Shanna, celebrate New Year's Eve on the grievous anniversary of the beginning of colonization.[22] This date is clearly important to Niro's art and she significantly links this date to the geography of New York State, the homeland of her people. On this date, their land was already threatened, even as Mohawk territory was not the initial site of the invasion.

The ironically referenced "short 500 years" of genocidal colonization in *It Starts with a Whisper* is picked up in Niro's photographic work. The title *500 Year Itch* on Niro's triptych of photographs (figure 4.1) spoofing Marilyn Monroe and the idea of "America" is also the title that Niro chose to echo in her career retrospective at the National Museum of the American Indian in New York.[23] The title *500 Year Itch* humorously refers to the film *The Seven Year Itch*. Monroe appears in *The Seven Year Itch*, and the famous skirt-blowing scene occurred when she was posing for photographers during the making of that film. The idea of *The Seven Year Itch* is that, after seven years of marriage, husbands and wives each start to hanker for someone new. Niro's humorous twist on the title suggests playfully and powerfully that Indigenous North Americans are tired of the forced "marriage" with settler colonialism and are ready to move on to something better.

In the triptych, the image of Niro dressed as Monroe is to the left, while a tender archival photograph of Niro's mother is at the center, with the artist in work clothes facing the camera on the right. The "romance" of colonization is a bitter one, suggests Niro in her blonde wig and goofy Marilyn pose. The contrast of this image with that of her youthful, elegant mother and herself imaged as the serious working artist deeply accentuates a problematic of settler culture: its epitomization of femininity as powerless. By contrast, Haudenosaunee femininity, displayed by Niro's mother and Niro herself in work clothes, is centered and focused and matrilineal. The mother is at the center of the triptych because she is at the center of the meaning of collective identity and power, including identity and power harnessed in Niro's art. Articulating the power of Mohawk women, Niro creates art that does battle—subtly and brilliantly—with settler colonialism. The work's title, *This Land is Mime Land*, plays on the line "this land is my land" from Woody Guthrie's problematic anthem "This Land is Your Land" (1940).[24] Niro's title points out that the land was stolen from America's original people (New York State stolen from the

Haudenosaunee). By twisting Guthrie's "my land" to the spoofy "mime land" in her triptych title, Niro pointedly refutes the song's claim that the American continent rightly belongs to settlers. She counters this settler acquisitive gaze with her Mohawk gaze. Looking hard at the absurdity of settler culture, Niro mimes its tropes. Her art is activist in the tradition of satire but also brings a haunting sense of poignance to its critique. The images of Chiquita Doxtater and her daughter, the artist, counterpose against a fabricated Marilyn Monroe with the mother's vivid presence a centerpiece for the daughter's steady, stable, ability to work and create original art. The self-portrait shows the artist as a working artist. As Niro notes, "Marilyn is compared to 'Mother' [that is, Niro's mother] and reflects on the artist becoming a triangle of social and historical dilemma, in feminist discourse."[25]

A virtuoso of subtle satire, Niro refers to the brutal genocidal process of colonization as a love story gone so wrong in her film *Honey Moccasin*.[26] There, she uses the lyrics to Peggy Lee's song "Fever" to make her point by playing the words over images of residential school deportations and other atrocities committed against Indigenous Americans. This conceit of

Figure 4.1. *The 500 Year Itch* (1992), triptych photograph, gelatin silver print heightened with applied color, mounted on Masonite, 182 cm × 121.5 cm. *Source:* National Gallery of Canada, gift of Victoria Henry, Ottawa, 2003. Used with permission of the artist.

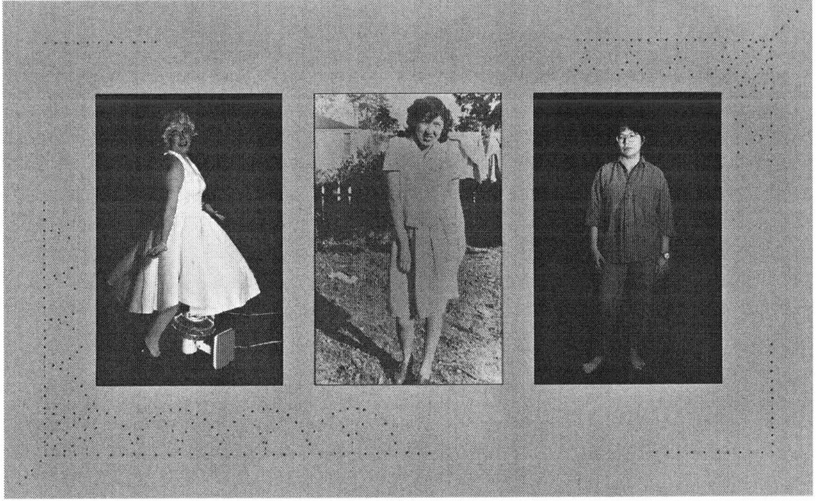

colonization as a hideously twisted love story runs through Niro's oeuvre. But the love that is untwisted, that is pure and real, is the love for the land of New York, the homeland. In returning through her art Niro cares for this land.

In bringing her young *It Starts with a Whisper* protagonist, Shanna, out of Toronto and to Niagara, Niro brings her to the place that is a border and also a stronghold, where spiritual and geological forces converge. Niro sets the young woman's confrontation with Indigenous genocide (as indicated by the chanting of the names of nations that have survived and including those that have not survived) in *this* place, Niagara, because it is a place where the spirits speak, a sacred place. The return to Niagara is necessary for Shanna's ability to thrive; this place protects her with its strength (much as a quarter century later the sacred force of Niagara protects Shelley Niro when the artist returns to create the elegiac film *Niagara*, discussed previously). As the aunties and Shanna celebrate the arrival of the new year, 1993, they mystically and humorously cut into their cake, reversing the colonizing gaze over their land and spoofing the settler-colonialist paradigm of world dominion.

The return to face New York is a return to the Mohawk source of power: their ancestral land. Niro created the film *It Starts with a Whisper* (1993) in the aftermath of the Oka Crisis.[27] Also known as the Kanesatake Resistance, this was a "78-day standoff (July 11–September 26) between Kanien'kehá:ka (Mohawk) protesters, Quebec police, the Royal Canadian Mounted Police and the Canadian Army. It took place in the community of Kanesatake, near the town of Oka. . . . The crisis was sparked by the proposed expansion of a golf course and the development of townhouses on disputed land in Kanesatake that included a Kanien'kehá:ka burial ground."[28] As Abenaki filmmaker Alanis Obomsawin's magisterial documentary film *Kanehsatake: 270 Years of Resistance* makes clear, the Oka Crisis erupted after centuries of colonialist theft of Indigenous land in this area. Settler colonialists' belief that Indigenous graves are less valuable than an expanded golf course starkly reveals the corrupt values of settler colonialism. Niro's response to this crisis was to create art that obliquely and deeply referenced not just this crisis but the broader conditions of oppression and genocide that spawned it. *It Starts with a Whisper* responds to the Oka Crisis very differently than a documentary film would: it focuses on a young girl's coming-of-age experience. Shanna is disheartened and saddened, finding it hard to move forward because of the treatment of her people and the overwhelming weight of Indigenous history. In response to the Oka Crisis, Niro creates an intimate family story: three aunties and a young woman going to Niagara for a vacation they won playing bingo.

This characteristic move of Niro's at once responds to the immediate political moment, deepening awareness of it, and making that knowledge permanent. Her political guerrilla tactics are subtle and deeply empathic. *It Starts with a Whisper* tells the inside story of the effect of the Oka Crisis on a young woman and her family, even as it never explicitly and overtly references the crisis. In making the effect of the crisis intimate, Niro's film reaches through the immediate moment and ties into deeper themes of time, family, and Mohawk culture. The Oka Crisis is an event that spurred Niro's political awareness, but the film she creates in response is not set in Oka. It is set in Niagara. The film is about return, the meaning of return to New York for the Mohawk. The answer to crisis, for Niro, is to connect the present—and the future—to the past. In Niro's work the past is never forgotten; it is never dead but vivid and intensely potent in the lives of the living in the present. The Mohawk knowledge of the past is a different modality of knowledge than the settler-colonialist epistemological regimes. In the next section, I look deeper into that difference.

Resistance and Resurgence

It Starts with a Whisper is a companion film to Niro's photographic triptych *500 Year Itch*, which was released in 1992, the five hundredth anniversary of what is typically considered the beginning of colonization and genocide in North America.[29] As noted, Niro opens *It Starts with a Whisper* by framing the problem of lost knowledge through a young woman's longing to know about the Tutelo, a tribe of Siouan people who suffered a population collapse caused by one of the many disease epidemics brought on by colonization in the eighteenth century. Though a few Tutelo survivors joined the Haudenosaunee, and some of their rituals were thus retained, the people themselves persist as a haunting memory of loss, an active, potent presence of one sliver of the vast cultural richness, languages, and knowledge systems, that coloniality attempted to extinguish. It is not just coloniality's territorial violence that Niro's films critique; they also target the willingness to desecrate and destroy other cultural and conceptual worlds in order to assert the monolithic one-world of coloniality's drive for material goods.

The young protagonist, Shanna, remembers that "so much [of Indigenous knowledge] has been lost"; as she stands alone, facing the river a place called Tutela Heights, the loss of knowledge is potent and extensive, haunting her. And yet, the voices speaking Mohawk that open the film, as beadwork and wampum are displayed as living objects, imply that this lost knowledge is still there, somewhere. Later in the film, when Shanna, in the company of her aunts, reaches Niagara Falls, the young woman hears comforting ancestral voices. And within these voices, the aporia and spaces of unknowing coloniality (i.e., rejecting settler definitions of time and history) are articulated as Shanna hears the ancestors soothingly and mysteriously tell her: "Don't be sad, we made it through another year, a short five hundred years." The sense of the long pain and threat and terror of five hundred years of colonization, despite which Indigenous Americans still persist and thrive, is at once vivifying and also desolate, highlighting what it feels like to survive against great odds.

Five hundred years and one year become the same length in the surreality that is coloniality's relentless attempt to destroy and erase Indigenous knowledges and peoples. To not know the difference between one year and half a millennium is an accurate reflection of both the pain and the ultimately meaningless knowledge system of coloniality's force. The voices in Niro's film reassures: "Little One, Shanna, don't be afraid, the voices of the past are calling you; the voices of the present urge you on; the voices of the dead tell you their sorrow."[30]

In *It Starts with a Whisper* (1993), the problematic of submerged practices and histories of Indigenous knowledge is articulated through oblique interrogation of the ways that coloniality steals and alters land. The problem is not merely that of seeking to disrupt coloniality's knowledge, an emphasis that would ultimately be acquiescence to coloniality; instead, the filmmaker focuses on Indigenous knowledge and re-accessing that knowledge by elliptically *muting* the knowledge fields of coloniality. Here, Indigenous knowing is not about responding to coloniality's interlocking systems of knowledge-power; rather, the work of the film is to excavate Indigenous knowledges, even as their incompleteness stands hauntingly at the centers of the films. Importantly, this incompleteness of knowledge is not problematized in the film as a weakness, in contrast to purported colonialist completeness of knowing. Instead, the haunting and pregnant spaces of incomplete Indigenous histories are thrown back through lens-based technology to illuminate gaps or hollows at the center of coloniality's drive to take over Indigenous material resources by capturing these resources in wall-to-wall discursive colonization. Knowledge (of Indigenous peoples, languages, and cultures) that has been lost through genocide is mourned in the film, yes; but this mourning is itself a source of resurgence as the film consistently suggests that sources of knowledge continue to emerge that fill in the gaps of what has been lost. I connect this approach to Niro's work, discussed in chapter 3, of photographing fossils at Cayuga in her series *Resting Place of Our Ancestors*. Her art entails a fierce determination to find what has been lost and to reclaim it.

The problematic of settler culture's defining extractive economic resources as the only site of meaning, with capitalism negating cultural memory as a viable site of wealth, places the film *It Starts with a Whisper* in oscillating tactics of resisting coloniality. It is an anticolonialist film that critiques capitalist excesses, and the subtlety of the film's confrontations with capitalism occurs along the axes of temporality and memory, where these axes are rendered unstable in the filmic medium, full of caesurae, gaps, pauses. It is these elements that articulate the film's contestation of coloniality. Through these moments of incompleteness, the film contests capitalism—the bulwark of coloniality.

It Starts with a Whisper begins with the invocation of water and moves into cosmological considerations of loss, suppressed knowing, and—to draw on Gerald Vizenor's (Ojibwe, White Earth Reservation) term—*survivance*. The effect is one of marked temporal estrangement in scenes that emphasize fragmentation and resilience—resilience emerging from loss. The family ties between the aunties and Shanna are crucial to the film and recuperate and parallel Shanna's connections with the ancestors she shares with her aunts.

"From the silence we speak to you," say the voices of the ancestors, just before the film cuts from the bucolic Tutela Heights riparian zone to the busy and noisy city of Toronto. These moments of unsettlement, of being unsettled, establish the film's subterranean protest. The ancestors stay with Shanna throughout as Niro's film creates a sense of an ongoing estrangement from the bourgeois and capitalist strategies of wrapping family ties into the gathering of material possessions are absented. The film likewise undoes Western colonialist suppositions of gender when the aunts and Shanna sharply make fun of Western ideas of women's burlesque.

In oblique patterns that invoke how Indigenous resurgence depends on unknowing coloniality, Niro uses magical realism and temporal estrangement so that even as *It Starts with a Whisper* seems like a "road trip" movie, Shanna and her aunts are pictured as driving not in the world but through a vista of unsettling black-and-white reel footage (as noted), as if they were lost in filmic time rather than driving from Toronto to Niagara Falls, New York. The scene of the women's journey illustrates that we do not entirely know where they are; where they are both is and isn't *Onguiaahra*, because in coloniality Niagara both is and isn't itself. The three aunts resist the losses of coloniality when they—as their niece disparagingly puts it—continue to *talk, and laugh, and eat* (i.e., continue to be fully and joyfully alive). Though aware that they inhabit the haunted atmosphere of coloniality, they do what they must to survive and thrive in this surreal space of coloniality to which unknowing colonialism is a tactic of resurgence. As scholar and educator Jeff Corntassel (Cherokee) argues, "Being Indigenous today means struggling to reclaim and regenerate one's relational, place-based existence by challenging the ongoing, destructive forces of colonization."[31]

The aunties in *It Starts with a Whisper* embody resurgence and illuminate Vizenor's theory of Indigenous survivance; they vivify survival and resistance in the face of coloniality. Vizenor argues that Indigenous Americans move beyond the positionality of what he terms "victimry" and instead respond to the history of genocidal violence that is colonization with a simultaneous awareness of the history of violence and a refusal to reinscribe onto themselves the position of the victimized Other. In Niro's *It Starts with a Whisper*, resistance, survival, and thriving are entwined through the film's capacity to bend time, to bring into the present the voices of the past. The ancestors' voices that soothe Shanna emerge from the film's originary aesthetic of magical realism and temporal estrangement. We believe these voices because they speak with poetic concision and poetic logic; they tell the exhausted and saddened young woman that it will be okay because "we made it through another year, a short five hundred years. Next year will be better." The five hundred years of colonization that continue now, as we still live within the system of coloniality, is a very long year indeed; and, as the postscript to the film makes clear, it is in the still moments of observing colonialist violence that we can begin to see paths of survivance.

Film is, of course, definitively not a still medium. And yet, in Niro's film, aesthetic force—the recurrent pulse of stillness—is paramount. It is in the moments when narrative flow is broken, when the diegetic spell of the moving image stills—that is, in the fracture of narrative movement—that resistance comes to the fore. In *It Starts with a Whisper*, there is a spectral fragmented narrative of womanly lineage. When Shanna confronts the loss of so many Indigenous memories, languages, and knowledge ways, the film moves toward a cosmological viewpoint; standing near the force of Niagara Falls, Shanna hears the names of tribe after tribe, nation after nation, of Indigenous North Americans, many who are still here, some who are not. That force of loss combined with persistence, of survival as itself the essence of resistance, co-occurs with the film's moments of stopping. When Shanna arrives in Niagara Falls, she is confronted with the tawdry neon signage of settler-colonialist capitalism. The trash that settler colonialism creates is repeatedly pointed to in Niro's work: far from representing settler-colonialist culture as "civilization," she represents it (accurately) as the great creator of trash.

In response to this trash—the tourist junk of Niagara Falls—Shanna is stunned, and yet it is through this moment of fracture, the stillness of being stunned, that she begins to hear the ancestors comfort her. It is here that she meets Elijah Harper, a figure of guidance and survivance. At the film's close, when she and her aunts eat the globe-shaped teacake that represents the world, Turtle Island, they turn the trope of settler trash as dominion on its head. As the film closes, the Mohawk women have the world in their hands. It is here that Niro weaves, deep into the fabric of her films of political resistance, the act of *de*coloniality as a process of *unknowing* coloniality. As Patrick Wolfe persuasively makes the case, coloniality functions as a structure of knowledge, making us feel as if settler-colonialist civilization is the only place we are allowed to live—with the ever-present capitalist imprimatur to buy and consume. In such a system, to unknow coloniality is a form of protest.[32] By unknowing coloniality, we can eschew being reinscribed into the circle of coloniality where the oppressed are marked as victims within a system that remains intact.

Niro's Shanna and her aunts inhabit realms where the unknowing of coloniality is expressed as resistance, hence resistance occurs—in the structure of the film—with the act of breaking repeatedly the diegetic press of the narrative so that moments of unknowing become the unstable but ultimately comforting, healing, and truthful telos of the film. The incantation of the names of Indigenous nations in the film fragments the flow of action, preventing the linear, enclosing grasp of settler-colonialist epistemology. The ancestors cannot be contained or restrained in colonialist-capitalist discourse, and their force of the active resistance that is unknowing capitalist colonialism persists throughout the film.

This abiding sense of the loss, fragmentation, and unanswerability of Indigenous survivance and resurgence builds as the film focuses on moments of womanly connection albeit intercut with palpable grief. These connections between women—aunts and niece—provide integument in the face of coloniality's violent uncanniness. Within the invoked spaces of not knowing is the pregnant force of resisting coloniality, not because coloniality—here—is yet again the locus of attention, but on the contrary because coloniality is doubly *negated* in Niro's film. The uncanny juxtaposition that closes the film depicts Shanna and her aunts eating the cake shaped like the world as New Year's Eve fireworks for 1993, the 501st year of colonization, fly behind them. This indicates a profound vision of protesting colonization, as Raheja notes the fireworks take the form of the Celestial Tree. Showing the illogic and contradictions of the structures of coloniality, this film, early in Niro's oeuvre, presents the subtle guerrilla tactics that Niro develops and deploys throughout her career.

Indigenous Feminist Resistance

There is vigorous contestation of how and if feminist resistance instigated by settler culture (putative white feminism) and Indigenous feminism connect.[33] Niro anchors her resistance in Mohawk traditions and also welcomes connections with women (including this author) who are not part of that tradition. There is stable epistemological ground for connecting across feminisms, even if in practice these connections are rarely sincere. Feminist philosopher Silvia Federici argues that capitalism works not only by stripping land from those who, thus rendered landless, become the proletariat but also by controlling, punishing, and violating the female body.[34] In this sense, she makes a case for feminist connections between Indigenous and settler proletariat. It was in response to the economic crisis of the late Middle Ages, argues Federici, that "the European ruling class launched the global offensive that in the course of at least three centuries was to change the history of the planet, laying the foundations of a capitalist world system, in the relentless attempt to appropriate new sources of wealth."[35] As Federici explains, Karl Marx includes in "the chief moments" of early accumulation "the discovery of gold and silver in America, the extirpation, enslavement and entombment in mines of the Aboriginal population [of America]."[36] But moving beyond classical Marxist theory, building on its foundational awareness of the coterminous contiguous trajectories, Federici further contends that the creation of the capitalist world order depended on not only the genocidal theft of Indigenous property but also the "accumulation of differences and divisions within the working class" so that the ideology of differences of gender and race severely dampened unity and resistance within the proletariat.[37] Importantly, the cultural manufacture of the concept of the female body as an eminently punishable body is at the core of the creation of the capitalist world order, argues Federici. The brutal expropriation of the peasantry from its land, in Europe, set the pattern by which the land of Indigenous North Americans was genocidally taken from the original people of North America, and Federici argues this pattern of violence is most deeply inflicted on women, all women.

Notes Federici, "The drive to maximize the exploitation of labor put in jeopardy the reproduction of the work force. . . . This contradiction exploded most dramatically in the American colonies where work, disease, and disciplinary punishments destroyed two-thirds of the Native American population in the first few decades after" contact.[38] Federici rightly states that this destruction of Indigenous North Americans reached "genocidal proportions," and she connects this ruthless destruction of human life with the systemic punishment of the female body as constitutive of the creation of the capitalist world order.[39]

Niro's art is feminist art, especially in the places where it critiques the capitalist desecration of North America, and particularly New York State. This theft began, as Niro's work signifies, five hundred years ago. Federici notes, "In Europe, privatization of land began in the late fifteenth century," along with early colonization and colonial expansion.[40] She posits (drawing from Cunningham) that, before 1494, European warfare was waged on a smaller, local scale. It is with the emergence of horrific new scales of war that colonization and the regularized punishment of women co-occurred, thus reshaping the world. The enclosures taking place in Europe connect directly to the untrammeled theft of Indigenous land in North America.[41] Niro's insistence on her vision as a woman who returns to the stolen land of her people is doubly a rebuke of settler colonialism. Her art emerges as the vision of a Haudenosaunee *woman*, refusing settler-colonialist beliefs in women's secondary status, as well as refusing the silence and invisibility that cloaks the history of settler-colonialist theft of Indigenous lands in New York State, as elsewhere in the Americas.

Notably, the Europeans who came to Haudenosaunee land in the seventeenth century were coming from a Europe where hunger reigned.[42] Contrast this endemic European hunger with the abundance of Haudenosaunee resources at the time (noted in this book's opening chapter). The

European settlers and speculators brought their hunger to the Haudenosaunee, inflicting starvation on Niro's ancestors where the Haudenosaunee had before contact stewarded the land to create abundance. As Taylor notes, Sullivan's genocidal expedition of 1779 against the Mohawk found and ruined an abundance of Mohawk agriculture: "Every few miles his army stopped to destroy a great quantity of corn and a great many fruit trees." Moreover, Sullivan's army found miles and miles of fields planted with corn and an array of vegetables as well as miles of cleared land and "fruit trees surrounding villages such that at times the abundance was so great Sullivan's army did not have the man power to destroy it."[43] This Mohawk abundance was due to the relative lack of power that capitalism held in their culture (by the late eighteenth century, the Mohawk had long been trading with European settlers but had not been thoroughly forced to accept the European lifeway and economy). Mohawk abundance (prior to expulsion) was also due to Mohawk women, who were traditionally the ones who planted and maintained the fields and orchards around their villages.

This place of abundance, Mohawk ancestral lands, became a series of battlefields in capitalist settler colonialism, reaching a high-water mark of violence just after the American Revolutionary War. But the violence of colonization began, of course, with first contact; in the century that followed, there was a population collapse of Indigenous people so severe that it is rightly called the "American Holocaust."[44] Recent studies conclude that approximately 55 million Indigenous North Americans, from a population of 60 million, died as the result of war, disease, and famine in the first century after contact.[45] The vast scale of settler-colonialist destruction of Indigenous populations also, argues Federici, added to the brutal control of the female body in what became capitalist economies.[46] Niro's *Battlefields of My Ancestors* (see chapter 2) returns to the scenes where her ancestors were massacred, and to the places where a culture—the Mohawk culture—in which women were equal was supplanted by a culture in which women were violently subjugated.

Niro's ancestors, then, are not only Haudenosaunee people as such but also Haudenosaunee women (the women from whom Niro descends) and are substantial forces in tribal governance. Exposing the battlefields that settler colonialism created and then covered up, Niro also reveals the punishment of women under settler-colonialist cultures. In returning to New York State in *Battlefields of My Ancestors*, she exposes the crime of settler land theft and the weakness of the legal protection of Aboriginal title. In *It Starts with a Whisper*, Niro anchors resistance in connections between women. Shanna's aunts are portrayed by Niro's own sisters, and it is the aunts who show Shanna a way and a reason to survive through resistance and toward joyful resurgence. In their resistance is a powerful refusal to submit to settler-colonial sexism with its punishment of the female body. The aunts in *It Starts with a Whisper* are ebullient, clever, and humorous, slyly poking fun at settler expectations of women and above all refusing and entirely refuting settler notions of female powerlessness.

Niro's Mohawk Feminist Gaze

The feminist force of Niro's work is inescapable. Women and their powers to resist, thrive, and surge forward against all obstacles are at the center of almost every work of art Niro creates. The women characters in her films and the female subjects in her photographs are always Indigenous women. This insistence on Indigenous feminist power is a key way that Niro indigenizes visual culture. As Maile Arvin (Kanaka Maoli), Eve Tuck (Unangax̂), and Angie Morrill (Klamath) argue, "Native feminist theories offer new and reclaimed ways of thinking through not only how settler colonialism has impacted Indigenous and settler communities, but also how feminist theories can imagine and realize different modes of nationalism and alliances in the future."[47] The history of racism within feminism is well known, and I have noted it in my discussion of Judith Butler's work earlier in this book and in my essay "Roland Barthes, Ana Mendieta, and the Orphaned Image."[48] And yet, white-feminist racism does not mean that feminist resistance is itself colonialist; on the contrary, in response to coloniality and racist feminism, Indigenous feminism articulates strength because it is only in undoing coloniality that we undo a central origin of heteropatriarchy. As Mishuana Goeman (Seneca) and Jennifer Nez Denetdale (Diné/Navajo) contend, "We desire to open up spaces where generations of colonialism have silenced Native peoples about the status of their women and about the intersections of power and domination that have also shaped Native nations and gender relations."[49]

In the photographs of *Battlefields of My Ancestors* (chapter 2) created across three decades and continuing into the present, Niro's images heal wounds of colonialist alienation forced onto Indigenous women who have been torn from their land. Her images of the land function both as rebellion against racist visual ideologies and as a formal practice of healing.

Niro's images of Mohawk women and Indigenous North American women generally also function as visual sites of resistance and healing. As Patrick Wolfe argues, the fabular social category called "race" is an image created by settler colonialism.[50] States Wolfe, "Race . . . is a trace of history: colonized populations continue to be racialized in specific ways that mark out and reproduce the unequal relationships into which Europeans have co-opted these populations."[51] As Wolfe elaborates, these social imaginary structures of race (which is always already a form of racism) cut to the core of how the state dictates identity.[52] Niro not only photographs other women but also is a genius of the self-portrait genre. In Niro's self-portrait triptych "Abnormally Aboriginal" (see figures 1.10–1.11), the artist subtly instates a return to the land of New York State, although this return is implicitly encoded as a rebuttal to the settler-colonialist state's claim to dictate the artist's identity.

At the artist's retrospective in 2023, a massive rendition of the three-image self-portrait photographic triptych, *Abnormally Aboriginal*, faced the museum visitor as they entered the exhibit *500 Year Itch*. Confronting the viewer, whomever they may be, with Niro's face formally structures the entire retrospective as the artist's active return to New York. In the first frame of the triptych, she faces us, wearing cat's-eye glasses and a black T-shirt that states ABNORMALLY ABORIGINAL in skewed letters, a DNA helix, and the pattern of the buffalo nickel's profile, sculpted by James Earle Fraser (a composite portrait of three Indigenous North American men). The faces of these three men were merged to create the image on the buffalo nickel, as if they were only one person. The portrait subjects, however, are Two Moons, a Cheyenne warrior who fought against the United States in the Battle of Little Big Horn; John Big Tree, who was Haudenosaunee (Seneca); and Chief Iron Tail (Oglala Lakota), a performer in Buffalo Bill's Wild West Show.[53] Niro's self-portrait echoes and corrects this merging of three men into one by unfolding herself as one woman into three. The first frame of Niro's self-portrait cleverly attacks settler language that codifies Indigenous people as "other" than the "norm" of Euro-settlers.

As legal scholar Rebecca Tsosie (Yaqui) notes, there is a comic—notwithstanding very destructive—side to settlers' restive presumption of naming and renaming Indigenous peoples:

Pow-wow pundits often joke that in the 1940s, "Indians" were classified by U.S. census takers as being of the "Mongolian race," and then, by the 1960s, they had their own "American Indian" category, until the 1980s, when they became "Native American." However, that term became somewhat discredited in the 1990s when Native political activists disclaimed "American" identity in favor of the more globally politically correct term "Indigenous peoples." "Today," the joke continues, "I'm Other." This joke has always inspired enthusiastic howls from the crowd, most of whom understand themselves in the context of a particular tribal identity—Diné, Tohono O'odham, Lakota.[54]

And to her list, we might add Mohawk. Niro's triptych deftly confronts the absurd power imbalance that generates the capacity for settler colonialists to constantly change what they name America's first people.

Returning to New York by placing her self-portrait here, in this place, Niro also returns by claiming herself in the self-portrait process—her self as an Indigenous New Yorker. In the middle frame, she has donned sunglasses, and the T-shirt now says NORMAL ORIGINAL. Here, Niro looks askance at the visitor, daring them to question her originality. But in the final frame of the triptych, *Abnormally Aboriginal*, Niro wears no glasses. No words appear on the T-shirt. The viewer is provided no frames of reference, technologies of seeing. Instead, there is the woman artist, the Mohawk artist, looking directly and astutely at the viewer. It is she who sizes us up. This is Indigenous feminism: Shelley Niro's gaze looking at us.

As scholar and theorist Glen Sean Coulthard (Yellowknives Dene) argues, it is not the goal of Indigenous activism to be seen as equal by settler society, not the goal to be assimilated.[55] Rather, the aim is sovereignty, and sovereignty cannot have meaning without the materiality of land, which includes the deep recognition of self. Coulthard shifts the gaze of coloniality, enabling us to see that Indigenous "belonging" on the American continent is interpreted not as something settler states can grant Indigenous people, but as inherent to the condition of indigeneity. He draws from the work of Frantz Fanon to argue that resistance means turning "our attention to the cultural practices of critical individual and collective self-recognition that colonized populations often engage in to empower themselves, instead of relying too heavily on the colonial state and society to do this for them."[56]

In returning to New York, through her art, Niro instates her right to be present and to be seen in this land that was stolen. Her triptych self-portrait *Abnormally Aboriginal* is a feminist act. Niro's feminism is neither clearly poststructural nor essentialist (as is often the charge made against Luce Irigaray). Niro insists, rather, on a historical, embodied continuation of Mohawk femininity (not necessarily heterosexual or cis-gendered). In staging returns to traditional Mohawk lands, whether those returns are imaginary, evoked through ceremony and memory, or literal embodied returns to take photographs of places in New York State, Shelley Niro engages and displays Haudenosaunee values. As historian Daniel Richter notes, the Haudenosaunee vehemently disliked the "competitive and acquisitive" values of the settler colonialists.[57] In contrast to settler sociality, traditional Haudenosaunee sociality holds significant power for women, that power distinctly connected to the land.[58] Niro's return to claim the land of her ancestors, then, is both a refusal of settler values and an expression of Mohawk femininity.

Niro's work *The Iroquois Is a Highly Developed Matriarchal Society* (figure 4.2) is a tongue-in-cheek photograph poking fun at the typical white anthropological discourse describing the Iroquois (Haudenosaunee) as matrilineal. In the photograph, we see Niro's mother, Chiquita Doxtater, having her hair done in the kitchen of one of her daughters. The photograph is domestic, open but also cautious. In the photograph's gentle humor is the point that Mrs. Doxtater and the daughter doing her hair are not exactly looking and acting like fierce matriarchs. The artist's mother is photographed here—as in all Niro's photographs of her mother—with great respect and love. In Canada, where Niro grew up and where she

Figure 4.2. *The Iroquois Is a Highly Developed Matriarchal Society*, 1989, hand-colored gelatin silver prints, triptych, 22 in. × 37 in. *Source:* Courtesy of the artist.

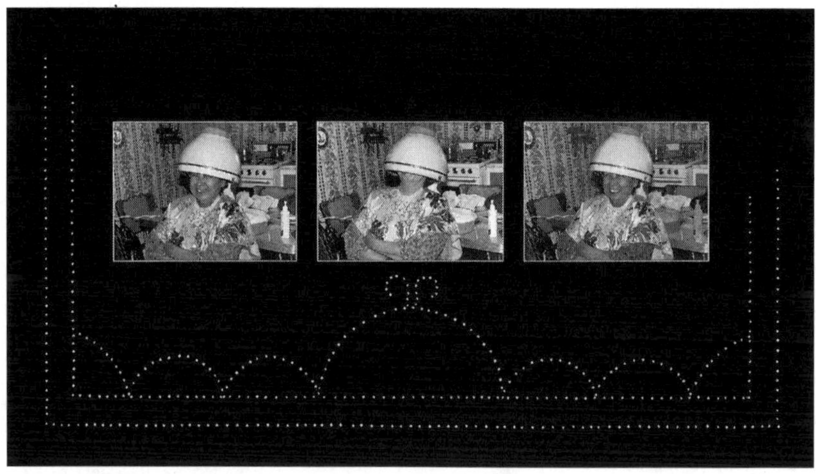

and her extended family now live, the Indian Act determined that one's legal status as Indigenous was inextricably tied to masculinity. As Indian Affairs Minister Jean Chrétien stated (in 1969): "To be an Indian is to be a man."[59] By portraying her mother having her hair done in a Canadian kitchen, Niro reflects not only on how settler culture diminishes the tradition of female power in Haudenosaunee culture, but also reflects on the place—the where—of her mother's and sister's domicile. The Mohawks in this photograph are a displaced people: they are in a kitchen in Canada, not New York. The word "Iroquois," deployed humorously in the photograph's title, is not the people's name for themselves. Rather, the word indicates a group of people displaced from their homeland and named "Iroquois" by those who displaced them.

In Niro's *The Iroquois Is a Highly Developed Matriarchal Society*, we see the artist's mother laughing. The space appears cozy and middle class, neither a space of abject poverty nor of overweening wealth. In this comfortable space, the middle frame of the triptych shows Chiquita Doxtater laughing so hard her face almost disappears into the hair-drying bulb, the implication being she is laughing at the context of the "highly developed matriarchal society" "anthro" lingo. Traditional Haudenosaunee beadwork patterns support Doxtater, as they run beneath the images. The beading patterns suggest the stability of Mohawk spiritual belief in contrast to, and as antidote against, settler violence. The symbolic traditional pattern contests settler naming. Not only is Niro spoofing anthropologist jargon, but she also makes the serious point that violence against Indigenous women is rampant, and this is so because settler colonialism brought in a system of entrenched sexism in which sexism and racism combine to make Indigenous women frequent victims of patriarchal violence and gender-based abuse.

In the essay "Being an Indigenous Woman Is a High-Risk Lifestyle,"[60] scholar Mary Eberts argues: "The staggering amount of violence against Indigenous women is a product of colonialism."[61] Eberts notes that not only law—which in settler nation-states is written to protect settlers, not Indigenous people—but also social constructs of gender cause this astronomical rate of violence against Indigenous women: "The stereotype of the 'squaw' is described by Métis scholar Emma Laroque as *a being without a human face* who is lustful, immoral, unfeeling and dirty."[62] In creating her self-portrait series *Abnormally Aboriginal,* Niro places her human face in a space where it cannot be ignored. In creating *The Iroquois Is a Highly Developed Matriarchal Society* she shows her mother's face being gazed at with love.

Niro has discussed the irony that Mohawk culture is considered, by white anthropologists, to be matriarchal (matrilineal), when the effect of colonization has been to foment gender-based violence against Indigenous women.[63] Niro's activist art subtly and substantively insists on nothing less than a complete shift in how Indigenous women are seen. Her work's response to gender-based violence, here, is paramount because coloniality brought an epidemic of gender-based violence to Indigenous women. Niro's feminist statement here is to show love and deep respect through the gaze of her camera. Contrasting with Niro's feminist Indigenous gaze that shows Indigenous American and First Nations women with respect and love, the statistics of Indigenous women's victimization by gender-based violence (including sexual violence and murder) are horrifying. Eberts points out that, between 1997 and 2000, Indigenous Canadian women were seven times more likely to be murdered than non-Indigenous Canadian women, while more recent (2020) statistics indicate that 84 percent of Indigenous women have experienced violence in their lifetime and nearly half have survived rape.[64] The epidemic of missing and murdered Indigenous women has a long history and continues today in Canada and the United States. Statistics from 2023 indicate that, in the United States, murder is the third leading cause of death for Indigenous women.[65] Niro's *The Iroquois Is a Highly Developed Matriarchal Society* at once spoofs anthropologists' terminology and also focuses on the pressing problem of gender-based violence that afflicts Indigenous women in settler-colonialist nations.

Niro's photographic series *M: Stories of Women* is another example of how Indigenous feminism is expressed in her art. In the title, the initial *M* stands for Monster, referencing the monstrous representations of Indigenous women that are typical in the mainstream media. This 2011 series "is composed of ten digital photomontage portraits of women facing the camera to confront the burdens mainstream society" (settler society) has placed on them, notes curator Wanda Nanibush (Beausoleil First Nation, Ojibwe). Nanibush continues, "Niro assertively presents the resilience each woman holds in parallel with the trauma each has experienced and holds inside. Building on Sky Woman's narrative, the Haudenosaunee Creation story, the series directly confronts present-day burdens."[66] Niro powerfully connects the series with genocide and the epidemic of missing women and views her photography as a path to see Indigenous women anew, stating: "With this exhibition, my goal is to create another kind of image of Native North American women. Our legacy starts in the Skyworld."[67] Centrally, the power that Niro shows in each of these portraits invokes the history of Sky Woman, with a tender portrait of Niro's elder daughter, pregnant with her daughter (Raven), as a figure of the pregnant Sky Woman anchoring the series.

Sky Woman's Ambivalence

Sky Woman (discussed in the introduction to this book), who plays a crucial role in the Haudenosaunee creation story, is central to Niro's presentation and understanding of Mohawk women.[68] Her series of photographs "Flying Woman" interprets Sky Woman as an ambiguous figure, neither of the earth nor of the sky, circling human places but neither leaving them nor joining them. Niro presents Sky Woman as a form of survivance, the term created by theorist Gerald Vizenor for Indigenous thriving in the face of genocidal violence. Niro creates an unsettled gaze across the landscape that Sky Woman crosses as her art interrogates the legacy of genocide and violence against Indigenous women, a silenced space in our culture, one that contemporary white feminism largely ignores. Niro's films *It Starts with a Whisper* (1993) and *Kissed by Lightning* (2009), read together with her series of photographs *Battlefields of My Ancestors* and the mixed-media sculpture *1779*, contend with the near erasure of the Mohawk people from their homeland. Her art resists that erasure of place by emphasizing female resilience.

Her series of photographs "Are You My Sister?" is a group of portraits of Indigenous women, which also includes a photograph of the artist's shadow and two images of a woman's outlined silhouette. The series draws the viewer in, asking her if the viewer can be the sister of the Indigenous women photographed, and ultimately of the photographer herself, the shadow presence made manifest at the series' center. In "Are You My Sister?" spectral figures of a woman's outline flank the series, while at the center there are elegant photographic portraits of Mohawk women. Asking the question "Are You My Sister?," Niro makes the case for inclusive feminism but also contests the white-feminist habit of dominating by acting, and writing, as if everyone is white or fits into a rubric controlled by whiteness. Sisterhood, Niro's work suggests, must be *earned*—not taken. Sky Woman's ambivalence in falling to Earth is also, perhaps, Shelley Niro's ambivalence in creating art that is primarily for Haudenosaunee women but also celebrated by a settler artworld that is not anchored by Haudenosaunee values and beliefs.

Animacy: The Eloquent Acts of Shelley Niro's Camera

Her haunting and mournful film *Niagara* (2015, originally titled *Ongniaarha*), an elegy for her younger daughter, fuses the feminine line of three anonymous speakers—a mother, daughter, and grandmother—within the site that is considered by the Haudenosaunee to be a gateway to the spirit world, Niagara. Female lineage here is threatened with silence and erasure, and yet the voice and vision of the filmmaker perseveres, speaking and creating survival even in the face of a trauma. Instead of silencing, the film presents voice. In the haunted place of Niagara, then, Niro exposes unacceptable loss but counters this loss with the force of continuation, condolence, and female survivance. Femininity and indigeneity, the meaning of being a woman and Haudenosaunee, are at the heart of Niro's art of return to New York, a mode of survivance in genocide's aftermath.

Returning to Coulthard's emphasis on the work of Frantz Fanon, I suggest that Fanon's theory of colonization—as an instantiation of violence masked as social hierarchy—provides an important heuristic for understanding Shelley Niro's work that resists coloniality. Fanon's *The Wretched of the Earth* helps us understand the decolonizing force of Niro's art. Her work intercedes in the space where the pressure of Indigenous North Americans to assimilate shapes the discourse of citizenship. Niro's films and photographs remove the mask placed across Indigenous people in the oppressive history of racism and white dominance. Consider philosopher Jean-Paul Sartre's notion of the social power encoded in "the look" as a condition of alienation that can aid us in interpreting Niro's portraits of her sisters and mother and her self-portraits. Argues Sartre, "These differences are born of colonial history, in other words, of oppression."[69] The entwinement of settler artworld practices creates an ambivalent space for Niro's art that assuredly strives for visibility but is primarily aimed at Indigenous audience.

Philip J. Deloria (Standing Rock Sioux) and Marge Bruchac (Abenaki), working separately, theorize animacy in objects held in museums, theorizations that I suggest can also help us interpret the space that Niro's art creates in settler-controlled galleries and museums.[70] Animacy of the object illuminates ways that Niro's art resists, refuses, and overturns the colonialist gaze. Deloria argues persuasively that settler-colonialist culture sees objects of art and of archaeological museum collections as items that are mute and without animacy, objects that are fetishized to trophy-like status, whereas Indigenous culture perceives such objects as living with stories to tell and connections through history. I interpret Niro's photography and film works as "animate" visualities that transcend the category of fine art even as they inhabit that category within settler discourse. Niro's penchant for combining photographs with mixed-media pieces makes her work a hybrid space where the visual and the haptic merge.

Troubling traditional museum boundaries and categories, Niro's sculptural photographic projects, such as the three-photograph set *Chiquita, Bunny, Stella* (figures 4.3–4.5), create a relationship with the viewer that alters the museum and gallery space, making it not a cabinet of curiosities but a living, vivid realm of ideation and beauty. Combining photography with patterns of traditional Haudenosaunee beadwork, feathers, and cornhusks, in this trio of photographs, Niro creates a space of animacy—and of intimacy—in which she reclaims contemporary perspective, refusing the oppressive structures of Western time that consign Indigenous peoples to a primordial time-before. For theorist Mel Y. Chen, animacy is a political designation, a heuristic concept that explains racism by theorizing the imputation of being less alive to those who are colonized and oppressed

Figure 4.3. *Chiquita, Bunny, Stella*, 1995, Frame 1 of three gelatin silver prints on fiber-based paper, 48 × 36 × 23⅝ inches / 122 × 91.4 × 60 cm. *Source:* Courtesy of the artist.

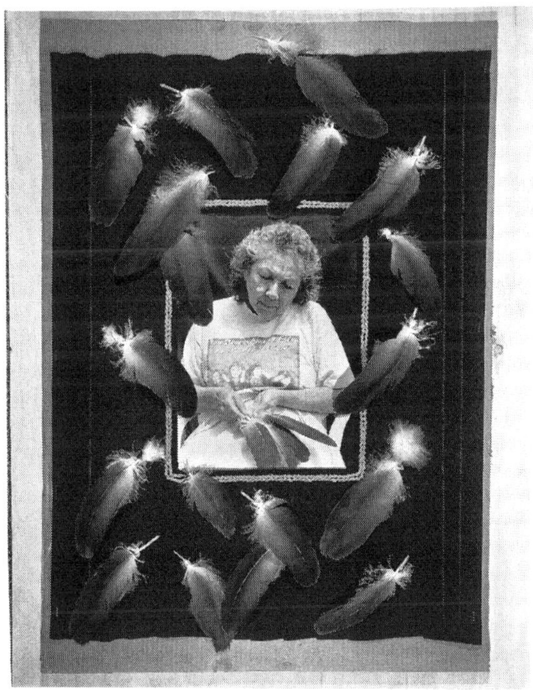

Figure 4.4. *Chiquita, Bunny, Stella*, 1995, Frame 2 of three gelatin silver prints on fiber-based paper, 48 × 36 × 23⅝ inches / 122 × 91.4 × 60 cm. *Source:* Courtesy of the artist.

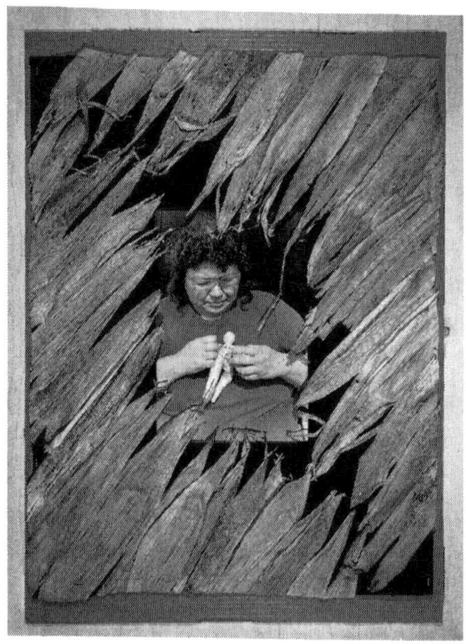

Figure 4.5. *Chiquita, Bunny, Stella*, 1995, Frame 3 of three gelatin silver prints on fiber-based paper, 48 × 36 × 23⅝ inches / 122 × 91.4 × 60 cm. *Source:* Courtesy of the artist.

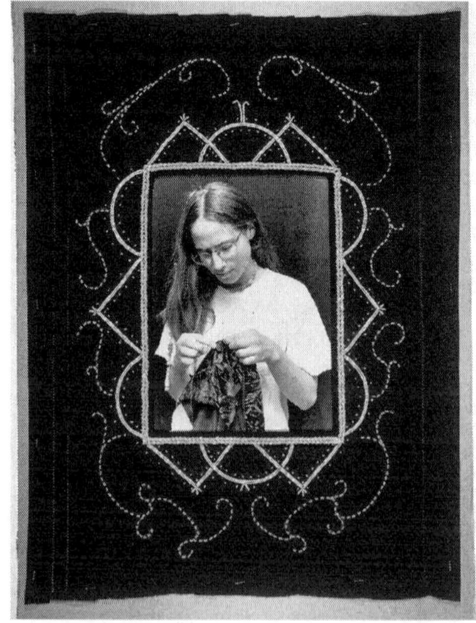

by racism.[71] Niro's art subverts the persistent myth that Indigenous culture is in the past—dead history—and demonstrates that these traditions are alive in her twenty-first-century art as she extends animacy through her photographic work.

In the photographs of *Chiquita, Bunny, Stella*, Niro's mother, sister, and daughter are shown doing fine work; Chiquita works with feathers, Bunny with cornhusks, Stella with cloth. The women's faces are intent on their work in the photographs so that we see a kind of mythopoetic transformation crossing between the still photographs and the gallery or museum space. By framing the images with cultural living materials—feathers, husks, beads—Niro clarifies that the women in her family create living Haudenosaunee art and that, in turn, the photographer also creates living works with her camera, continuing, extending, and making new Haudenosaunee tradition.

The photographic work implicitly extends into the gallery or museum space as, visually, the feathers, corn husks, and stitching are extended through the picture frames of the women's forms so that images of feathers, corn husks, and traditional pattern work, as living objects, spill vividly toward the viewer. The tenderness and trust that run through the photographer's gaze and the faces of her mother, sister, and daughter add to this sense of animacy. The women are not looking at the photographer; they are intent on their work. But her work is to look at them, and this one-way gaze is predicated on immense trust. The photographs attest to and repay that trust. The mother's (Chiquita) worn face is revealed in the beauty of the contours of her bone structure; the sister's (Bunny) centrality as she creates the cornhusk doll positions her as the heart of the family tableau. The daughter's (Stella) delicate build is accentuated by the bodily position she holds in the final photograph of the group. Unlike the artist's mother and sister, who hold their hands close to their bodies as they work, the artist's daughter, Stella, holds her hands slightly away from her body so that they move into the foreground of the image, as if they were reaching toward the viewer. The effect is such that her hands become a site of implied shared touch with the viewer. Through Stella's hands we are brought into the intense work of art as living object. The artist's mother, sister, and daughter, like the artist, are Turtle Clan. In these works invoking women of the Turtle Clan, Niro rebuilds the place of the Mohawk in New York State. Forced out of their homeland of the Mohawk Valley, Niro re-places—re-creates place—through the living act of creating photographs of the physical acts of traditional arts. Through photography of care, she leverages her forceful political statement of claim.

Chapter 5

Indigenous Resurgence against Colonialist Capitalism

Coloniality as the system emerging in temporal and cultural entwinement with Renaissance and Enlightenment ideologies is now buttressed and sustained by global capitalism. In capitalist coloniality, land is commodity, and one that is forcibly created through the violence of stripping Indigenous people of their ancestral land, whether by displacing them, murdering them, or starving them. By contrast, Indigenous conceptualizations of land encode the idea of reciprocity, of human beings caring for the land, which reciprocates by nourishing, sustaining, and sheltering human stewards. Indigenous conceptualizations of land encode notions of the land's meaning rather than its value as capital. As Shelley Niro (Six Nations of the Grand River Reserve, Bay of Quinte Kanien'kehá:ka Mohawk Nation, Turtle Clan) writes in the multimedia photographic work *For Fearless and Other Indians*: "In my culture/there are no monuments/ no man-made structures/no tourist sites/one visits/burns tobacco/says a prayer/think of our elders/and ancestors/remind ourselves/the importance/ the significance/this space holds/we don't need reminders."[1] Niro here makes clear the absolute incompatibility of settler-capitalist notions of land and Mohawk notions of land. For the Mohawk, the meaning of land is deeply saturated with cultural ancestral meaning. Space (i.e., land) holds significance through millennia of culturally specific meaning imparted by the people long in that place. In this sense, the land of New York State is still Haudenosaunee land since the meaning of the land hasn't changed just because the people have been displaced.

By contrast, settler-capitalist notions of land interpret it through a legal framework that conscripts land for its market value, as capital. To own land in capitalist terms is merely to own a type of money; land can be turned into money, and that is its only value in capitalism. That is not to say that people living in settler-capitalist regimes do not, at times, feel strong emotions that tie them to land or place. Rather, it conveys that, within the system of settler capitalism, land is solely *legally* structured as commodity.[2] Historian Michael Leroy Oberg notes the nefarious fusion of capitalist "growth" and dispossession of the Haudenosaunee, writing that in the aftermath of the Treaty of Canandaigua (1794), "The lands the Seneca lost . . . represented a massive share of their homeland. The State of New York, meanwhile, took every opportunity it could . . . to acquire lands belonging to the Cayugas, Oneidas, Onondagas, Mohawk, and Tuscororas."[3] New York State was created through the machinations of settler-colonialist speculators who used deceit, proffered alcohol, and altered laws whenever it seemed the people of the Six Nations might be able to use the law in their favor, so as to strip the Haudenosaunee of their lands. Argues historian Laurence Hauptman, "The Great Peace and Power the Iroquois League had from the seventeenth century operated in this manner to provide protection . . . and establish a buffer against white settlement pressures."[4] However, as Hauptman goes on to make clear, "For New York State to arise as a major force in the new nation, its borders had to be secure."[5] Borders, in nation-state discourse, are nothing but capitalist structures despite the mythology in which they are typically enrobed. This need of the settler-colonialist nation-state to establish a space for untrammeled capitalist commerce meant that the Haudenosaunee were again and again cheated of their land during the decades following the Mohawk expulsion. But the land is still, in its essence, Haudenosaunee land, as Niro demonstrates in her artworks that return to and evoke New York State.

It is worth recalling that roots of decolonization theory, in the work of Frantz Fanon, are clearly and explicitly critical of capitalism. Fanon writes:

> Capitalist exploitation and cartels and monopolies are the enemies of underdeveloped countries. On the other hand, the choice of a socialist regime, a regime which is completely orientated toward the people as a whole and based on the principle that man is the most precious of all possessions, will allow us to go forward more quickly and more harmoniously,

and thus make impossible that caricature of society where all economic and political power is held in the hands of a few who regard the nation as a whole with scorn and contempt.[6]

In other words, as Fanon rightly perceives, untrammeled capitalism is the enemy of decolonization. Decolonization cannot happen in the context of capitalist economics precisely because racial capitalism and coloniality are entwined systems that developed together and mutually reinforce colonialist social, economic, legal, and environmental practices.

The concept of "colonial unknowing" (discussed in chapter 4) that Manu Vimalassery, Juliana Hu Pegues, and Alyosha Goldstein describe as a response to the conceptual "entanglements" of racism and settler colonialism extends from the seminal theoretical work of Patrick Wolfe and seeks ways beyond these comprehensively entangling cognitive structures of coloniality.[7] The validity of this approach inheres in its ability to bring to the surface the potency with which the entire structure of knowledge that forms the mythos of coloniality saturates epistemic and economic belief and action. That is, coloniality contains, paradigmatically, a structure of knowledge as punitive power, hierarchical knowledge systems that hold sway and control without ethics and have direct material and economic consequences because they shape the material economy of coloniality.

We are, of course, still living in the context of this system of the veneration of hierarchical Western traditional knowledge that historically emerged in tandem with systems of racist thought, and violent programs of colonization, and the imposition of nearly universal capitalism. And yet, if we are to *unknow* these systems, we must be aware—and beware—that their very structure will punish any declarations of their nonnecessity. To unknow structures of colonialist thought is to place oneself in spaces of unrecognizability, for coloniality only recognizes its own structures. Within coloniality, we can claim identity as injured parties, but we can only legibly "unknow" coloniality by taking refuge in other knowledge systems that make visible coloniality's incompleteness of knowledge.

In other words, unknowing as an intellectual stance can reveal the *ill*ogic of coloniality's ideological frame, but the process of unmasking and unknowing constantly risks the erasure of its own protest, a subterranean and suppressed corollary to the signal habit of coloniality's suppression of the knowledge of its real history. As Fanon makes clear, the fundamental structure of colonialist power is all-out war and extreme, even genocidal, violence in the initial phases of contact, followed by aggressive discursive colonization—myths, and knowledge systems as myths—that *cover up* and render secret and unspeakable the violence of settler colonialism. Deploying irony, he argues: "Violence in the colonies does not only have for its aim the keeping of these enslaved men at arm's length; it seeks to humanize them. Everything will be done to wipe out their traditions, to substitute our [the colonizer's] language for theirs and to destroy their culture without giving them ours. . . . Starved and ill, if they have any spirit left, fear will finish the job."[8] Fanon as noted uses the word "humanize" with irony. This covered-up violence is the core of coloniality itself. It is the forgotten real that must remain submerged and silenced for the project of coloniality to continue. To accept the North American continent as a European culture—English, Spanish, and French its languages—is to uphold profound and ongoing acts of forgetting. But speaking of this forgetting also risks encountering acts of re-erasure (of being re-erased). Remembrance, however, is not merely verbal. It is also geographical. Fanon contends: "If we examine closely this system of compartments . . . its ordering and its geographical layout will allow us to mark out the lines on which a decolonized society will be reorganized."[9] Niro's brave and virtuosic acts of remembrance are visual contestations fighting geographic displacement.

The most fundamental structure of coloniality is land theft from Indigenous peoples and the subsequent organizing of that stolen land to structure resource access (and lack of access)—access for those wealthy and white, lack of access for the colonized and impoverished. It is important to also note that land access in Canada and the United States is overwhelmingly correlated with wealth. The vast majority of settler descendants (the putative 99 percent) have little capital and less land. That reality of capitalist exploitation through class structure makes it all the more urgent to confront the reality that North America *is* Indigenous land. This recognition is foundational to unsettling capitalist legal structures that create the land as property. Niro's series *For Fearless and Other Indians*, discussed in the following section, is a work she made twice, emphasizing its critical importance in her oeuvre. Niro contests the loss of land and asserts sovereignty in this work of subtle brilliance that clarifies differences of settler and Indigenous understandings of land's meaning.

For Fearless and Other Indians: Shelley Niro's Statue of Liberty

In her 1998 series of photographic works *For Fearless and Other Indians* (figures 5.1–5.7), Niro confronts an icon of Americana: the Statue of

Figure 5.1. *For Fearless and Other Indians*, 1998, Frame 1 of seven color photographs on paper and decorated mat, 121.9 cm × 83.82 cm each. *Source:* Courtesy of the McIntosh Gallery and the artist.

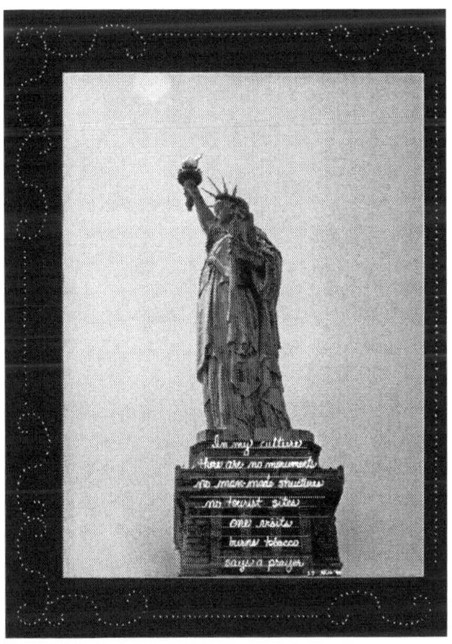

Figure 5.2. *For Fearless and Other Indians*, 1998, Frame 2 of seven color photographs on paper and decorated mat, 121.9 cm × 83.82 cm each. *Source:* Courtesy of the McIntosh Gallery and the artist.

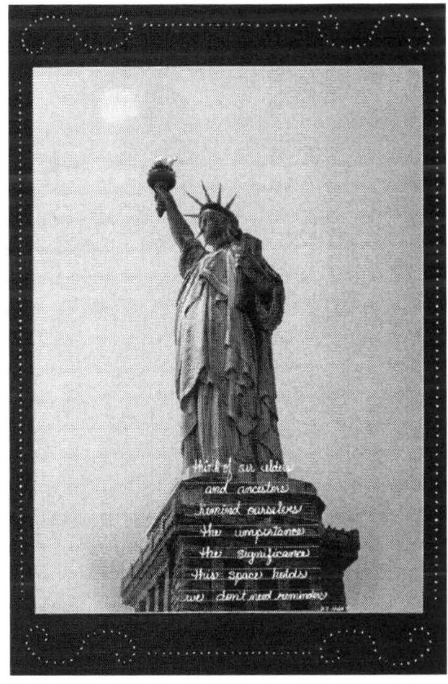

Figure 5.3. *For Fearless and Other Indians*, 1998, Frame 3 of seven color photographs on paper and decorated mat, 121.9 cm × 83.82 cm each. *Source:* Courtesy of the McIntosh Gallery and the artist.

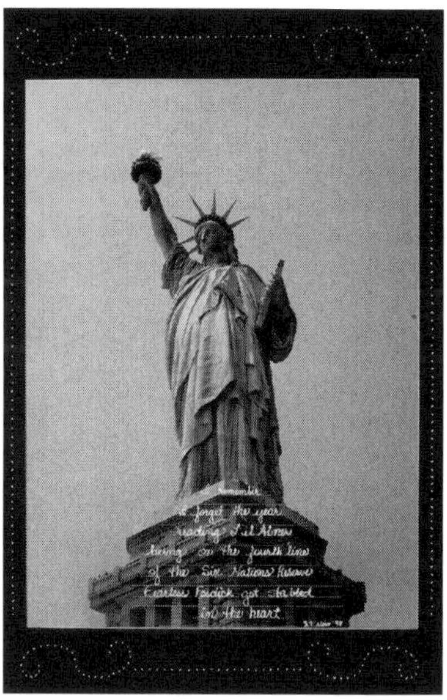

Figure 5.4. *For Fearless and Other Indians*, 1998, Frame 4 of seven color photographs on paper and decorated mat, 121.9 cm × 83.82 cm each. *Source:* Courtesy of the McIntosh Gallery and the artist.

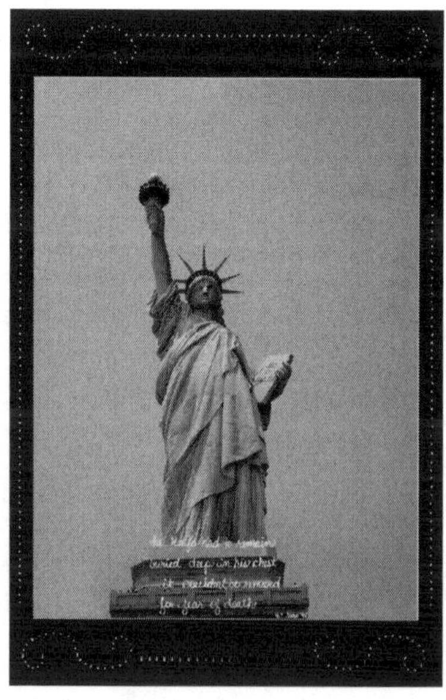

Figure 5.5. *For Fearless and Other Indians*, 1998, Frame 5 of seven color photographs on paper and decorated mat, 121.9 cm × 83.82 cm each. *Source:* Courtesy of the McIntosh Gallery and the artist.

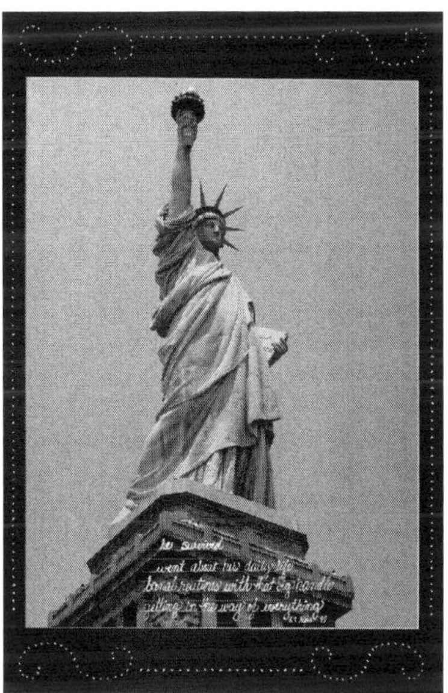

Figure 5.6. *For Fearless and Other Indians*, 1998, Frame 6 of seven color photographs on paper and decorated mat, 121.9 cm × 83.82 cm each. *Source:* Courtesy of the McIntosh Gallery and the artist.

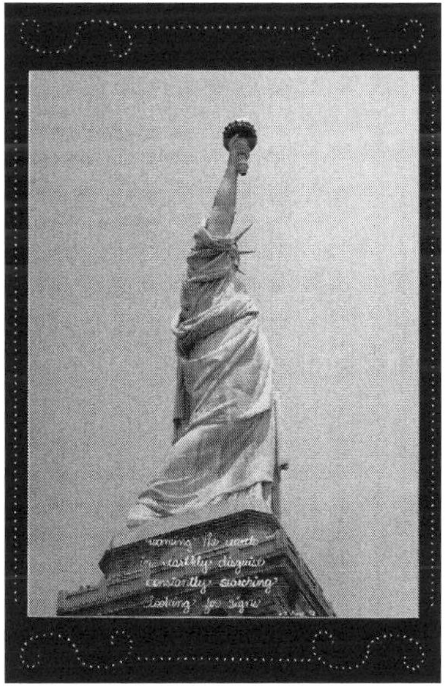

Figure 5.7. *For Fearless and Other Indians*, 1998, Frame 7 of seven color photographs on paper and decorated mat, 121.9 cm × 83.82 cm each. *Source:* Courtesy of the McIntosh Gallery and the artist.

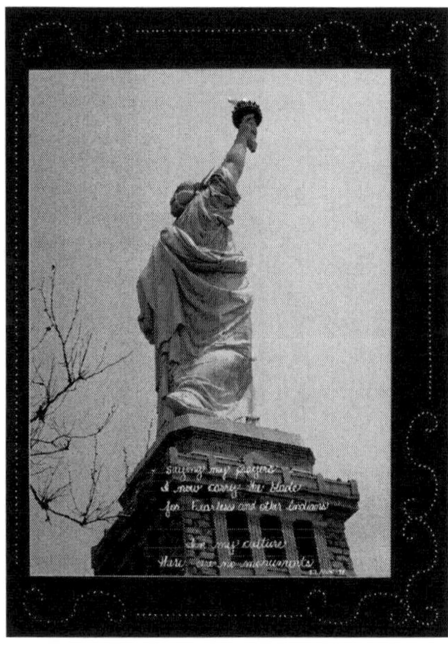

Liberty. This series of seven photographs shows the Statue of Liberty against a field of blue sky juxtaposed with handwritten text contrasting the "democracy" of America. The series performatively pivots by contrasting symbolic settler-colonialist nation-state monumentality—the Statue of Liberty—with traditional Mohawk (and more broadly, Haudenosaunee) systems of making political decisions, remembering ancestors, and participating in communal, ethical ways of life. Niro's series deconstructs the very premise of iconic emblems of colonialist democracy as a false front. In *For Fearless and Other Indians*, Niro subtly takes apart the premise of American exceptionalism as a leader of democracy, positing that, instead of a shining "city upon a hill," the elided history of settler atrocities against Indigenous Americans is the primary fact and act of the United States' formation. My discussion of the work follows Niro's lead in excavating the history of American democracy as linked to the process of monumentalization. I consider how her work is important now as we encounter a crisis of democracy in the United States.

For Fearless and Other Indians addresses how colonialist violence is reified in what we might broadly call "war monuments": a topic that became a flashpoint in North America some twenty-five years after Niro's initial creation of her work. The early twenty-first-century debate over monuments takes the form of arguing over who should *not* be memorialized. In Charlottesville, Virginia, for example, statues for Robert E. Lee and Stonewall Jackson were joined by a sculpted rendition of Lewis and Clark in which Indigenous Americans are shown crouching beneath the white men, until 2021 when they were finally taken down. Niro's seven-frame photographic and word series *For Fearless and Other Indians*, however, plumbs deeper than the practical remedy of removing offensive statues. In seeing the Statue of Liberty as comparable to Civil War monuments I draw from theorists who contend that the United States bases its power on continual colonialist proxy wars in addition to the extensive and formative history of its overt wars of conquest.[10]

Niro's *For Fearless and Other Indians* takes on this most iconic of American monuments, deconstructing the framework and idea of monumentality and revealing the practice of monumentalization as itself a foundation of oppression; it sees monuments themselves as key markers of hegemonic ideology. In seven photographs contrasting a blue sky with images of the statue viewed from below, Niro handwrites a counter-politics to monuments. Mohawk culture, she asserts in the seven-stanza poem printed across the photographs, does not create monuments. Mohawk ways of showing reverence for history, ancestry, and culture take place through the practice of memory: one says a prayer, burns some tobacco, and remembers one's ancestors, remaining aware throughout of the sacredness of place itself. By contrast, Niro's photographs of the Statue of Liberty emphasize the metal monument's lack of human tactility and intimidating form, with its up-thrust arm and monstrous size.

The Statue of Liberty is not shown in Niro's photographs as part of a human community but rather cast into a cold sky. The statue cannot satisfy or shelter the kind of sacred enactments that Niro describes as intrinsic to her culture's notion of reverence. The words of Niro's poem contrast with her intimidating images of the Statue of Liberty, making viewers aware of just what a nation-state monument does: it demarcates and commandeers space, telling the person looking at it whether they do or do not have the right to be there. The presence of the Robert E. Lee statue in what was long called Lee Park sent a message to African

American residents of Charlottesville; it communicated that the city viewed as noble and just the Confederacy's efforts to preserve the enslavement of people of African descent. Living in Charlottesville for nearly fifteen years, I was struck by the irony that most of the daily visitors to Lee Park were African American men experiencing houselessness, with nowhere else to go. Their continued subjugation to racial injustice was symbolized by Lee's statue, visible from the makeshift beds of coats upon which the men slept.

Niro's description of Mohawk ways of carrying cultural memory contrasts sharply, then, with the ostracizing control of social space that statuary monuments produce. Around a monument, vulnerable citizens can be humiliated and excluded. A prayer, the practice of remembrance, burning tobacco—these acts do not command space; rather, they respect it, asserting not domination and demarcation but the continuation of the sacredness of spaces as known by citizens of the Bay of Quinte Kanien'kehá:ka Mohawk Nation. These are often communal activities and they are always community based, even if performed alone, because they signify collective memory, knowledge, and belief.

As Niro's series of photographs *For Fearless and Other Indians* circles the impassive, unyielding statue, her handwritten poem reflects on a comic strip, Al Capp's *Li'l Abner* (1934–77), and its metafictional strip-within-a-strip, *Fearless Fosdick*. The action of the sub-story in the comic strip was briefly set at the border of the Six Nations Reserve. Here, at the boundary of colonialist space commandeered by settler-speculators (that is, reserve space into which Indigenous peoples were displaced), Fearless Fosdick, the title character in the metafictional strip, is stabbed in the heart in an attempt to assert justice in his typically un-self-protective way. Throughout the strip-within-a-strip, Fosdick is portrayed as a detective who tries to preserve justice and mostly ends up getting wounded. He is not an Indigenous character. Why did Al Capp describe Fosdick, who is not imaged as Indigenous, as an "Indian"? The comic strip did have an Indigenous American caricature character named Lonesome Polecat, offensively portrayed.

The comic strip's painfully racist depiction of a supposed Indigenous American (labeled a Kickapoo by Al Capp, the comic strip's creator) cries out for incisive critique. But Niro's series *For Fearless and Other Indians* isn't primarily about racist stereotypes. It is about monuments and the violence inherent in their symbolic apportioning of space. Her work reveals how democracy is bent by the practice of monumentalization. Recalling that the character Fearless Fosdick is stabbed in the heart at the boundary of the Six Nations Reserve, one notes that this reservation is also a symbol, a forcefully enacted demarcation of social space. Demarcations of this kind lie at the heart of colonization. They structure the social space of coloniality.

This stab wound to Fearless Fosdick is a permanent one, a haunting parallel to the experience of genocide and violent colonization that is the history of North American Indigenous peoples. Niro's *For Fearless and Other Indians* suggests that the knife of colonization cannot be taken out because the damage is so extensive. It is not just a wound; the knife is still in the collective social body of Indigenous Americans. Pulling a knife out of a stab victim must be done with surgical care or else the person will hemorrhage. The parallel that Niro establishes, in her description of Fearless's knife wound, is that of colonization as a wound to the heart of Indigenous people, an injury with the weapon *still in place*. In *For Fearless and Other Indians*, we notice that the Statue of Liberty's up-thrust arm looks like a weapon, as Niro photographs the monument. The spikes of Liberty's gloriole (headpiece) also look deadly.

To be sure, Niro does not appear to be critiquing the theoretical position of the Statue of Liberty: welcoming the outcast to American shores. Yet her photographs of the statue present it as unfeeling, harsh, metallic, weapon-like. Rather than welcoming the poor and the hungry, the statue manifests as a barrier (a problematic with which the United States continues to wrestle, with many politicians concerned more with exclusion than with welcoming).

Niro's narrative in *For Fearless and Other Indians* explains that, although Fearless Fosdick survives, the knife handle protrudes, and the blade is always in him. The handle gets between Fearless and his daily activities while the threat of instant death is constantly asserted by the knife in his heart. As this meta-reality is explained, Niro's script crosses the plinth of the statue in the photograph. Recall that Fearless Fosdick is a metafictional comic strip, a strip-within-a-strip. We are deep in the realm of metaphor here, and yet the reality of physical pain, danger, and damage is vivified not by images culled from Capp's comic strip but by Niro's photographs of the Statue of Liberty.

The Statue of Liberty is presented in *For Fearless and Other Indians* as the physical representation of the knife of colonization that remains lodged in the collective social body of Indigenous Americans. The Statue of Liberty is the knife thrust into the collective body of America's original people. As Niro's series continues, Lady Liberty begins to turn her back on us; she turns away from the viewer as the series closes. Here, the narrative describes the plight of the injured Fearless, who wanders across the Earth. He is exiled from the living world in that, having come to the boundary of an Indigenous reservation, he was stabbed and now internalizes that line, carrying with him always the boundary of life and death in the aching metaphor of a knife that cannot be pulled from his heart.

In the final image of the seven-photograph series, the Statue of Liberty entirely turns away from the viewer. We see her back only. Here, the photographer reveals herself as a double of Fearless Fosdick, noting that she—the artist—carries a wound, the wound of her people's displacement and the genocidal violence they survived. Just as *Fosdick* is a strip-within-a-strip, Niro positions herself as an emblem within a story through the words of her photographic and written text artwork: "Saying my prayers/I now carry the blade/for Fearless and other Indians."[11]

Claiming the role of the artist as the carrier of the wound radically recenters the project of Niro's photographs of the Statue of Liberty and the tale of Fearless Fosdick. Whereas the creator of the Statue of Liberty, Frédéric Auguste Bartholdi, shaped an icon of ideology, "Liberty Enlightening the World," Niro's photographic work is antimonumental, and her juxtaposed words reflect on her reconceptualization of the role of the artist. She is *not* one who creates massive objects before which others bow down; instead, she stands with those who suffer wounds and survive anyway. In this sense, she posits her art as the true democratic (*of the people*) alternative to the Statue of Liberty.

Whereas the statue stands at the boundary of colonial domination and the turning away of many who seek refuge, Niro states that she will carry the knife wound of suffering for all those—Indigenous, ancestors, and other peoples wounded by the processes of colonization: stabbed in the heart by the violent apportioning of lived public space that is a core act of colonization. At the heart of the project of colonization is taking control of who may and may not enter various socially symbolic domains within the nation-state. Reservations are an enduring result of the genocidal legacy of white-settler violence. But, as historian Donald L. Fixico (Shawnee, Sac and Fox, Muscogee Creek, and Seminole) notes, Termination Policy—the mid-twentieth-century effort in the United States to erase the legality of tribal claims to exist—and contemporaneous efforts to force Indigenous peoples to leave reservations were policies that masked genocidal intent—that is, the intent to erase the very notion of indigeneity.[12] The goal of Termination Policy was a continuation of Thomas Jefferson's effort to assimilate all Indigenous Americans so that no Indigenous culture would remain. The erasure of Indigenous culture, the genocide of Indigenous people, is foundational to the concept of US nationality. Extending from this originary erasure, attaining US citizenship has long been circumscribed in ways that directly contradict the Statue of Liberty's role as "mother of exiles." The Chinese Exclusion Act, US law in force from 1882 to 1943, restricted Chinese immigration and prevented Chinese immigrants from attaining citizenship. Indigenous Americans were not afforded citizenship until 1924, just ten years before Capp launched his *Li'l Abner* strip. Trump-era (2016–20) clamor for a southern border wall was more of the same. As I write in early 2024, Trump is again running on a platform that grotesquely misrepresents the meaning of the United States' southern border and extolls violence and barbarism against those families who attempt to cross this border. Indeed, Leslie Marmon Silko's (Laguna Pueblo) *Almanac of the Dead* envisioned Indigenous resurgence as deeply entwined with Latinx resurgence.

Niro's *For Fearless and Other Indians* contends not only with the politics of who is allowed full citizenship but also and, fundamentally, with the structure of settler-colonialist domination. Niro's art illuminates and disputes how settler coloniality shapes social space. As Natchee Blu Barnd suggests, "The stories of connection to land are not just observations but actions."[13] In *For Fearless and Other Indians*, Niro presents a relationship to land. The series is anchored in New York City and clarifies why the theft of Indigenous land, through settler-colonialist actions, is a knife wound to the heart of indigeneity. Niro contrasts monuments, in their purposively conspicuous role of demarcating social space, with Indigenous conceptualizations of land, which cohere with sacredness and ancestral memory. Monuments as active symbols of dominance and power stake a claim on space. Monuments are nation-state ideological rhetoric made visible.

The rhetoric of monuments is not incidental but fundamental to settler colonialism, Niro's *For Fearless and Other Indians* makes clear. As philosopher Ernesto Laclau argues, "Rhetoric, far from being a parasite on ideology" is the "anatomy of the ideological." So too is the Statue of Liberty; it is the figural anatomy of an ideology.[14] Laclau further notes that representation (which of course includes fine art) "takes place in a terrain already partly sedimented and partly penetrated by relations of power."[15]

Refusing settler sedimentation, Niro closes her visual and poetic meditation on the Statue of Liberty by again reminding the viewer that, in her Mohawk culture, there are no monuments. For the Mohawk, deep cultural memory is held intact through the actions of living bodies, through prayer, remembering ancestors, visiting a sacred place that has no marker but is known by memory passed through generations. This supple, vivid, Indigenous way of retaining cultural memory is the spectrally conjured body that Niro evokes with the metaphor of sustaining a knife to the heart. By contrast, the Statue of Liberty is presented in her photographs as cold, against an empty sky, metal, impenetrable. Made of heavy-gauge metal that is nearly impossible to "stab," the monument appears instead as a knife itself. The "anatomy" of neoliberalist beliefs that enshrine violence as a right (European settler regimes enacted genocide on North America's original population and therefore now have control of most of the geography of the United States) is given embodied form in metal and stone monuments: the Statue of Liberty, Robert E. Lee on his horse, Lewis and Clark with their feet on the backs of Indigenous people. Niro's metaphor, her deployment of the meta narrative of Fearless Fosdick, deconstructs Lady Liberty's visual rhetoric of cold, metal flesh.

The Statue of Liberty is womanly, but she is a hard person. Liberty is called a mother, but one questions the way she allows men in power in her nation to abuse children in the name of freedom. By contrast, it is Niro herself who performs feminist resistance in the context of *For Fearless and Other Indians*. The artist performs a transformation, imagining her own body and psyche as the site of the construction of a people, those wounded by settler legacies and continued colonialist strategies of control, domination, and degradation. As Laclau argues, "The construction of a people is the main task of radical politics today."[16] The knife is already in, and the capacity for survival depends on bearing it while doing the work of resistance.

Deconstructing the Statue of Liberty, Niro's series of photographs and juxtaposed seven-stanza poem bring forward the pain of colonization not just for Indigenous Americans who have survived genocide but for all excluded by the boundary drawn by Lady Liberty. What is a democracy? It is the people, not the monument. The collective voice and body of humanity with our vulnerability to wounds is a democracy, not the anthropomorphic statue of stone or metal. Niro's art suggests that the wounded body of Indigenous people wanders without a safe and stable space to heal. This is the condition of exile and the terrible paradox of being in exile in one's ancestral homeland.

Here, Niro's work reveals the crux of settler-colonialist use of land: intrinsically it is always aware of its own instability and therefore requires monuments to shore it up. Settler nations fear losing what has been violently gained; hence, monuments and edifices as ossified cultural memory express this fear, revealing a system's fundamental incapacity to be truly plural, to engage through embodied cultural memory with the sacred. By contrast, Niro describes Mohawk cultural memory as extending through the bodies and minds of the people—visiting unmarked sites known to be sacred, burning tobacco, saying a prayer—indicating a sense of confidence that the sacred belongs to the people who carry it. Yet, the Statue of Liberty is not shared by all people inhabiting the land that is now the United States. It is not shared by Indigenous Americans who, through genocidal violence, were exiled from their homelands, wandering, bearing the knife wound. Also, as Niro's feminist pluralism attends, the welcome of the Statue of Liberty is not shared by those turned away from this country, or by those oppressed within it, whether by racist, sexist, or other cultural caste regimes.

Philosopher and historian Patrick Wolfe writes, "Confined Natives, relatives and descendants . . . remember their dispossession. That memory inscribes the foundational violence of settler democracy."[17] As Wolfe argues, for Indigenous people to resist settler colonialism is a dangerous act "given the power imbalance involved [between settler and Indigenous peoples,] resistance entails the most hazardous degree of risk-assessment."[18] Niro's continued artistic acts of resistance—through her creation of art and her stalwart willingness to bring her artwork into the public forum, to stand visibly as an Indigenous woman who, through her art creation, resists settler power structures—are an ongoing act of fearlessness. As she notes in the handwritten script of *For Fearless and Other Indians*, she carries the knife (of settler colonialism) in herself not only because she is a Mohawk woman, but, moreover, because she is an artist. The role of the artist, Niro continues, is to take responsibility to speak for her people. The artist, here, is antithetical to the dominant settler-colonialist vision of the isolated genius to whom the culture must bow as he creates his work. For Niro, the role of the artist as a Mohawk woman is to shoulder the injustice and oppression of Indigenous North Americans and to speak eloquently and fearlessly the truth of settler-colonialist violence.

The connection that Niro's work *For Fearless and Other Indians* makes with New York State is more elliptical here than in *Battlefields of My Ancestors, Niagara* (2015), and *Kissed by Lightning* (2009). Whereas those works show the land itself and—in the words of Solomon King in *Kissed by Lightning*—dramatize the way that the Haudenosaunee return to their homeland, walk the earth of their ancestors, and connect with those who came before, in *For Fearless and Other Indians*, Niro's confrontation is not only with New York State but also with the Statue of Liberty as a salient symbol of the myth of America as a promised land that shelters the dispossessed. The part of New York State that the Mohawk traditionally stewarded is the eastern region; the Mohawk, among the Haudenosaunee, were known as the "keepers of the Eastern Door." In the area that is now New York City, where the Statue of Liberty stands, the Algonquin were the predominant peoples before contact.[19] When Niro returns to New York to create *For Fearless and Other Indians* she confronts the symbol of American morality and ethics: the image of the Statue of Liberty standing for the ideal that the United States shelters those who have been displaced and treated violently by malign regimes elsewhere. As Emma Lazarus's poem reads, "Give me your tired, your poor, your huddled masses yearning to breathe free."[20]

And yet, as Niro's artworks make clear, settler-colonialist nation-states—far from being beacons of ethics and morality—are founded on genocide. The United States is founded on the attempted eradication of Indigenous Americans, very much including the Haudenosaunee who were a prime target of the new nation. Niro photographs the Statue of Liberty to expose the false front of the settler-colonialist nation-state that is the United States of America, a country that has yet to reckon with the reality of its own history. Shelley Niro creates art that enables us to begin to see ourselves as we really are. As she describes the difference between settler-colonialist monuments and Indigenous North American ways of honoring ancestors and place, Niro creates a pan-tribal unity that is anchored in New York. This unity among all Indigenous North Americans is powerful even as it encodes pain. To return to New York, for Niro, is to confront the way that the land of the Mohawk, the Lenape, and other Haudenosaunee and Algonquin peoples was brutally stripped from them. This history of settler-colonialist barbarity is a knife wound carried by Indigenous North Americans, as Niro expresses in *Fearless*. It is the role and the job of art, contends Niro in this important work, to stand up for those who carry the injuries of oppression. In this sense, her art is intensely political.

Although Niro originally created *For Fearless and Other Indians* in 1998, she remade the series for her 2023 retrospective in New York City. The new version of the piece (completed in 2022) was requested by the curators of the retrospective because of condition issues with the earlier version. In recreating the work, Niro made some meaningful changes. The photographs (prints created from the original negatives) and the verbal text remain the same, but the frame and typeface were altered to significant effect. Whereas the original photographs emphasize a clear and hauntingly blue sky, and there is a spare frame that includes a Haudenosaunee beading pattern: the 2022 version features a blanched sky and an elaborate border with images of embroidered flowers and the Haudenosaunee bead pattern of the Celestial Tree—an image that is bountiful and significant in many of Niro's works. In the 2022 version, rather than being handwritten, the words that help structure the multimedia project are typed. The effect of the profusion of flowers on the border of the Statue of Liberty photographs softens the blunt and painful narrative and images. The sense of starkness that is so salient in the 1998 version is muted and replaced with a sense of the artist offering viewers comfort in the updated piece, as if Niro, twenty-four years later, not only wants the viewer to absorb the message of the horror of colonization and settler nation-states but also seeks to comfort the viewer's grief in this confrontation. Oddly, in the retrospective exhibit in New York City, this important work was sidelined to a hallway where only the most dedicated visitor would find it. Yet, within that hallway, it filled the space with a sense of majesty, ushering the viewer into a new understanding of the relationship between the United States, New York State, and the Haudenosaunee.

Scholar and cultural theorist Audra Simpson (Kahnawà:ke Mohawk) pinpoints the vicious intersection of settler coloniality and gender oppression in Canada's nation-state policies creating categories of indigeneity. Contends Simpson,

> Race and sex became meaningful categories for determining membership in the consciousness of Kahnawà'kehró:non when resources were threatened and Mohawk became "Indians." . . . Beyond the boundaries of the reserve was white society and, with this social fact in mind we might infer that Kahnawà'kehró:non might not have wanted white men to affect the distribution of power within the society of the Kahnawà:ke. Extinguishing the rights of the Mohawk women may have been less of an attempt at discriminating against their own people than at protecting the community from a possible takeover by non-Indian men.[21]

In other words, Simpson sees the creation of gender oppression both as a move directly imposed by settler society and as a reaction, from within Mohawk society, of attempting to self-protect against further violation by white society. Notably, Simpson connects the stripping of rights from Mohawk women with the violent altering of their relationship to the land: "It was Mohawk women who paid the legal price for some sort of broader political protection through their disenfranchisement and legal exile from their natal homes, which must have been an enormous cost to the traditional structure of the community given the clan-bearing, clan-transmitting, and property-owning status of women." Simpson continues: "The powerful role of [Haudenosaunee] women had been forgotten for some," and "the territorial history of the Mohawk Nation shapes the central question of membership."[22] This refers to the ways that not only settler laws but also Mohawk self-governance as impacted by the strictures and violence of settler law denied membership to Mohawk women who married out. The generalized movement of denuding women's traditional power, then, is interpretable as the Mohawks' effort to retain power of any kind in the face of violent and endless settler territorial and juridical invasions into Mohawk place, space, and society.

We can see the force and courage of Niro's *For Fearless and Other Indians* as part of Mohawk tradition, women's traditional power in that culture. Facing the erosion of traditional ways caused by the centuries-long settler invasion, the artist rearticulates the meaning of place, space, and land. It is the meaning of place that anchors the act of the sacred in the language of *For Fearless and Other Indians*. The artist's pain, described in the series, is borne for the sake of her people. She takes on this role as part of the tradition in which women determine the political shape of the community by choosing who will lead and by keeping the fields, orchards, and villages. In other words, the traditional social role that we might mistranslate as "caregiver" signifies women who traditionally hold communal knowledge and power; this is also the space from which Niro inhabits the role of artist.

The gendered dynamics of *For Fearless and Other Indians* are striking. The photographs show the Statue of Liberty, a purportedly feminine figure who appears distinctly not sustaining. While Lazarus's poem intones that Lady Liberty, as the statue is sometimes called, says "give me your poor," the statue itself, in Niro's photography of it, appears not sheltering but violative. The narrator in *Fearless*, whose words run through the photographic and written text work, is not identified by gender. Fearless

Fosdick is distinctly masculine in the comic strip, but of course, being a comic-strip character is only an image of masculinity. Niro's narrator's own neutral gender juxtaposed with Liberty's eerily bellicose femininity and Fosdick's literally two-dimensional masculinity makes us aware, in the series, that what matters in this parable of how to be human—how to be a human being who cares for the land, the ancestors, and the community—is that gender is not of the essence. Niro's perspective, her frame of seeing, emerges from her place in a lineage of Mohawk women, but the series *For Fearless and Other Indians* strategically deemphasizes the series' speaker's gender. One can interpret this move in connection with Simpson's argument that "the powerful role of [Haudenosaunee] women had been forgotten for some."[23] Niro reminds us of that power quietly and forcefully.

Niro's *For Fearless and Other Indians* assumes the traditional power of Mohawk women to speak expertly about politics and asserts the artist's ability to shift between genders and to critique rigid settler gender designations. Aesthetically, the photographs distinctly critique settler femininity as a false front; that is, the images suggest that settler femininity often acts as a mere cover for settler violence. Linguistically, the series suggests that the narrator, in the role of artist, inhabits a space between genders, with Niro, who identifies as a cis woman, identifying herself in this series with Fearless Fosdick, a male comic-strip character. The series, then, corrects settler-colonialist encroachment on Mohawk territory in multiple ways. *For Fearless and Other Indians* asserts that settler nation-state monuments are part of land theft—they mark land stolen. It also leverages the power of a Mohawk woman who uses her art strategically as a mode of fighting to reclaim place, ancestral land, for her community. The work, like the process of commemoration it describes, is processual and profound.

Colonizing the Moon

To celebrate the opening of her career retrospective at the National Museum of the American Indian in New York, Niro was scheduled to be interviewed by the curators who collaborated on the show. However, when the curators and Niro arrived on the stage, she turned the tables by stating that *she* would interview them. The humorous moment turned serious when Niro playfully asked each curator how they would curate an art show on the moon, after it's been colonized.[24] The curators gamely spoke to the question, with only Mohawk artist and curator Greg Hill pulling away the curtain (so to speak) and saying that art wouldn't hang well on the moon.[25] At this comment, Niro jumped into the conversation and explained that she thought it was immensely sad that ultra-rich entrepreneurs are now trying to find ways to colonize the moon (and nearby planets).[26] Her awareness, signified in this playful exchange that turned serious, that colonization continues because it is a structure of social violence pressed forward by capitalism, is reflected in Niro's photograph titled *Final Frontier* in which Niro dons a *Star Trek* costume (figure 5.8).

On the left side of the triptych, the artist is dressed in a bright yellow-colored *Star Trek* costume; in the center, a little girl (the artist's younger daughter) is holding a skateboard, shielding her eyes from bright sun in the family yard; and on the right, the artist is dressed in work clothes. Through these juxtapositions, Niro troubles received colonialist notions of the frontier, notions that are fundamentally instrumental to settler violence displacing Indigenous peoples. In wearing a *Star Trek* costume, Niro pokes fun at the American obsession with the frontier (the putative "Frontier Thesis" having been for decades a key explanatory model in American

Figure 5.8. *Final Frontier*, printed 1992, triptych photograph, gelatin silver print heightened with paint, gelatin silver print, toned, gelatin silver print in hand-drilled overmat, 56 cm × 94.1 cm. *Source:* National Gallery of Canada, gift of Sandra Jackson, Bramalea, Ontario, 1995. Used with permission of the artist.

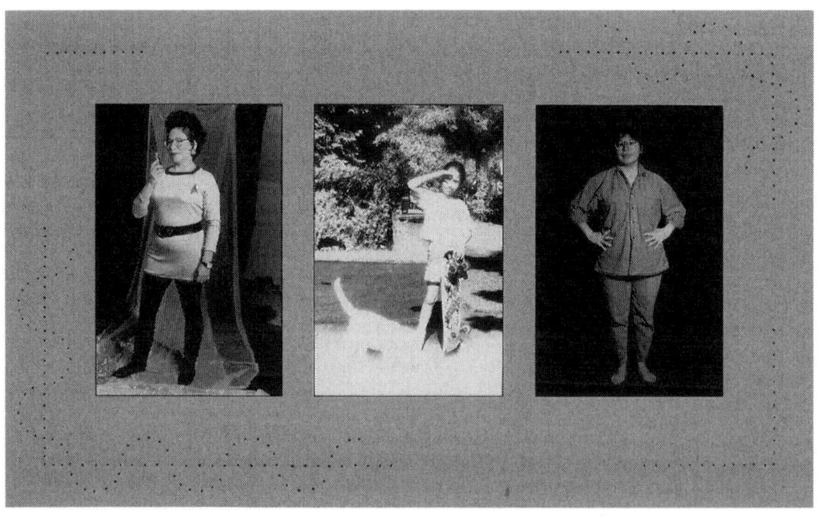

studies academe). She creates a visual joke, ribbing *Star Trek*, juxtaposing through the use of triptych her daughter's innocence—shielding her eyes from the sun—and her own stable identity as the working artist. In this way, the images combine to sharply critique the idea that a frontier is a good thing, and here Niro critiques the very eventuation we are now (some thirty years later) experiencing, with large sums of money being put toward the fantasy of occupying other planets.

The frontier is the effect of settler-colonialist capitalism's ceaseless push to expand markets and the exploitation of the resources that feed markets. Indeed, an endless need for more raw materials that presses capitalism to continue colonizing, philosopher Rosa Luxemburg argues, is the signal that capitalism is *not* a balanced self-regulating system but, on the contrary, can only continue by feeding vampirically off newly colonized resources.[27] That the periphery of capitalist societies—raw material, including labor and land—is the source of value means that capitalist settler-colonialist cultures *cannot stop* colonizing. Niro recognizes this rapaciousness in her initially humorous interview question that adroitly condenses the problematic fit of the art world and capitalist-colonialist expropriation of value from the periphery. Just as the Mohawk lands in New York State were once the periphery (in capitalist terms) and were violently pulled into the economy that became New York, so the moon is the new periphery, and Niro envisions the tragedy of its colonization as a space that, as Greg Hill (the only fellow Mohawk on the panel) caught, would not be suited for human art. To create art in the face of capitalist colonization's brutality is to create art, as it were, on the moon, Niro indicates in her interview question. Her artistic vision is expansive in that she does not see colonization as a past fact that is over; rather, she deeply understands how the past, present, and future flow together and how resistance must address all three.

Chapter 6

Twenty-First-Century Peacemaker

Shelley Niro's (Six Nations of the Grand River Reserve, Bay of Quinte Kanien'kehá:ka Mohawk Nation, Turtle Clan) imagined evocation of an art exhibit on the moon (discussed in chapter 5) participates in Indigenous futurism. Similarly, her films often play between past and present and invoke the future as a place of contestation. In *The Incredible 25ᵗʰ Year of Mitzi Bearclaw*, Mitzi's hallucinatory vision of the Earth from outer space as she sees the Earth dying from pollution draws together the deep past of Mohawk history, the recent past of television history, the present of Mitzi's young life, and the future of an increasingly sickened and damaged Earth. Even as the scene playfully gestures at *Star Trek* (the final frontier!), it deploys temporal estrangement and layering to bring home the profound loss that is not only the experience of Indigenous genocide but also the knowledge of coloniality's continued trashing of our planet. The distinction between settler culture and Haudenosaunee culture is intensely revealed in this temporal play. Niro emphasizes the urgency of the need to return lands to Indigenous peoples precisely by showing how an Indigenous concept of time disallows and closes down all the excuses for destroying the natural environment that are so prevalent in settler culture.[1] This tactic—part of her guerrilla strategy against coloniality—occurs in many of her works.

Niro's feature-length film *Kissed by Lightning* (2009) invokes the Peacemaker (Deganawida/Tekanawite) who brought the Condolence Ceremony to Hiawatha (Aiionwatha). Through Hiawatha, the Peacemaker's message of peace and conciliation spread to all the Haudenosaunee, leading to the founding of the Five Nations (later the Six Nations, when joined by the Tuscarora) and the Great Law of Peace. The Haudenosaunee Confederacy's contemporary (2023) website describes the history of the Peacemaker, a description I quote in full because the story is not one to truncate, and it is the Haudenosaunee who tell it:

> The Peacemaker was sent by the Creator to spread the Kariwiio or good mind. With the help of Aiionwatha, commonly known as Hiawatha, the Peacemaker taught the laws of peace to the Haudenosaunee. Travelling from community to community they both succeeded in persuading the Chiefs of each nation to join in the Great League of Peace and founded the only government with a direct connection to the Creator. Asking the Clan Mothers of each tribe to present their Chiefs, [Peacemaker] placed deer antlers on each of their heads to symbolize their authority to the Five Nations. The Mohawks had nine Chiefs of the bear, wolf and turtle clans, the Oneida also had nine of the bear, wolf and turtle clans, Onondaga presented fourteen of the turtle, snipe, bear, hawk, deer, wolf, eel, and beaver clans, Cayuga had ten from the heron, deer, turtle, bear and snipe clans and finally Seneca presented eight Chiefs from the bear, snipe, turtle, wolf and hawk clans. The Mohawk, Oneida, Cayuga, Seneca and Onondaga accepted the longhouse as a symbol of their unity. In the Onondaga community the Peacemaker planted a tree naming it the Great Tree of Peace.

The Haudenosaunee Confederacy continues:

> He [Peacemaker] directed the Chiefs of the council to sit beneath the shade of the tree and watch the council fire of the confederacy of the Five Nations. He told them that all issues concerning the confederacy would be discussed and deliberated under this tree. The roots outstretching from the tree reached north, south, east and west and were labeled the Great White Roots. The Peacemaker declared that any nation choosing to follow the guidelines of the Great Peace should follow the Great White Roots and make themselves known to the Chiefs of the confederacy. If they promised to obey the laws of peace they would be welcomed beneath the shade of the tree. Above the tree an eagle was placed to see far and alert the confederacy of approaching enemies. Beneath the tree

the Peacemaker asked that all men throw in their weapons to bury any greed, hatred and jealousy. Finally the Peacemaker took an arrow from each of the Five Nations and bound them together. In this way the nations were united in their powers and the union was complete. Each nation retained their own council with Chiefs chosen by Clan Mothers of families holding hereditary rights to office titles. The rights and duties of Chiefs are explained to them as they stand up as Chiefs and it is the Clan Mother who maintains his moral obligations and keeps him in a straight line. One by one the Peacemaker took wampum strings, one for each of the laws of the Great Peace and described what each signified. With this action the Great Confederation of the Five Nations was formed. With his mission fulfilled the Peacemaker vanished promising that if the Great Peace should fail the people were to call his name in the bushes and he would return.[2]

In her 2009 film *Kissed by Lightning*, Shelley Niro not only alludes to but also quietly and reverently reenacts Peacemaker's and Hiawatha's connection and the message of peace. *Kissed by Lightning* tells the story of Haudenosaunee artist Mavis Dogblood (played by Kateri Walker) mourning the loss of her first husband, Jessie Lightning, and growing to find love with Solomon King (nicknamed Bug). As the film unfolds, Niro uses a technique of temporal estrangement to draw together the narratives of Mavis, Jessie, and Solomon with the history of Peacemaker and Hiawatha and to suggest a future return of peace. Jessie Lightning, who appears throughout the film in grief-filled flashbacks, is the Peacemaker, a brilliant musician and composer who brings a sublime music to the world but dies suddenly and very young when struck by lightning. Jessie Lightning disappears abruptly and yet also remains a constitutive part of the lives of Mavis, Solomon, and Kateri (his first wife, with whom he had a son). By revisiting and bringing to life in the present day the stories of Peacemaker and Hiawatha, Niro decisively brings her film—primarily shot in Canada but often set in New York State—home to New York, to the Cohoes area where Peacemaker originally emerged. Weaving together the time of the Peacemaker, the time of the Revolution, when the Haudenosaunee were pushed from their homeland, and the present day—the lives of the ancestors and the living—Niro's *Kissed by Lightning* returns to New York State and, in parallel, Haudenosaunee history.

The film works through the centering trope of the journey, as artist Mavis Dogblood ferries her paintings—which show the Peacemaker's history and the origin of the Haudenosaunee, the Great League of Peace—from Canada to a gallery in New York City where they are eagerly awaited. The journey that Mavis and Solomon take together retraces the route by which the Haudenosaunee were expelled from New York in 1779. In this, the film has a clear connection to Niro's photographic series, *Battlefields of My Ancestors* (discussed in chapter 2). Along their journey, Mavis and Solomon see warriors and realize that, in returning to New York, they are returning to the place of their ancestors and feel their presence.[3] As Niro recalls the scene: "They are outside at night and they are lost, and they can feel that the spirits are reaching out to them. They can see those warriors of the past at the moment of their being lost too. Maybe their village left while they are gone to war, so they are still wandering, wondering where everybody is."[4] Niro describes the sense of being lost that permeates cultures victimized by genocidal colonization, writing a film in which her characters are lost in their own homeland. She also, importantly, writes a film in which those characters find their way home.

As Mavis and Solomon make their way from Canada to New York City (where Mavis's paintings will be exhibited), the long-reaching effects of Mohawk displacement rise to the surface in a racially charged moment in an upstate New York diner. When they enter the diner, where white people stare at them and make heinous comments about their grandfather having a collection of Indigenous people's scalps, Mavis and Solomon also meet a group of African American gospel singers. Mavis is subsequently serenaded by these singers, who thank her and Solomon for being the "Mohawk people" (alluding to the Mohawks' role in the Underground Railroad). This signifies that Mavis is coming home, even though the region feels like hostile terrain because of the racism of whites in the area. The deepest turn of the movie occurs later when, during a snowstorm, Mavis and Solomon spend the night with Jessie Lightning's grandmother in a small house in what was Mohawk country, in the Cohoes region. Niro indicates that this grandmother is also a figure for Jikonhsaseh, who advised Peacemaker on the foundation of the Haudenosaunee Confederacy and who had earlier poisoned young men but was taught by Peacemaker to nourish them.[5] Hence, the nourishing meal that Jikonhsaseh/grandmother of Jessie Lightning/Peacemaker gives Mavis and Bug (Solomon King) in her home late at night is a symbolic meal of peace and sets the stage for the foundation of the couple's union and their child's anticipated birth.

This geography of return is essential to the film. It is the entire point of the work—to explore how Mavis's art stems from her connection to the Peacemaker and to New York. In this sense, Solomon King is like the Hiawatha figure, but so also is Mavis, since it was Hiawatha's role to translate to the Haudenosaunee the wisdom of the Peacemaker, and Mavis, as the artist who paints Peacemaker's story, is the translator of his story for the public.

Mavis, as a woman artist, brings to the Peacemaker tradition the innovation of a woman translating for the Haudenosaunee the Peacemaker's message. In this aspect, the film is mythopoetic, for it is Niro, a woman filmmaker, who translates the story of Peacemaker in *Kissed by Lightning* so that contemporary Haudenosaunee audiences understand his message. The links between Niro and Mavis are clear: both are artists, both are Mohawk women. Niro herself painted all the paintings of Peacemaker's saga that appear in the film, and in this act, Shelley Niro and Mavis Dogblood literally are the same artist. When Mavis returns with Solomon King to the Mohawk homeland, Niro—the filmmaker recording the scenes—also symbolically returns home. In this next section, I look deeper at that return, reencountering the thumbnail sketch of the film I've given here and expanding its discussion.

Crossing the Border

Niro's film begins by recounting, in words displayed across the screen, the origins of the Confederacy of the Six Nations. The film's first ninety seconds show a traditionally dressed Haudenosaunee man on a corner of a busy street in New York, merging temporalities in the first instance of magical realism used in the film. Jessie Lightning, the contemporary Peacemaker, is a musician, setting art and music at the heart of the production. Jessie plays the viola and composes music. Niro points out that the viola is called the "Peacemaker" in an orchestra "because it's between the violin and the cello."[6] Just as across the film we see Mavis creating the series of Peacemaker paintings, the narrative of which comprises the substructure of the film, we also repeatedly hear the voiceover of Jessie Lightning (Peacemaker) speaking of the Peacemaker and saying "this story took place right here, in our own territory," meaning, of course, in what is now called New York State.[7] As Mavis's memories of Jessie Lightning play through her mind as montage flashbacks, the paintings she is creating are superimposed across these images so that Mavis's art of painting and Jessie's art of music are conjoined with the history of Peacemaker and the foundation of the confederacy, a founding that took place in traditional Haudenosaunee territory in what is now called New York State. Throughout the film, the images from the paintings return, as history replays itself as palimpsest with the present. When Kateri (Jessie's first wife) asks Mavis to take Zeus's (Jessie's son) school photograph to Jessie's grandmother in New York, the image becomes a conduit, drawing Mavis and Solomon to the heart of Haudenosaunee territory, the Cohoes region of what we now call New York.[8] Dreams interweave with art throughout the film so that the past enters the present, connecting the dreams' knowledge with art.

To cross the border from Canada to the United States, for their journey to New York City, Mavis and Solomon must pass through customs. There, they are detained because Solomon is on prescription painkillers after sustaining serious injuries in a fall (Solomon, we learn, is clumsy). In the film, Niro shoots the scene in the Border Patrol office so that US flags frame Mavis and Solomon to devastating effect, while Mavis is grilled by an officer (and Solomon falls asleep). The customs officer offensively asks Mavis if her paintings are pornographic, when they are representations of the Peacemaker, a sacred visual text. While she is held at the crossing, an older Indigenous man reminds Mavis that the Jay Treaty (1794) guaranteed Indigenous North Americans the right to cross freely between Canada and the United States; yet it is only Indigenous people who are stopped at the border, as the scene is shot in *Kissed by Lightning*.[9] In contradiction to the Jay Treaty, Mavis and Solomon are held at the border, not *despite* their being Haudenosaunee but *because* they are Haudenosaunee. Within the border authority's building, the American flags surrounding Mavis help us recall the Haudenosaunee flag seen earlier on her house. Here, the border crossing is emblematic of the control that settler-colonialist nation-states continue to exert over Indigenous peoples. This theme of borders runs throughout the movie.

The return to New York State, then, is traumatic and difficult and occurs only by contending with settler-colonialist systems, a nation-state apparatus, and racial prejudice. Yet Mavis maintains her calm and escapes this trap, and she continues driving through a snowstorm, with the somnolent Solomon beside her as they enter the traditional heartland of the Mohawk. The drive into New York is in heavy snow, as if Mavis were moving through the weight of history made manifest as material substance.

Settler colonialism, at once a form of haunting and a materialized force of destruction, is metaphorized here as heavy snow. As Kimberly Tallbear (Sisseton Wahpeton Oyate) notes, "The United States has established the right to inherit everything from Native peoples."[10] Niro's film vigorously contests this right.

Niro deploys the affective (emotive) register of snow, and of being lost in the snow, to evoke the affective realm of coloniality, the deathliness and erasure that coloniality brings. As theorist Patrick Wolfe writes, "Our analyses of colonialism need to go beyond the quantifiable positivities of law, economics, military capacity and government policy to include the affective dimensions of settler subjectivities, considering what it means, how it feels, to be a colonial subject in all domains of social life . . . recognizing the Indigenous presence as an absent center that structures settler discourse even in contexts that do not manifestly concern things Indigenous."[11] Niro's filmic vista of Mavis and Solomon returning to Haudenosaunee homelands contends with the "affective dimensions of settler subjectivities" precisely by returning to the place of the "absent center" of indigeneity, that is, the heartland of the Mohawk where in contemporary times the Mohawk are largely absent.

When Mavis and Solomon return to the land from which the Mohawk were cast out by settler-colonialist nation-state wars and deceit, they fill in the "absent center," placing their bodies, Mavis's art, and their eyes, ears, and voices back in the space of the Mohawk homeland. Filling in the absence, Mavis and Solomon, carrying the message of the Peacemaker, return to the place of origin. Very much alive, these characters change the landscape of contemporary Mohawk absence, in the Mohawk Valley, to one of Mohawk presence. As historian Eric Hinderaker reminds us, "The Mohawks guarded the eastern 'door' of Iroquoia which extended from the Mohawk River Valley some two hundred miles west to Seneca country on the Genesee River."[12] It is to this landscape that Niro's characters in *Kissed by Lightning* return.

Mavis and Solomon drive into New York State and, as music envelops them, Solomon describes a trip he took in boyhood to follow the footsteps of the Peacemaker. He then describes to Mavis how the Peacemaker created a way of living based on peace. While he is speaking, Mavis is driving them deeper into New York. As they reach the areas of their ancestral territory, Solomon recounts the saying: "When your feet touch the earth, your soul mixes with the souls of your ancestors."[13] As images of Mavis's paintings and of Mavis and Jessie Lightning in an embrace are superimposed, we hear Jessie again saying, "This story took place here, in our territory," emphasizing the significance of the land of New York.[14]

In their homeland, now called New York, when Mavis and Solomon encounter overt racism from white people and meet a friendly African American man, he asks them where they are from because he assumes they are Asian. Mavis laughs because their "original place of origin," as the man frames the question, is right here, New York, where they are.[15] In being told they are Mohawk, the African American man says, "You are from here, you are from this land, you are right where you should be!" and calls them the "real Americans."[16] When Mavis is invited to sing with his gospel group, she sings a song created by Jessie Lightning about home, being at home, being lost from home: "Where is my home, how long have I been away?" And so, again, Niro uses art to guide her Haudenosaunee characters home, both symbolically and diegetically, to New York.[17] As they continue driving deeper into New York, we again hear the voiceover of Jessie saying, "This story took place right here, in our territory," emphasizing the importance of Mavis's return to New York with the Peacemaker paintings. The repetition of Jessie's voice stating "right here, in our territory" is Niro's claim on the land.

Likewise, when Niro film's actors Eric Schweig (Solomon King) and Michael Greyeyes (Jessie Lightning) as Hiawatha and Peacemaker, respectively, she invokes traditional Haudenosaunee land.[18] Just after this scene, which brings to life Peacemaker and Hiawatha, we see Mavis and Solomon lost in the snow in New York. Yet, it is at this juncture that Solomon remarks: "Those people in the restaurant were right; this *is* our home."[19] He then reminds Mavis, "You know those paintings in the back? Well, that [Peacemaker's saga and the founding of the Haudenosaunee Confederacy] all took place right here. The Mohawk River is right over there, and we can't be too far from the Hudson."[20] Here, with Solomon echoing Jessie's words, Niro deepens the importance of Haudenosaunee traditional land and its entwinement with her people's art—and of course also its entwinement with her art. As they sit in the van, lost at home, suddenly Mavis and Solomon see a mysterious vision of Haudenosaunee warriors crossing the road. Like them, the warriors are lost. Niro uses temporal dissonance to hold both times as one, as they occur in the same place.

Lost, Mavis and Solomon are in the Cohoes region of New York when they hear on the radio a piece of Jessie Lightning's.[21] As the radio plays "The Hiawatha Sonata," Mavis describes to Solomon how deeply she still grieves for Jessie. And then, in another turn of magical realism, they happen upon Lightning Road, where Jessie's grandmother lives. They find her house and give her the photograph of her great-grandson and she invites them in. It is in this house, and on this night, that the sense of being lost is dispelled and Mavis and Solomon experience home, in the heart of their people's traditional land. In Josephine's (Jikonhasaseh's) house, photographs of Indigenous hero Chief Joseph of the Nez Perce, Dr. King, and a painted print of the imagined face of Jesus Christ cluster on a table and wall alongside family photographs and keepsakes, a kind of Peacemaker shrine.[22] Josephine then takes out the family photo album, with many pictures of Jessie, and gives it to Mavis to comfort her.

The history of the Haudenosaunee, and the Mohawk specifically, in their traditional homelands of New York State is as complicated as it is deep, and Niro's multilayered film carries this complex depth. Mavis Dogblood and Solomon King take a journey that leads them to the heart of the place of Mohawk losses, and to the heart of the place of Mohawk sustenance. The Mohawk did not lose their traditional lands just once, in 1779; rather, those lands were brutally contested throughout the period of colonization leading up to that fateful year. The Mohawk and the Six Nations fought and negotiated for centuries, brilliantly navigating a path to retain their lands up until the American Revolution when George Washington's barbarous decision to attempt to eradicate the Haudenosaunee caused wholesale displacement. The Haudenosaunee called George Washington "town destroyer" because his genocidal acts were so horrifying the people were afraid to speak his name.[23] The settler violence of this campaign was, however, not an entirely new tactic, but rather a steep worsening of ongoing settler-colonialist practices of violence.

A century before the Sullivan-Clinton genocide, Hinderaker notes that "in the last half of the seventeenth century, the Mohawk lived in a land of shadows, between a dream of peace and a nightmare of warfare, disease, death, and destruction."[24] He explains that the traditional "mourning war" played a prominent role in Haudenosaunee decisions during the bitterly difficult years of early colonization, when so many were dying: "As contact with Europeans triggered devastating cycles of epidemic diseases, mourning wars took on a new importance."[25] The tradition of mourning wars stems from the deeply tender belief that the death of a beloved member of the family can only be survived by those who mourn the lost one if a new life is provided to replace the dead. It was women's responsibility to demand captives, from other peoples, to fulfill this task. These captives were procured through mourning wars. The League of the Five Nations (now Six Nations) is founded on the good news of peace, emerging as I've discussed from the knowledge of the Peacemaker (Deganawidah) and the Consolation Ceremony he created. The League was established in response to war; Hinderaker estimates the time of the League's founding as the second half of the fifteenth century, while other historians set the date as much earlier.[26] The head of Niro's clan, the Turtle Clan, is believed to have been the first to accept Peacemaker's message (as delivered through Hiawatha) of condolence and peace. The Mohawks, and the Turtle Clan in particular, then, have an especially strong tie with Peacemaker's message of condolence. Niro's photographic work *The Essential Sensuality of Ceremony* (discussed later) expresses vividly this deep tie, as does the entire movie *Kissed by Lightning*. We can understand many aspects of the narrative of *Kissed by Lightning* as an arc moving from death (Jessie's Lightning's sudden passing) to renewed life (Mavis's pregnancy). The mourning for lost land and lost people goes deep for the Mohawk, reaching almost to the earliest time of contact.

When Niro's film returns to Haudenosaunee territory, then, it is not merely a return to the wounds of the Sullivan-Clinton genocidal campaign but also a return to a territory that was contested and defended for centuries, after first contact, *before* the genocidal campaigns of 1779, and of course more deeply it is a return to the homeland before contact. As noted, during a snowstorm, when they are lost, Mavis drives—by a kind of magical realist chance—to the home of Jessie Lightning's grandmother. Seeing the name "Lightning" on the mailbox in this rural terrain with heavy snow closing in, Mavis finally meets the woman who holds so much knowledge and history about Mavis's disappeared love, Jessie. Mavis tells Mrs. Lightning that she has come to bring her a photograph of Jessie's son, Zeus. The photographic medium here becomes a signifier of peace, a renewed way to find peace. This theme continues as, inside Mrs. Lightning's home, we see a gallery of photographs not only of her family, including Jessie Lightning (Peacemaker) but also of other peacemakers, including Dr. Martin Luther King Jr.

The tapestry of cultures and peacemakers is significant in Niro's work, which—always deeply informed by and respectful of tradition—continuously recognizes the complexity of the so-called postcolonial nation-state world. As Niro makes clear in her artist statement to *La Pieta* (chapter 2), the Haudenosaunee are not isolated from the world but very much aware of the multiple ways that the era of European barbarity, expressed through settler colonialism (as Silvia Federici notes; see chapter 4), profoundly altered the course of world political and environmental history.[27] The Lightning house, which holds memorabilia of Jessie Lightning, is a home that holds remembrance of many peacemakers—many who, like Dr. King, strove and gave their lives to undo and diminish the violent effects of settler colonialism. Long before decolonization became a buzzword in academia, Martin Luther King noted "Our nation was born in genocide . . . We are perhaps the only nation which tried as a matter of policy to wipe out its Indigenous population."[28]

Weaving together cultural and personal tragedy, and return to life, the film will end with Mavis pregnant, carrying Solomon King's child; Niro's filmic meditation on genocide and displacement also becomes a work of art that instates Indigenous resurgence.[29] Niro's *Kissed by Lightning* draws on techniques of magical realism and temporal estrangement to pull together the historical and contemporary threads of the characters' journey, circling back and forth through past, present, and anticipated future.

"From This Land": Art and Land In *Kissed by Lightning*

As noted, *Kissed by Lightning* (2009) is structured by a journey that is a return, this trip that Mavis and Solomon take into the heart of New York, their traditional homeland. The journey, however, is simultaneously Mavis's errand, so to speak, to bring her paintings of Peacemaker's saga to New York City, where the opening of her exhibition will be celebrated; and. it is also a journey of reencountering Haudenosaunee history and ancestors and bringing continued life to this inheritance. When Mavis breaks down in tears and tells Josephine that she doesn't know if she has survived Jessie's death, Josephine again brings art into the picture, telling Mavis: "If you can make paintings, and drive them somewhere, you're surviving."[30] Shelley Niro echoes this idea when she mentions, in conversation, that what gives the Haudenosaunee strength to survive now is the art that the people are making.[31] Generously, she does not focus on her own art in this comment, but instead expands the notion, indicating that because there is a resurgence of Indigenous artmaking, the people are thriving. Art, then, is at the heart of survival, and art, in *Kissed by Lightning*, is anchored in New York; it is what brings Mavis to New York and to Josephine, and it is what Mavis's art is about.

When Mavis celebrates the opening of her exhibit in New York City, near the end of the film, Haudenosaunee ancestors gather with Mavis,

Solomon, and all the people there to see the exhibit—the dead with the living—in the chic contemporary YouMe gallery. The ancestors walk through the exhibit of her art, looking at Mavis's translations of Peacemaker's life and message of consolation. The journey to New York is one of consolation, as it enables Mavis to make her peace with the loss of Jessie Lightning and to accept the life she has—with her art, with Solomon King, and with her new expected baby. The loss of Jessie Lightning represents the grave loss the Haudenosaunee have suffered through the centuries of settler colonialism that have stripped the people of their homeland and killed so many. The genocide of Indigenous Americans is one that has yet to be fully reckoned with by any North American nation-state. In Niro's art, subtle threads of remembrance and confrontation work together to offer healing from this horrifically violent past. One may even suggest that not only Indigenous Americans but everyone who shares in this brutal history needs some kind of healing. Niro's expansive vision offers that by drawing deeply and repeatedly on the knowledge of Peacemaker.

In *Kissed by Lightning*, art within art is a key structural element to the narrative. In the film, Mavis labors to create the painting series of Peacemaker's story. When she has completed the series, the journey to carry the paintings to New York begins. It is the creation of the paintings and their being carried to New York that structure the overt diegetic arc of the film. The paintings themselves oscillate between times, being at once contemporary and also ancient (they depict deep history but exist in contemporary times and contemporary art). When Mavis exhibits the paintings in the New York gallery, and Haudenosaunee ancestors arrive and view the paintings with her, the art becomes a conduit between histories. Time becomes whole in the paintings: past, present, and future. Mavis's labor in creating the artworks is how she gives a home to Kateri, Jessie Lightning's former wife, and to his son, and it is also how she remembers Jessie Lightning (Peacemaker) and how she, Mavis, becomes the Hiawatha figure who spreads the message of peace. Shelley Niro, as the painter of the works used in the film, creates the images that convey Peacemaker's message of condolence and peace, and Niro also creates the film that conveys to wide audiences these paintings' message of peace. The paintings are the instigation for Mavis and Solomon's journey to New York to deliver them to the gallery. Driving through the state of New York, they reencounter and move deeper into Haudenosaunee territory.

Bringing her Peacemaker paintings to New York, to the fictional YouMe Gallery in the city, Mavis is not simply on an errand to make money for her family; she is returning home, bringing the story of Peacemaker back to its geographic origin. Her paintings in the film stage a return to the homeland and also Niro's film itself stages this return. Fittingly, then, in this movie where Mavis and Solomon see Haudenosaunee warriors who are spirits of the ancestors inhabiting New York, when Mavis opens her exhibit, the ancestors attend, as Niro extends the magical realism and temporal dissonance that gives such power and depth to *Kissed by Lightning*. At Mavis's opening, the film shows us Niro's paintings in detail, and so art—showing the Peacemaker in New York—draws the film together. In Niro's filmic lexicon, art is integral to the healing that decolonization can bring.

Decolonizing Means Giving Land Back

In sharpest contrast to Peacemaker, who healed divisions and suffering, the Haudenosaunee have long referred to George Washington as *Hanadahguyus*, meaning "town destroyer," because he ordered his generals, Clinton and Sullivan, to destroy the Haudenosaunee.[32] Niro suggests that this moniker is too kind a descriptor for Washington who, in his actions against the Haudenosaunee, expressed and enacted genocide.[33] The Revolutionary War temporarily pulled apart the Six Nations in that the Oneida and Tuscarora sided with the colonial Americans, while the Mohawk, Seneca, Onondaga, and Cayuga sided with the British. While the 1784 treaty at Fort Stanwix established peace between the new nation of the United States and the Haudenosaunee, it also stripped the latter of almost all their remaining lands in New York State. During the next ten years, the United States forced the Haudenosaunee to sell most of the few lands remaining to them in New York. Although the Canandaigua Treaty (1794) established the right of the Haudenosaunee to their remaining land, the forced and illegal "sales" (theft) of Haudenosaunee land continued unabated despite the treaty.[34]

For Niro, to return to New York State, then, is to return to land that wasn't stolen just once but repeatedly, in pieces, over and over across decades and centuries. She returns to set together the fragments and to assert the continued importance of Haudenosaunee presence. As pedagogical theorists Eve Tuck (Unangax̂) and K. Wayne Yang remind us, Patrick Wolfe correctly makes the case that "settler colonialism is a structure not an event."[35] And yet each episodic event of Indigenous displacement and erasure is part of the structure of settler colonialism.

Land's theft is essential to colonization; therefore, land's return will be essential to *de*colonization. As Tuck and Yang make the case, "in our view, decolonization in the settler-colonial context must involve the repatriation of land."[36] Niro's artwork that reconnects to New York State is, on the one hand, not direct repatriation of land. The land of New York State is still, after decades of Niro's brilliant art, securely owned by settler-colonialist speculators. However, decades of Niro's art have made it clear that the Mohawk have not forgotten this land that is theirs; for the Mohawk, the land is still their land. Her art is a step toward the necessary return of some of New York State's lands to the Mohawk. It is her guerrilla tactic of bringing forward into the public domain the rightness of the return of land. The ideation of return sets the stage for its actuality.

Tuck and Yang contrast the decolonialist theory of Frantz Fanon with that of Paulo Freire, arguing that "Fanon positions decolonization as chaotic, an unclean break from a colonial condition," while Freire "positions liberation as redemption, a freeing of both oppressor and oppressed through their humanity."[37] To be clear, Tuck and Yang establish this duality to critique Freire, yet one can salvage Freire's theory of inclusive decolonization in connection to Niro's artistic message of decolonization as a structure built through events of resistance that will likely unfold slowly across time, and that, of necessity, may include alliances with those who are not Haudenosaunee, and possibly even those who are not Indigenous North American. As Wolfe points out, the question of whether it is accurate, and useful, to draw a sharp and inflexible line between who is colonized and who is a settler, in the chaotic and economically violent space of our contemporary sociality, is at the heart of any effort to decolonize. On the one hand, Wolfe contends, the sharpness of the line is essential. If we extend this line of analysis to Shelley Niro's work, we see that her identity as a Haudenosaunee woman is entirely necessary to her work's connection to the land of New York State. This is the land where her people lived for millennia. This is her homeland. I, who am not Haudenosaunee, feel sympathetic to and supportive of the idea of the Mohawk regaining meaningful tracts of land in New York, but since I am not Mohawk, my subject position in this desire is ineradicably different from Niro's.[38] Land is the dividing line of history; the history of the land's occupancy is the dividing line. Niro, who is a Haudenosaunee artist, writer, and thinker, and many other Haudenosaunee artists, writers, and thinkers along with various settler-descended artists, writers, and thinkers may all agree about key aspects of decolonizing theory, but the return of Haudenosaunee land to the Haudenosaunee only has meaning if it is returned *to the Haudenosaunee*. Hence, binarism is of the essence for this fundamental aspect of decolonization: the meaningful return of lands.

And yet, even in the embrace of binarism to protect against the slippage of historical forgetting and to make meaningful and substantive the term *decolonization*, Wolfe notes that a "third space . . . and a *bricoleur* style of binarism is often strategically necessary."[39] Tuck and Yang likewise suggest that "in U.S. educational research in particular, Indigenous peoples are included only as asterisks, as footnotes," indicating that precisely the kind of cultural paradigm change that Niro's art offers is an essential step toward decolonization.[40] As philosopher Cornelius Castoriadis contends, it is the social imaginary that shapes the material conditions, including land possession, in which we live.[41] For land to be returned, it may be necessary for those who now possess the land, having gained possession through settler colonialism's military violence and egregious manipulation of laws, to come to the belief that it *should* be returned. While Fanon argues that coloniality can only be overcome by violent rebellion, the present-day situation of settler colonialism's extreme militarism tends to block that path. Because settler-colonialist nation-states, including the United States, depend on an implicit, ongoing state of war to maintain their boundaries, the wealthy US military would likely suppress any Haudenosaunee attempt to forcibly (through violent rebellion) regain their land.[42]

We have seen this tragic reality of settler-colonialist military violence in the Oka Crisis, which at the close of the twentieth century showed yet again that settler-complex state violence is always implicitly prepared to silence and stop Indigenous efforts to protect the meager lands they still have, much less to take back stolen lands by force.[43] The US military budget, for example, in 2022 (the most recent year for which information is available) was larger than the next ten costliest military budgets in the world, dwarfing all other nations' expenditures on warfare.[44] Niro's art is essential in that it eloquently shows the meaning of the land, the memory of the land, the Mohawk tie to the land that has not been broken despite five hundred years and counting of settler invasion and total war against the Haudenosaunee. In coloniality's social space, wherein Indigenous military action to regain stolen lands will bring the war apparatus that is the core of settler nations to bear against those who seek the return of their lands, Niro's path of eloquent art that testifies to the meaning of the land and the history of its theft is no mere metaphor. It is a political act of demanding justice.

Her work, in this sense, expresses what scholar Gina Starblanket (Cree) summarizes as the power of Indigenous feminism: "Indigenous feminism has the potential to nuance and advance the way in which we think about Indigenous resurgence. . . . Indigenous resurgence refers to political strategies and cultural practices that are grounded in Indigenous visions and freedom and autonomy."[45] Starblanket further connects such Indigenous feminist resurgence with the renewal of Indigenous cultural memory.[46] Niro's practice of returning to New York State literally, in some photographic and filmic works, and figuratively, in other works, is a practice of Indigenous feminist resurgence.

The Essential Sensuality of Ceremony

In Niro's series of five black-and-white photographs, *The Essential Sensuality of Ceremony* (2002; figures 6.1–6.5), the return to New York State is oblique, and yet the series' invocation of Peacemaker indicates that in this artwork Niro is returning, metaphorically, to New York. Here, the Condolence Ceremony created by the Peacemaker and given to the Haudenosaunee, performed and photographed in Canada, signifies the connection to New York State. Niro accentuates this connection to New York State in an alternate presentation of the same group of photographs, *Haudenosaunee Senses* (2001). Here, the photographs of *The Essential Sensuality of Ceremony* series are displayed on a sketched background of purple wampum while sketched DNA helixes adorn the top of the frame and beneath the images the Six Nations are listed in hand-inked script: *Mohawk Oneida Onondaga Cayuga Seneca Tuscarora*. In this earliest iteration of the series, Niro makes clear the relationship of the Condolence Ceremony to the land of New York through the people of New York, the Haudenosaunee. Here, she invokes the deep ties to their land that the Haudenosaunee still hold.

The loss of Haudenosaunee lands to settler-speculators, as I have argued, did not occur just once in 1779, though that is the most egregious and blatantly genocidal moment in the history of settler-colonialist relations with the Haudenosaunee. The loss of land began before and continued after 1779. As lawyer, writer, and philosopher Vine Deloria (Standing Rock Sioux) makes clear, in 1779 the Mohawk lost their essential role as keepers of the Eastern Door, and the retrieval of this role is vital to their long-term prosperity.[47] The loss of this role occurred in 1779 with the

Figure 6.1. *Sense of Smell, The Essential Sensuality of Ceremony*, 2002, series of five black-and-white gelatin silver prints, 40 in. × 30 in. *Source:* Courtesy of the artist.

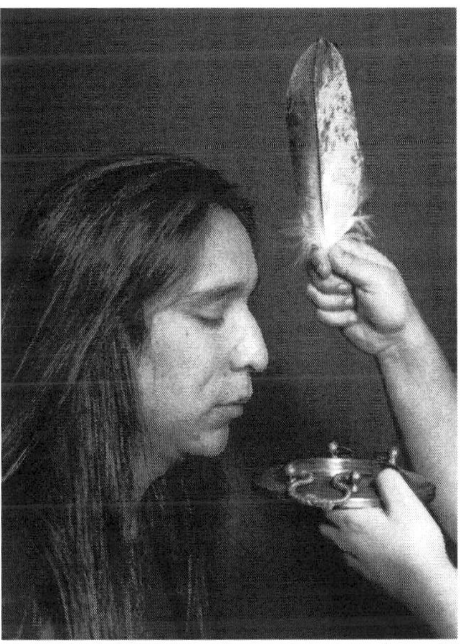

Figure 6.2. *Sense of Sound, The Essential Sensuality of Ceremony*, 2002, series of five black-and-white gelatin silver prints, 40 in. × 30 in. *Source:* Courtesy of the artist.

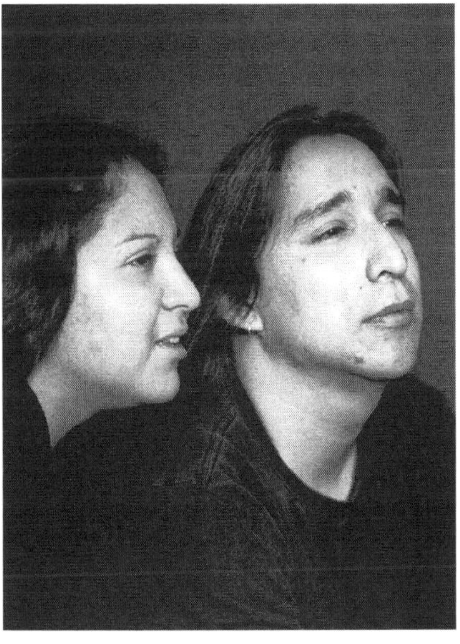

Figure 6.3. *Sense of Touch, The Essential Sensuality of Ceremony*, 2002, series of five black-and-white gelatin silver prints, 40 in. × 30 in. *Source:* Courtesy of the artist.

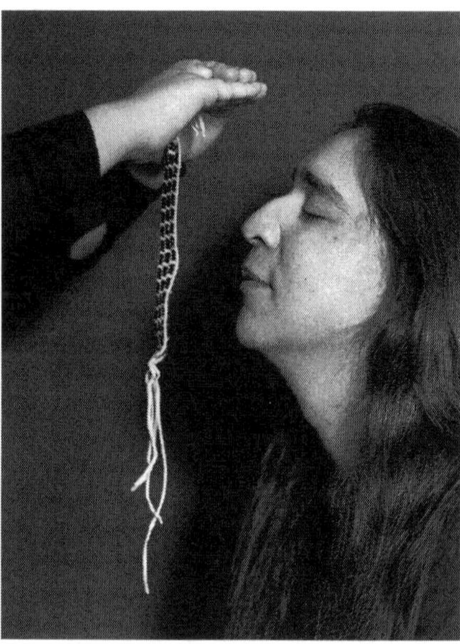

Figure 6.4. *Sense of Sight, The Essential Sensuality of Ceremony*, 2002, series of five black-and-white gelatin silver prints, 40 in. × 30 in. *Source:* Courtesy of the artist.

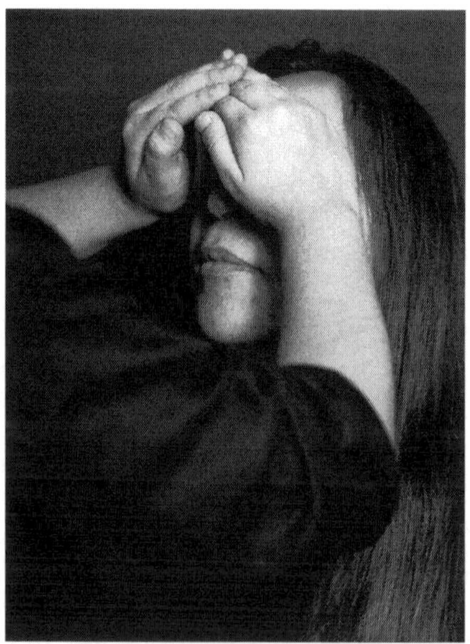

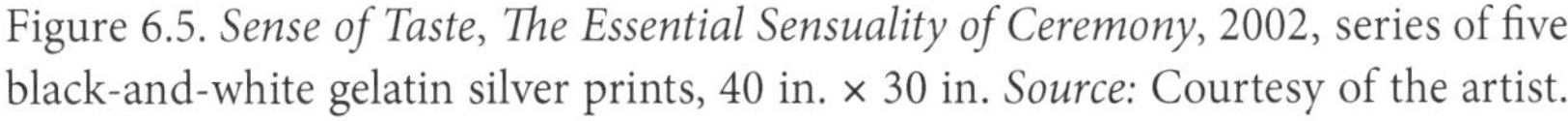

Figure 6.5. *Sense of Taste, The Essential Sensuality of Ceremony*, 2002, series of five black-and-white gelatin silver prints, 40 in. × 30 in. *Source:* Courtesy of the artist.

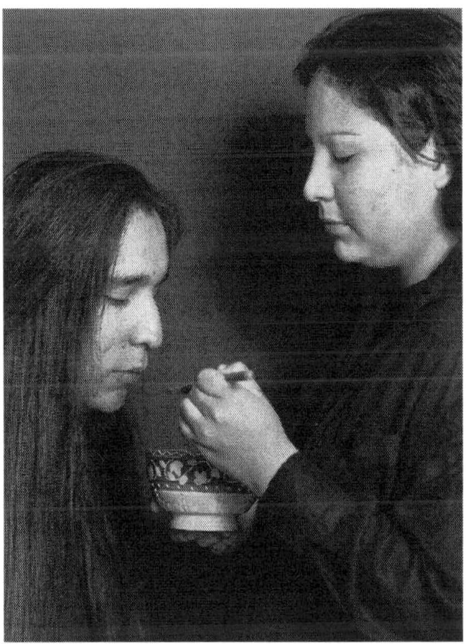

forced removal of the people by the genocidal Sullivan-Clinton campaign, but continued throughout most of the eighteenth century, as historian Laurence M. Hauptman notes.[48] While the terms "settler complex" and "coloniality" are typical descriptors for settler colonialism, in the case of New York State, as in many other instances, "speculator colonialism" would be more accurate.[49] Once the genocidal Sullivan-Clinton campaign pushed the Haudenosaunee out of New York State, settler-speculators greedily, and illegally, gobbled up most of what land was left to the original people. Notes Hauptman, in the late eighteenth century, Irish American surveyor Christopher Colles defined Haudenosaunee lands as " 'waste and unappropriated lands,' in need of state development, arguing on political, economic and national security grounds."[50] Along with Colles, speculator Elkanah Watson pushed through the goal of making Haudenosaunee lands a conduit to the west by creating canals, while Philip Schuyler was "without doubt *the* major player in securing Oneida lands for the evolving transportation networks."[51] After the Revolutionary War, settler-speculators cut illegal channels through Haudenosaunee territory, eating into the little land that remained to the Haudenosaunee, creating thoroughfares for settlers and settler speculators.

This theft was justified by grotesquely racist ideology. As Hauptman notes, in the opinion of New York's governor DeWitt Clinton (1817–23, 1825–28), Indigenous Americans were "much like wild beasts [that] had to give way to progress."[52] Digging canals throughout Haudenosaunee lands brought tourists, settler agriculture, and a massive, illegal, and irreparable (so far) influx of settlers, and forced the Haudenosaunee permanently (at least so far) out of Buffalo and much of New York State.[53] The speculators' close ties with government facilitated the construction of transportation networks through Haudenosaunee territory and was, as geographer Richard H. Schein argues, fundamental to the process of colonization.[54] The theft of land occurred not only through military genocidal violence but also through speculation, through the aggression of capitalist expansion, which continues to know no limits. The government of New York repaid the Oneidas' loyalty to the nascent United States by stealing their land. In this bitter historical context, the Condolence Ceremony offers healing.

In contrast to settler-speculator greed and treachery, the Haudenosaunee Condolence Ceremony is very much about honesty, fidelity, and accepting the real and reciprocal relationship between the people and the land, between ancestors and family; it is about accepting the limitations of the mortality of being human, accepting the ethical limits of using so-called natural resources. As Niro creates her photographic series *The Essential Sensuality of Ceremony*, she emphasizes the tactile quality of the Condolence Ceremony. Five images in black and white, framed in lilac, accompanied by a sumptuous purple cloth and mirror set beneath the photographs, show two young people, a man and a woman, enacting a tender ceremony. The young people's skin reveals lives of high stress, acne, and worry lines, but their facial expressions are placid. They arrive in the viewer's eyes as real: here are the real people. This is the first part of the essential sensuality of the piece: that photography here is used to see what is present, what is real, not to photoshop out those elements of human being, being human, that commercial images routinely elide. Wolastoqew artist rudi aker writes, "In her 2002 photographic series 'The Essential Sensuality of Ceremony,' Shelley Niro offers a visceral vision of grief and illustrates the importance of relationality in ceremonial practice to confront loss and sorrow."[55] aker further notes,

> Each image features a young man and woman, engaged in a sequence of ceremonies: the woman aids the man in his healing journey through smudging, singing, and nourishing while tending to his tears and offering her teachings. These figures reflect details of the Haudenosaunee legend of the Peacemaker—the prophet sent by the Creator to bring peace amongst nations and to teach his people to live well—and his relationship with Hiawatha, he who assisted the Peacemaker in the transmission of his teachings.[56]

aker points out that Niro alters typical presentations of the Peacemaker by giving the role of Peacemaker to a woman in this case.[57] As she does in *Kissed by Lightning* (2009), Niro invokes Peacemaker and reinterprets the connection between Peacemaker and Hiawatha so that Mavis Dogblood is the messenger whose art brings to the world the guidance of Peacemaker. In this sense, Mavis is like Hiawatha: her art speaks. Moreover, Shelley Niro as the filmmaker also functions in the Hiawatha role, for it is her film that brings to the public audience the message and story of Peacemaker, just as Mavis's paintings do. Niro is herself the artist who created Mavis's paintings, and in this act she doubles her role as the Hiawatha-like figure who brings to the people the message of Peacemaker. Similarly, in *The Essential Sensuality of Ceremony* Peacemaker is represented as a woman.

Picturing a woman in the Peacemaker role intensifies the revolutionary force of peace in Niro's *The Essential Sensuality of Ceremony*. We are so sadly accustomed to seeing women as the ones on whom others act, but here a woman is the agent of action. As aker makes clear, the revelation of vulnerability and the care needed to protect and heal is necessary for the recuperation of historical losses, a recuperation that *The Essential Sensuality of Ceremony* actively offers to viewers. Writes aker, "Charged with what Niro names as 'whispers of history,' 'The Essential Sensuality of Ceremony' offers a retelling of the Haudenosaunee legend of the Peacemaker and moves beyond to a place unhindered by time to epitomize the deep kinship ties between those who care for one another, in community and ceremony."[58] The recuperation of history is also, here, the return to land. The Condolence Ceremony always expresses the reciprocal relationship that the Haudenosaunee have, not only with each other but also with their traditional lands. aker rightly sees Niro's *The Essential Sensuality of Ceremony* as a critique of the "colonialist, capitalist regime."[59] As scholar Aileen Moreton-Robinson (Goenpul woman of the Quandamooka) contends, "Colonization morphologizes in multiple ways as it continues to operate discursively and materially within cultural formations, institutions, and public culture."[60] The continued effect of the loss of land on the Mohawk is not a one-time event but an extensive and ongoing loss. Likewise, Peacemaker's ceremony is also extensive and ongoing, continuing to offer healing and peace to the Haudenosaunee people.

As the series *The Essential Sensuality of Ceremony* begins, we see the mourning man's face with eyes closed as the Peacemaker's healing hands smudge his face, cleansing him. Niro titles this frame *Sense of Smell,* indicating that the five-image series will address consolation through the five senses. In the next frame, *Sense of Sound,* Peacemaker sings to the mourning young man a traditional song, which begins to alter his expression so that, in addition to sorrow, he starts to express comfort. In the third frame, *Sense of Touch,* gentle hands hold wampum to the man's face so that the message of peace encoded at the foundation of the Five Nations (now Six Nations) is conveyed to him through knowledge and tactile contact. Here, in the third frame, his face begins to show even more of a sense of moving through mourning toward peace. The fourth frame, *Sense of Sight,* is striking in what appears to be a contradiction, for here the Peacemaker covers the young man's eyes, wiping away tears. Through this image, though, we come to realize that internal vision is a powerful way of seeing, and that we do not awaken to our interior knowledge until we see, as it were, with closed eyes. Likewise, we do not fully see a photograph until our eyes are closed and we remember it. The Peacemaker here is wiping away tears, allowing the mourner to see clearly again.

The sense of trust here is immense. Allowing Peacemaker to touch his eyes, the mourning man indicates how deeply he respects and trusts the condolence she brings him and the process through which she brings it. In the final frame, *Sense of Taste,* the mourning man who has undergone the healing process of the Condolence Ceremony accepts food from the healer, for we must eat to be healed. The series, in its starkness and gentleness, is achingly poignant and also can be hard to look at for someone like me, an outsider to Haudenosaunee culture, but this long looking that the series requires yields an awareness of peace that is available not only to Haudenosaunee viewers, who will certainly be the best positioned to comprehend the work, but also to those outside the community. As author-activist Leanne Betasamosake Simpson (Mississauga Nishnaabeg) notes, "I believe that the ancestors and the spiritual world . . . love us unconditionally and that they are brilliant. I believe that they are benevolent. . . . I believe that it is important to reclaim our foundational ethics of consent."[61] The ethics of consent are at the core of Niro's photography.

In Niro's series *The Essential Sensuality of Ceremony*, the photographs are not merely images, they are image-acts—that is, images that create intention, mind, knowledge in the viewer and thereby change the viewer. The series, which does not show the land of New York State, reminds us of what is at stake with the loss of that land. Because the series returns to the Condolence Ceremony that was created in a specific place for a specific people in that place, it invokes the reciprocal relationship of care not only among human beings but also between the land and human beings, reminding us of how deeply this ethos of care has been lost in the ongoing world of speculator/settler colonialism. It invokes the reciprocal relationship of care between the Haudenosaunee and their traditional ancestral lands.

This sense of care is entwined with the care for the land and the need to return to the Mohawks' ancestral land of New York. The need for return to Mohawk land signifies the deep and inextricable ties among the land, people, history, and tradition in Haudenosaunee culture. As Douglas M. George-Kanentiio writes: "Ever since the Mohawks had been compelled to leave their homes in the Mohawk Valley of Central New York during the American Revolution, the Confederacy's Grand Council had to function without the Mohawks having a national capital."[62] The theft of Mohawk land by settlers/speculators was not just a change of scene for the Mohawk. It stripped the people of their fundamental role as keepers of the Eastern Door and robbed them of their geographic center. Shelley Niro's numerous artworks invoking Peacemaker and the Condolence Ceremony instigate the essential steps toward return to and reclaiming this land.

Conclusion

Returning

Shelley Niro's (Six Nations of the Grand River Reserve, Bay of Quinte Kanien'kehá:ka Mohawk Nation, Turtle Clan) art is fundamentally connected with New York State, the place of her birth and the ancestral homeland of her people. As I have discussed throughout this book, this intergenerational haunting of lost homeland that Niro's art dramatizes and illuminates is a significant enlightening heuristic through which we can interpret the artist's oeuvre. Her activist art repeatedly turns toward New York and, artwork by artwork, enacts guerrilla tactics toward the return of the land, the return to that land.

Decolonizing the gaze is central to Niro's activism, and encoded within this formal aesthetic of resistance is the instantiation of Haudenosaunee time—both as the Haudenosaunee concept of time and as in it is now the Haudenosaunee's time, a time of ascendency for this art. Time is central to Niro's artistic argument of the Mohawk claim and connection to their ancestral homelands in the area that is now called New York State. Drawing from Jodi Byrd's (Chickasaw) argument in *The Transit of Empire*, we can meditate on the way that Niro's mnemonic work decolonizes our collective images of culture in time. Argues Byrd, because Indigenous Americans are cast symbolically and function politically as "transit, the field through which presignifying polyvocality is re/introduced into the signifying regime, and signs begin to proliferate through a series of becomings—becoming-animal, becoming-woman, becoming-Indian," we need to create a new archive of symbols, one that does not facilitate settler-colonialist "becoming" through its enforced stasis.[1]

In *Mohawk Rebel: Shelley Niro's Art and New York State*, I suggest that Niro's art creates a counter-archive of symbols, an alternative to the

Euro-American practice of archiving images of Indigenous Americans and retaining Indigenous cultural objects as a form of conquest. Niro's connection to the New York region is essential to understanding her art, and in this conclusion I stress the importance of this relationship by framing Niro's characteristic emphasis on connections to land across time.

The Significance of Return

One can trace a trajectory in Niro's filmmaking and photography career in which return to New York is the central motif. Niro's early film *It Starts with a Whisper* (see chapter 4) follows a young Mohawk woman's coming of age, a transformation that requires the young woman to return (from Canada) to the border to face New York, for it is here that she encounters the spirits of her ancestors. The specific weight of geography is crucial to this early film; the meaning of the film occurs through the trope of geographical memory. The physical, psychical, and visual staging of returns to face the geography of the ancestral homeland is central to Niro's artistic practice. *It Starts with a Whisper* also acts as a kind of coming of age for Shelley Niro as a filmmaker. In the movie (made in collaboration with Anna Gronau), Niro herself is starting out as a filmmaker. She inaugurates her first film by sending its characters to the edge of New York: the main action of the film is Shanna and her aunties driving to Niagara and spending the night in a honeymoon suite that one of the aunts won at bingo night.

Nearly two decades after the creation of *It Starts with a Whisper*, Niro's feature-length film *Kissed by Lightning* contends with the importance of the New York State region for the Mohawk people through interpellation of the living and the ancestors in the film's diegesis. In *Kissed by Lightning*, a contemporary story of loss and renewal is mapped onto the traumatic history of the Mohawks' expulsion from much of the territory of New York State. As the heroine, Mavis Dogblood, travels back through the path her ancestors took in the eighteenth century when they were pushed out of their homelands, she repeatedly encounters spirits of the dead that remind her of her need for this land. The film's pivotal point occurs deep in the ancestral homeland of the Mohawk, in the small house of an elder member of the tribe. The border, the boundary, as the line demarcating the nation-states, the United States of America and Canada, is at once troubled and dematerialized in the film as Niro shows Mohawk people overcoming the nation-state through the creation of art, reconnecting with ancestors on ancestral land, and giving birth and nurturing the next generation of Mohawk people.

In the work of mourning that is her film *Niagara* (2015), Niro creates a powerful elegiac production, grieving her mother and her daughter. The power of the Niagara waterfalls is central to the work, where the photographer and filmmaker enacts key gestures from the Condolence Ceremony, wiping away from the camera's glass the spray from Niagara in a gesture contiguous with the wiping away of tears in the Condolence Ceremony. Here, the water of Niagara and the tears of a Haudenosaunee artist symbolically merge as the act of the film, its words and images, perform and offer profound condolence. In this film (see chapters 1 and 3), Niro also contends with Mohawk ideas of power, interweaving visions of Niagara (the film's original title was *Ongniaahra*) as a sacred place with a critique of the incursion of tourism and the violence of coloniality. She connects these acts of violence with personal familial losses. Here is a deeper elegiac tradition, one in which Niro does not merely mourn the immediate losses of mother and daughter but also ties them with her people's history of being expelled from their homelands. Settler pollution of the contemporary Niagara River must be interpreted in its connection to Niro's mournful work of honoring the place of her origins. In Niro's film, we see the crashing falls at Niagara, a sacred place where the spirit world and the world of the living are bounded. Overlaid on the crashing water, the film captions the dialogue between women, a dream about seeing a deceased grandmother. The film becomes, in effect, an elegy for all Indigenous women whom poverty and historical trauma have killed. As legal scholar Mary Eberts notes, "Indian women are easy prey for government officials, police and non-government actors."[2] And, importantly, the film is a performative space where Indigenous women are revivified, with incantatory words held aloft and made visible. It is a film that fiercely refuses the erasure of Indigenous presence. It is notable that Niro locates this short but very important film at the boundary facing New York. Here, facing the homeland of the Haudenosaunee, is the imaged healing, a healing that can only happen with return. Niro returns and claims her strength, and the strength of all Indigenous women, in this place of origin, a boundary, Niagara.

The Role of Art

In 1788–89, ten years after the removal of so many of their people, Haudenosaunee leaders complained to DeWitt Clinton, then governor of New York, that they were threatened with destruction, even extermination, from starvation.[3] The famine was exacerbated by very cold weather, but mainly Haudenosaunee starvation was triggered by settler migration and colonialist genocidal violence, which we now know was also a *cause* of the temporarily colder climate, as settler migration killed so many Indigenous North Americans that it altered agricultural patterns on the continent, leading to reforestation and a temporary drop in global temperature.[4]

As noted, in the initial phase of colonization, Haudenosaunee populations were reduced by European diseases at a factor of 90 to 95 percent, wrote Adriaen van der Donck (a Dutch colonialist who lived during the seventeenth century in what is now New York State); "they were ten times more numerous before the arrival of the Europeans."[5] In other words, long before the Sullivan-Clinton genocidal campaign, the Mohawk were very much under siege. Their ability to survive centuries of colonization stems from their preservation of a culture with deep resources of knowledge, and the preservation of a traditional religion with peace at its core.

Creating art that contends with such a massive level of grief and loss, Niro draws on the strength of Haudenosaunee history, beliefs, and traditions that were in place before contact. She draws on the strength of her people to give her art the power to encounter the darkness of a genocide so vast that it altered the world climate and ushered in an era of settler capitalism: this is an era that is itself shifting the world climate in a sinister way today (as we encounter global warming caused by patterns of settler-colonialist capitalist industries). In drawing on Haudenosaunee tradition, Niro taps into a culture going back thousands of years in the area now called New York State, a culture in which deference was shown to elders, competition was disapproved of, and the people "possessed no subordination."[6] In this culture, words—the gift of oratory—were highly prized, to "lift away the darkness."[7] As her 2003 work, the banner-sized photograph of a young Mohawk man (Jody Hill) with arms outstretched, states: *Surrender Nothing Always* (figure C.1).[8] At Niro's retrospective in 2023, this image stretched high above the transept as one walked between gallery rooms. The image was enlarged greatly, so that the young man's outstretched arms had a wingspan wider than that of any living human, a heroic wingspan, extending across the room and encompassing it with

Figure C.1. *Surrender Nothing Always*, 2003, digitized photo, 13 in. × 43 in. *Source:* Courtesy of the artist.

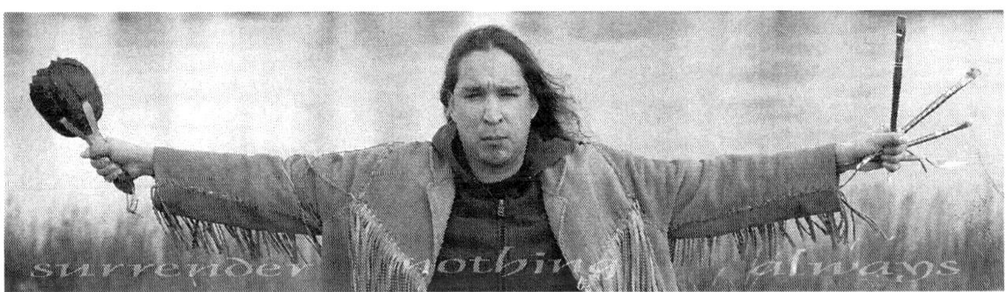

the powerful message of asserting and insisting on sovereignty. He holds a turtle rattle and paintbrushes (a turtle rattle is a ceremonial object and considered sacred). The presentation of the turtle rattle in parallel to paintbrushes is a radical contrast and one that makes Niro's point very clear: activist art is itself a sacred path to resistance and agitating for return of lands.

As scholar and curator Amy Lonetree (Ho-Chunk) reminds us, quoting from Waziyatawin Angela Wilson (Wahpetunwan Dakota) and Michael Yellowbird (Mandan, Hidatsa, and Arikara): "The first step toward decolonization then is to question the legitimacy of colonization."[9] Drawing from the work of Wilson, Lonetree emphasizes "the importance of truth telling [and] calls for a truth commission in the United States . . . to address the ongoing and systematic attacks on Indigenous bodies, language and sovereignty, and lifeways that have continued to occur."[10] Niro's work, of course, is not an official governmental truth commission, and yet, to see her retrospective in New York is to see a return with great meaning. A Mohawk woman's artistic truth telling taking place in New York is a return with meaning. Niro emphasizes the importance, for her, of Indigenous youths seeing her work, and she reiterated this frequently in discussions during the weekend celebrating the opening of her career retrospective.[11] She has been active in making sure museums that show her work secure funding so that groups of Indigenous youths can visit and view the retrospective. The point Lonetree raises, both in this essay and in her book *Decolonizing Museums: Representing Native America in National and Tribal Museums*, presses hard on the question of what role art and museums can play in real decolonization.[12] Yang and Tuck imply that this sort of cultural window dressing is inadequate when what is really needed is the direct return of stolen lands.[13]

And yet, Lonetree vigorously makes the case that art can and must be a vital part of decolonization, but she contends that such art cannot be created and cannot be presented in ways that elide confrontation with the violence of colonization. Echoing Wilson, she states that "the only way for Native people to heal from the historical trauma that we have experienced—genocidal warfare, land theft, ethnic cleansing, disease, and the attempt over complete destruction of our religious and ceremonial life at the hands of the government and Christian churches—is for us to speak the truth about what has happened."[14] In other words, only art that does not placate settler ideology, and museums that are created for Indigenous people as the prime audience, can do the work of decolonization. I suggest that *Surrender Nothing Always* is such work. It does not assuage, it confronts; it confronts us in a writ-large way combining language, image, space, and gesture. That this image is now represented in the New York State Museum and that it also appeared to such powerful effect in Niro's retrospective at the National Museum of the American Indian New York enacts a profound step. It is telling those in that significant space, in New York, that the Mohawk never surrender and always refuse to surrender.

Shelley Niro is often described, as I've discussed, as an accessible artist who uses humor deftly. Yet if we look at her work contending with New York State, its humor and accessibility are surface layers laid across pain, mourning, and resistance to and refusal of coloniality. Niro's art has impact, in fact, through immense complexity of signification. The work is densely historically allusive, referencing historical events with which most well-educated Americans, let alone people outside the United States, are not familiar. The history of the genocidal campaigns against Indigenous Americans is not well publicized in the United States because to have this knowledge as a bedrock of familiarity in American culture would be to undo the foundational myths of this nation. The national ideology of "freedom" and the nation-state myth of a new beginning for Euro-Americans in a land of plenty are sharply undercut by awareness of the nation's deeper history as a site of genocide.[15] New York State is a land of plenty because the Haudenosaunee had long stewarded the land, expertly developing abundance.[16] It is a land whose abundance was stolen from its original stewards.

Niro's intent and intense allusions to New York State history, as it concerns the Haudenosaunee, and to the traditions of her people layer the surfaces of her works. She speaks of her desire for her works to be available to audiences on multiple levels, so that people can connect with the art in different ways, depending on their vantage and background.[17] For example, someone might watch *Kissed by Lightning* as a romance, while someone else might view it as a complex, multilayered temporality play and a deep history of New York. It is especially in the context of New York State that her work contends with genocide, with the US government's attempt to destroy the Mohawk. In these returns home—whether literal returns to the land to photograph and film in New York, or figurative returns engaging Peacemaker and Haudenosaunee history of the place we now call New York—Niro creates art as a forceful decolonizing act. Reaching into and reshaping the mythology of the settler nation-states, the United States and Canada, her art allows us to see both what these nation-states really are and what they are not. Settler nations are not progress and destiny; rather, they are the results of old violence held in place by continued naturalized state violence. I do not mean to imply here that the artist is "against" America or Canada; she is a law-abiding citizen. What I mean, rather, is that her art allows us to see the substructure that holds settler colonialism in place, still, and that through this vision of clarity, her art decolonizes the gaze.

Consider again the photographs of the Mohawk Valley and of the Adirondacks (see figures I.2 and 2.9), respectively, in her two series *La Pieta* and *Battlefields of My Ancestors*. In these sublimely calm landscape images, a wealth of mourning is contained in tension with an insistence on claim. It is the tradition of settler landscape photography to lay claim to terrain. Landscape photography is a foundation and participant in the settler-colonialist gaze. But in *La Pieta* and *Battlefields of My Ancestors*, Niro reverses this gaze. Here, the landscape photographic claim on the land is through the eyes of a Mohawk woman, and the land she reclaims is her people's traditional homeland. The calmly mournful and forcefully claiming images of the Mohawk Valley and of the Adirondacks are placed within photographic series that sharply and clearly contest the theft of land that stands at the heart of settler-colonialist eliminatory practices (eliminatory of Indigenous peoples). The tenderness of her care for the land is eloquent in these images.

In *La Pieta*, the landscape of the Mohawk Valley occurs near the outset of the series so that, as the series' contemplation of war develops, the reference point is back to the Mohawk Valley as a place where the Great Law of Peace once held sway. Likewise, and in conversation with *La Pieta*, *Battlefields of My Ancestors* places the serene photograph of the Adirondacks at dusk between images of New York State and New Hampshire signage that proudly and horrifyingly commemorate the genocidal Sullivan-Clinton campaign. Both photographic series are meditations on war, and both anchor their visual narratives in reference points for the Haudenosaunee homelands. In these series, Niro insightfully connects the theft of Indigenous land to the era of endless, unstated war that settler-colonialist capitalism ushered in.[18] The legal framing that secured, and continues to secure, settler claims on Indigenous lands is profoundly suspect, reflecting treaties and agreements made almost invariably in bad faith—and almost invariably ignored—by the colonizers. Joseph Brant (Thayendanegea) rightly noted that, after the Revolutionary War, the British sold his people (i.e., sold their right to remain on their land) to Congress, and he further objected to the British giving eighteen hundred gallons of hard liquor to the Six Nations in an attempt to stupefy them.[19] Notes Taylor: "Both the British and the Patriots exploited alcohol to manipulate the Iroquois."[20] The governor of New York, DeWitt Clinton, also took advantage of the famine and starvation of 1789–90 to "radically reduce" the remaining Haudenosaunee territory in New York State.[21] In other words, tactics ranging from genocidal military campaigns to manipulation and opportunism were used by the settler government to strip the Haudenosaunee of their ancestral land. Niro's focus in *La Pieta* and in *Battlefields of My Ancestors* is centered on the violent military history of how the Mohawk were stripped of their lands, as both series contemplate the depth and breadth of settler-colonialist betrayal and unethical action that the Mohawk survived.

Writing of the painful struggles over Mohawk land claims in New York State in the late 1970s and 1980s, Douglas M. George-Kanentiio states: "Despite these challenges and distractions, the Mohawks continued to adhere to a collective identity defined by family, the bonds of a common ancestry, and the desire, however vague or muted, to preserve a distinct Aboriginal heritage."[22] Noting his people's cultural resilience, he continues: "On the surface, the Mohawks seemed to have become obscured and overwhelmed by a consumer culture, yet every lunar month the traditional faction gathered at the communal longhouse to carry on the most ancient of Iroquois rituals. Spoken exclusively in Mohawk, the ceremonies are meant to direct the attention of human beings toward the natural world, then engage in a series of prayers, dances, and songs meant to express gratitude for the infinite blessings of life." George-Kanentiio explains that the "Ohenten Kariwatekwen [Thanksgiving Address] . . . speaks to the Earth's waters, lands, plants, insects, fish, animals, trees, winds, birds, thunder, and medicines, each of which is told of the gratitude the Mohawk have for their being. Sun, moon, and stars (along with four spiritual beings) who watch humans from the horizons of the Earth are also thanked for their contentment to fulfill their instructions as given to them by the Creator."[23] This entwined emphasis on land and peace indicates how the Mohawk relationship to land is inseparable from their code of peace and gratitude. Niro's work honors the land, then, in her recognition of the profundity of the meanings of losing ancestral territory. As George-Kanentiio, paraphrasing Leon Shenandoah (Onondaga), writes: "Those who lived in the land were of the land; they spoke nature's language and moved to her rhythms. Displace them, silence them, integrate them and convert them at great risk to all."[24]

Art, photography, and film can contribute toward the movement to regain lost lands, to decolonize genocidal cultural structures foundational to the contemporary settler nation-state and still in place now. Niro's works contending with the history of New York State, in their lucid cultural specificity, manifest as decolonizing image objects. Scholar Brian Isaac Daniels argues that such cultural specificity of each tribe, each tradition, is at the heart of decolonizing art practices: "In the nineteenth century, nation states employed museums . . . to preserve particular aspects of culture in order to inspire a sense of a common history for the nation. By demarcating what was official history and culture and by training citizens to treat the past and its representative objects as official and definitive, states encouraged the formation of a homogenous, ideological community that could become a governable entity."[25] By contrast, as cumulative acts of resistance in a career-long guerrilla war against coloniality, Niro's art that contends with New York pushes against homogenization. In the films *It Starts with a Whisper* (1993) *Kissed by Lightning* (2009), and *Niagara* (2015), in the photographic series *Battlefields of My Ancestors*, *La Pieta*, and *The Essential Sensuality of Ceremony*, as in the multimedia work *1779*, Niro creates complex tapestries, weaving together New York State's real history. She shows that, as Taiaiake Alfred argues, decolonization is "a process of discovering the truth in a world created out of lies. It is thinking through what we think we know to what is actually true but is obscured by knowledge derived from our experiences as colonized people."[26]

The "process of discovering the truth in a world created out of lies" is what Niro accomplishes when her art confronts New York history. In her art, we learn that, deep in what was and still is the Mohawk homeland, Peacemaker's grandmother lives in a house filled with images of peace-makers. In Shelley Niro's art of New York State, we learn that this land, which settler-colonialist myth tells us was always meant to be inhabited almost exclusively by those of European descent, is actually Mohawk land. We learn that the Mohawk people continue to mourn those who were killed during the American genocide. We learn that the American genocide had many instances and moments, each carrying a searing weight into the future as coloniality remains the system in which we live. We learn that the early US government and its first president believed that only by destroying the Haudenosaunee in New York State could the nation be founded. In Shelley Niro's art, we learn the real foundations of New York State. We learn how beautiful and rich the land was and still can be. We learn to whom the land belongs.

Epilogue

"It Becomes a Beautiful Moment":
An Interview with Shelley Niro on New York

In midsummer 2023, Shelley Niro and the author met to talk about the relationship of Niro's art to New York State. This discussion took the form of an informal interview.

CLAIRE RAYMOND: So, maybe we'll start with a simple question that's not simple. What's your relationship to New York State?

SHELLEY NIRO: I was born in Niagara Falls, New York, which is just across the border. So it's kind of funny that I'm a US citizen—but I've been living in Canada for, let's say, sixty-four years.

So I'm a permanent resident. I have status on Six Nations Reserve. There was never really a border issue growing up, because in school we were always told that we had dual citizenship, US and Canadian. I never really put myself in a position of choosing. I see myself as both. And there's a lot of people who also feel that way.

CR: People in the Mohawk Nation?

SN: Yeah, people in the Mohawk Nation, people in the Six Nations, because of the history that we've lived through.

My biggest impact is probably my dad, talking about New York. Because he was a construction worker in Niagara Falls for many years. And he also shares that dual citizenship, although he was—although he's Canadian, you know? It's, like, kind of an invisible border there . . .

CR: At the Falls? That border.

SN: Yeah. I tell this story because I find it kind of funny. When I first started traveling, and I'd go with my passport and the person at the customs would say, "What's your citizenship?" And especially this one time, she asked me, "What's your citizenship?"

And I said, "Um, Mohawk."

She goes, "Uh, no. Your citizenship."

I go, "Uh, Six Nations."

"No, your citizenship."

"Um, Wakenyáhten [Turtle Clan]?"

"No"

Finally, I go, "United States?"

She goes, "Yes! That's it!"

Because we had it in our brains that we're Mohawks from Six Nations, and we're Turtle Clan, so that was my answer to that very simple question she was asking me. And she was probably thinking, *What a crazy woman. You know?* So I was being political, without knowing how political I was.

Now, when people ask me when I'm trying to cross the border, "What's your citizenship?" I just say "US." It's just, like, *Yeah, I just want to get out of here [the customs line].*

Of course, there's the Six Nations' history of coming from the Mohawk Valley, and why we left the Valley—we were forced to leave. I think it was in moments of terror that everybody was just running for their lives, Sullivan's campaign was coming through at the request of George Washington.

CR: Right.

SN: And I don't know if you had a chance to go through Native New York [an exhibit at the National Museum of the American Indian New York]. There was another exhibition in the same building [Niro's career retrospective *Shelley Niro: 500 Year Itch*, May 27, 2023–January 1, 2024] that we were in.

CR: Yes.

SN: George Washington, he was referred to as "Town Destroyer." And I just know a little bit about that whole period because there's just so much detail. But he told Sullivan and Clinton to go and destroy the Iroquois. Destroy the Mohawks. So they [the United States military forces] went through and, because of that, people [the Mohawk] were just so terrified of George Washington. And they called him the "Town Destroyer."

Which, to me, is a very gentle way of talking about him, because what he did was just horrible. And it wasn't just burning little villages. Ten houses, or fifteen houses. I've heard reports that those villages were up to fifteen thousand people. The crops were destroyed, the animals, as they just wanted to cut out the food supply.

So by the time they [the Mohawk people] go to Niagara Falls, they were starving. They were hungry, and they were hoping the British would be able to feed them, because they had nothing. They left with nothing, and they arrived with nothing. And when they got there, there was nothing for them to eat. And so a lot of them died.

Then, when you see George Washington's name, and he's looked at as this—*hero*, it's like, *Well, I don't know.*

CR: He does not sound heroic in that letter he sent to his generals telling them to destroy the Mohawk.

SN: No. He just wanted to be the president, and he wanted everybody to elect him again. But that whole history is so complicated that when you start reading one little part of it—it's, *Oh my God, that's just one tiny part.* And you start reading other tiny parts, and it can give you a migraine.

CR [recovering from a migraine]: Yes, and I don't want to jump in because this is your interview, but it does seem like it's just the opposite of the story that we were told in school growing up.

SN: Yep. And there's so many stories like that. And I just find that, when you start studying something, it leads you down this path. And then this path leads you down other paths. And then it's almost like you have to stop yourself, because you can't absorb all this stuff at once. You know? You can't absorb it, and it's almost like, I'm discrediting what I'm trying to do here by digging and digging and digging.

CR: Well, this history, it's potent. It's not just something that happened long ago that doesn't matter now . . .

SN: Yeah, when I was growing up, people my dad's age and older would talk about history all the time. It was something that people were trying to remember, through oral history, and they were just trying to patch things together.

And, you know, I wish I could go back fifty years or sixty years and be able to listen to those conversations again, because, you know, when people pass away, they take everything with them. And at that point, I don't think there were too many documentarians around. And if there were, there were mostly non-Native people who were writing down the stories, and so I think that they also missed out on stuff.

CR: Yes; your father would have been born in, what, 19—

SN: '21.

CR: 1921? To still have that memory 170 years later.

SN: And, he always talked about his grandmother, what his grandmother said. If only I could go back and say, "Okay, tell me more about your grandmother." Because a lot of their history was not written down either. So big chunks of family history are wiped out.

CR: Is she [Niro's paternal grandmother] the model for the grandmother in *Kissed by Lightning*, or is that more a composite grandmother?

SN: She's kind of like Jigonsaseh, who's in the legend of the Peacemaker.

CR: Oh.

SN: She was a pivotal character in that story. There are many versions of the story, but the one that comes to mind is that she was a woman who would feed warriors on their way to war. And sometimes she would poison them. She would invite them in, poison them, and then, the Peacemaker said, "Don't do that, because what you're doing is not helping the situation at all." So he had her change her mind about everything. And then she started taking people in, feeding them and nurturing them. So that's a bit of the character, but not the whole character.

CR: That's interesting. Because when they first come to her house, she does seem a little scary; but then the scariness changes and she becomes very sweet. And she feeds them.

SN: Well, she's a doubting Thomas, like, *What are you doing here? You know? You—you've never come here before, so* . . .

CR: Right.

SN: And Mavis goes, "We're just dropping off a photograph." You know? Goes, "We're not here to—to burn anything, really." Then it does get kind of sweet.

CR: Yes. That's an amazing night [in *Kissed by Lightning*, when Josephine Lightning shelters Mavis and Solomon].

And she is in the Mohawk Valley? Where the grandmother is? She's in New York.

SN: I made the location around Cohoes. Because, you know, it's storming out, and—they don't know where they're going to sleep; but she insists that they stay there, so, everything's fine.

CR: That's a nice scene.

SN: Yeah.

CR: With the works referencing New York State. There's *Kissed by Lightning* and *It Starts with a Whisper*, is that—so they stay on the Canada side?

SN: They stay on the Canadian side; but you can see it [New York] across the Falls. Yeah.

CR: And why did they need to go to Niagara? To the Falls.

SN: Mostly out of celebration. Just a celebratory situation.

CR: One of them wins [a hotel room] in a bingo game?

SN: Yeah, they win that hotel room. The four of them are together. And then Shanna, the young girl, she kind of begrudgingly goes along with them because, you know, they tease her, and they bug her, and they poke fun of her clothes, and all that sort of thing.

But, you know, she does go, and it becomes a very loving situation at the end. And, I just thought, well, the film was meant to be played at—or to end at five to midnight. New Year's Eve.

CR: Right.

SN: And it was done in a year where Christopher Columbus is being celebrated for his five hundredth year [after the] discovery of America. And to me, this was a time to say, after all *that*—after all that happened—we're still here to celebrate. We're still here, and we're still celebrating. So, it's where fireworks take off. They have their cake and tea.

CR: Oh, I love that cake! [The cake is in the shape of the world, like a globe]. And, what Shanna says to the aunts earlier, she's like, "Oh, all you ever do is, talk, laugh, and eat."

SN: Yes.

CR: And, yet, this is how they make it. You know?

SN: Yes.

CR: And those [the actors] are your actual sisters, right? Are they all your sisters, the aunts?

SN: They're all my sisters.

CR: They were really good. Really funny.

SN: They were good. But it's like, I'm not going to work with these guys again!

CR: You'll get some real actors [laughter from both].

SN: Going to get real actors.

CR: They were actually fabulous.

SN: Yes, they were pretty good.

CR: When they are looking at New York, and Niagara is that border zone. And, in your film, *Niagara*, you talk about it as a border—

SN: And I think it kind of encapsulates North America, essentially, you know?

CR: Okay.

SN: Because Shanna's walking around, and—she's at Niagara Falls, and she has all these words, almost like poetry going through her head, you know?

CR: It's really beautiful. The names of all these different tribal nations.

SN: Right.

CR: And then she meets Elijah—

SN: Elijah Harper. Yes. He's such a strong character in Canadian history. Because I think it was 1990 when they were having the Meech Lake Accord, and it was between the English and the French, and Elijah Harper stopped the whole thing. And he said, "You didn't have any Aboriginal inclusion here, so I'm going to strike this deal down." And because of that they couldn't go ahead with it. And shortly after that, that's when Oka [the Oka Crisis, July 11–September 26, 1990] took over. That's when the Oka thing happened.

SN: And that's when Mulroney sent in the army, and it turned into this big, ugly fiasco.

CR: And that—Oka—was a big influence on your work early on?

SN: Yes, it was. It was an influence on a lot of people, because every day in the newspaper, you'd read different things about the Mohawk Nation because that was taking place on a Mohawk reserve in Quebec.

CR: Right.

SN: But they had other statistics in the news articles, as well, which really made Native people look, you know, like bums and terrorists, and it wasn't great.

So after reading that on a daily basis, it's like, *Man, this is starting to have an effect on me!* And if it's having an effect on me, it must be having an effect on a lot of people.

And that took place in July of 1990, and then that's when I started doing the *Mohawks in Beehives* in 1991 [Niro's series of photographs of her sisters in bouffant hairdos playfully posed, sometimes in front of Joseph Brant's statue]. So, I asked my sisters. I took them out for lunch.

But, yes. That [Oka] took place.

CR: It was a horrible thing. One has this idea or narrative of, well, things *were* bad, and now they're better; but then something like that happens, and it's just, *Oh, no, they're not better.*

SN: Right. It's almost like propaganda. Well, it *is* propaganda. And the majority of non-Natives who read that will believe it. You know? And that's how they [settler-colonialist nation-state governance] gain power and get their votes and get reelected. Voters think, well, we're being protected, so let's get this guy back in here again.

CR: Right.

SN: Yeah, so it's just . . . it feels like you're a mouse in a cage, you know? So it's like trying not to be a mouse in a cage is, trying to get rid of that cage.

CR: Yes.

SN: I think comfort comes in knowing that people are making art and writing, and being creative in their own way. If people stopped being creative, then I think that we would really be in trouble.

But I think a lot of people are working in that vein, so it's really great to know. And once in a while, you see something [a new work of art by another artist] and you say, "Wow, that's pretty amazing!"

CR: That's right. And a lot of times, for me, that something is something that *you've* made. So, staying with New York State, in *La Pieta*, there is a photograph of the Mohawk Valley.

SN: Yes. Also [In *La Pieta*, the water photographs, frames 1 and 7] show how we come into the world and how we go out of the world. Water is essential, and it's something that is taken for granted; now it's not so beautiful in some of these places now. [The water images in *La Pieta* are not of the Mohawk River].

CR: Oh, yeah, that's true in a lot of places now.

SN: Yeah.

CR: But the Mohawk Valley photograph [in *La Pieta*] is so beautiful.

SN: That's from standing on the top of Whiteface Mountain. Lake Placid is below, and the valleys just go on and on and on. So it's like, *This is amazing!* No wonder we were chased out of here. It's so beautiful.

CR: That photograph is so calming and eternal looking—

SN: Yeah.

CR: What time of day was it when you took that photograph?

SN: It's in the afternoon.

CR: And it's summer?

SN: Yep.

CR: Do you always go there in the summer?

SN: I've gone in every season but winter.

CR: And the Adirondacks, in *Battlefields of My Ancestors*, those two images, to me, seem parallel. The Mohawk Valley and the Adirondacks. In these harsh series about sad things, there are these incredibly beautiful images.

SN: I know. When I talk to Mohawk people about being there—because they have the same history as myself—about visiting this area. And we've all experienced the feeling—it's almost like going through a time warp. And, I don't know how to explain it, but we've all felt it—I don't even know if it's an emotion. Your body just kind of like, *bows*. And what is that? I don't know. It's something real, but I don't have a word for it.

CR: In *Kissed by Lightning*, when their van is stopped in the snow and they say, "Oh" . . . How did you put it? I mean, you wrote the script. But it's something like, "When your feet touch the ground here, you touch the ancestors."

SN: "When your feet touch the ground, you're touching the ancestors."

CR: It makes sense, right? Because the Mohawk were there [in New York] for thousands and thousands of years, and you've only been gone for a couple hundred years, so the memory [of the land] is longer and deeper than that short time of being gone.

SN: Right. Not a time warp but almost like that.

CR: Yeah, I don't know the word for that, because in America it's unique to Indigenous people since all the rest of us don't have that memory of the land. Your photograph of the Adirondacks [in *Battlefields of My Ancestors*], it also looks almost aerial. They're very emotionally moving photographs; but they're also, in some ways, remote.

SN: Well, that one, [I was] standing on top of this mountain, and so this ability to see so much land around you . . . Now you're making me want to go and see it again.

CR: *Battlefields of My Ancestors* is an upsetting series, and then there's just this incredibly beautiful image, right?

SN: Yeah.

CR: And [in that series] you have a photograph of the Mohawk River, and one of where the Mohawk meets the Hudson, and those are both black and white. Why did you put those in black and white?

SN: They were analog films. While others are digital. So they are black and white for that reason.

CR: . . . because they look somehow grimmer than the rest. I don't know, but there's a lot of pollution in those rivers and, I wondered if the images were, sort of, reflecting on that?

SN: It looks lonely [in those photographs].

CR: Yes, it does.

SN: It's a very lonely looking landscape.

CR: Yes, it is. In *1779*, the film is of Niagara, right?

SN: It's the whirlpool. You can take a cable car over the whirlpool. You pay, like, fifteen bucks. And so I just videotaped it, because it's pretty dramatic and, I thought, that imagery will just fit right into what I'm trying to do with this piece here.

CR: It really does. I love the shoes on top of it. And that piece is reflecting on the year of the Sullivan-Clinton campaign?

SN: Yeah. And also in the video [version] of *The Shirt*, I have images of the Grand River going into Niagara Falls.

CR: I remember the river. I think you've said this before, but you've gone back there, over the years. For thirty or forty years you've gone back, sometimes with your sister?

SN: Niagara Falls, or New York?

CR: New York.

SN: Yes. Now, I've been doing research with other people there. We're doing research on Joseph Brant. He brought Six Nations to where we are now.

CR: Yes.

SN: Some of the population see him as a villain. He's been vilified.

CR: Why is that?

SN: They think he sold off a lot of the land for his own gain; but in doing research, he did sell off land, but it was to feed the people who were here.

And at the same time, we're supposed to get six miles on each side of the Grand River, from the source to the mouth.

CR: Right.

SN: And people would just come and squat and just stay there.

CR: You mean, settlers?

SN: Yes. So even now, those people are still there, and their families are still there. And, it just becomes a big, messy story. But because he's [Brant] been such a hard-done-by character in history, because he was looked at—he was kind of propagandized by non-Native people, especially before 1776. And, he was called a monster, Brant, because they credited him for massacres where women and children were killed.

But then years after that they were saying, "No, he wasn't the one who was responsible." So, it's [the research] going through, making these little corrections, you know? And, trying to see the story from a point of view that doesn't see him as being this horrible person that he's been put into history.

CR: It seems like—and God knows I'm not an expert—but it seems like he was trying to navigate and negotiate in an extremely difficult situation, to hold on to something so his people [the Mohawk and the Six Nations] wouldn't be wiped out.

SN: Yes.

CR: I think the British wanted to use him as their pawn. And then he was actually pretty good at resisting that, and not being their pawn.

SN: Yes. It's true. They wanted him to assimilate; but he became an infiltrator more than an assimilator.

And when the land was assigned to Six Nations, I think it was the British that said they only wanted Mohawks here. And he said, "No, we're going to leave it open for other—other [Indigenous] people as well." So I think, *Wow, that's pretty cool that he had this vision that land could be used by other nations, not just Mohawks.*

CR: Yes.

SN: So it's something that we have to keep reminding ourselves about, that he really came from a place of generosity, and not a place of exclusivity.

CR: It does seem like he was trying to find a way to survive when the Americans clearly wanted to basically commit genocide. And the British were not exactly reliable, right?

SN: Right.

CR: After they lost the war—I can't remember the exact quote, but it was something like, you know, "We'll just leave the Mohawk to the *softening influence* of their American friends."

SN: Right.

CR: I'm glad you're doing the [Brant] project. So you go down to New York with other people—

SN: Yes. We try to follow the path—those battlefield paths—and visit the important sites that had so much, uh, influence on today's Six Nations person. We've gone to Elmira, where the Battle of Newtown took place. So there's a lot of signage at that place.

CR: Are you still creating that series? *Battlefields of My Ancestors?*

SN: Probably. Because I find that when you start working on that sort of thing, it really—it becomes quite an emotional journey, because you're traveling to these places and you're trying to kind of remember things through your own body. And I just find that at a certain point, you just have to not do that [for a while].

CR: Right. It's too intense.

SN: Yes. I had my sister with me when I was taking some of those photographs, and she was really disturbed by the signage that we did come across. You know, I was just, like, "Hurry up, let's take this picture!"

CR: This is Bunny?

SN: Yes.

CR: That signage, it *is* horrifying.

SN: Yeah, really.

CR: The stone with that metal plaque that says, "Site of a very pretty Indian town of ten houses, burned September 21, 1779—see page 76 'Journals of the Military Expedition of Major General John Sullivan' Published by the State."

SN: I didn't find that sign, but somebody had posted it on Facebook. And I said, "Where is that sign?" So they told me, and I found it, and went there and took a picture of it.

CR: Was it in a field or something?

SN: It's on the road. It's just on the road. I just think, that's pretty crazy.

CR: Oh, God, it's like the world flipped inside out.

SN: Yes.

CR: So along those lines, of the world flipped inside out when you filmed *Kissed by Lightning*, and they go into the café—in upstate New York? The café where they sing to Mavis?

SN: It's supposed to be in New York State. It was filmed in a restaurant in Hamilton, Ontario.

CR: Yeah, because there's that wooden, you know, "wooden Indian" in the café.

SN: Right.

CR: And all the American flags. When I was teaching that film, one of my [non-Native] students who's from upstate New York said, "Oh, yeah, those carved figures, they're everywhere up there." I couldn't believe it. Still? Now? This kid is nineteen years old and it's 2023.

SN: Yes.

CR: So when she goes in the café and she looks at the carved figure and kind of laughs—tell me about that scene?

SN: Originally, I had written a scene where Mavis walks into this restaurant, and she can feel the racism. Of course, she flares up and she starts throwing cups, you know. She was really violent.

But then I thought, well, I'll just leave it in there for now, because I have to think about it. And then, it was a really cold winter day, and I had my dog, and I said, *Let's go for a walk*. So we walked out. It was super cold. And then we went out, maybe, fifteen, twenty minutes, came back in, and then the scene, sort of, appeared to me. And it came to me through two memories.

One of them is having a memory of being at church with my parents. My parents went to every church denomination on the reserve. And this one happened to be—I think it was Pentecostal.

There was a van of African American youths who showed up. And they jumped out and, you know, they had the big hair, and the hair picks in their hair. And they were really exciting to us because we—we don't usually see anything like this. And, then, in church, they were singing and clapping and there was just so much joy in them. So that memory came to me.

And then there was another—well, it wasn't a memory; but I had been in the National Museum of the American Indian [NMAI]. A few years ago where I was part of an exhibition at NMAI, and I had an installation, and I was there to talk about it. And there were school kids there. And a young Black man stood up and he asked, "Are you—are you angry?"

I ask, "About what?"

"About what happened to you in history?"

I said, "I guess so. But, you know, I don't think about it all the time. It's only when I start to work on stuff."

So those two ideas came to my mind. And I sat down, and I start thinking about being in this restaurant and then the quartet shows up, and they're on the way to the Martin Luther King Memorial. And, all those ideas started to converge into each other.

And so, I just thought, you know, *That's one way to solve that problem*, instead of having Mavis become this raging lunatic. She meets these people and she becomes more in tune with the history of the location she's at. Bug is already in tune with it; but the quartet, they're great.

And the song—I just wanted them to come in and go, *Ooh-la-la*, because, you know, we couldn't afford to pay for any rights to music. But when they were there on the day, they said, "We're going to write a song for that." And they did. That's what they did. They sang "Thank God for the Mohawk People." And when it screened at Imaginative, and they were singing "Thank God for the Mohawk People," [Mohawk] people just laughed their heads off.

CR: Yeah?

SN: And then somebody else said, "Well, can't we say thank God for, like, other tribes as well?" I said, "Well, this is the one they wanted to sing, so that's what they sung."

CR: I love that scene. And, Mavis, what is so appealing about her character is she sees everything, and then she just, sort of, rolls her eyes, and—

SN: Yeah.

CR: The song is beautiful, because it makes something that feels like it's going to be a horrible moment turn into something that's not horrible but transformative. Because when they first walk into that café, watching the film, you just think, *Oh, no.*

SN: Exactly, yeah.

SN: And you can feel their discomfort by being there.

CR: Those places are scary, and hearing a nineteen-year-old in the year 2023 say that it's still like that is a shame.

SN: Yes.

CR: Do you feel that it's important in your work—in general—when you reconnect with New York State?

SN: Yes. When I go through New York State, and I'm traveling through all the landscape, you know, I can't help but feel, like, a little bit possessive of it. Like, this is mine.

CR: Yes. It is yours.

SN: And of course, I know that, it's surely not mine; but, in a mindscape kind of way, it's like, this is my land.

CR: Yeah.

SN: And it becomes a beautiful moment, because I can be there, and I can claim it, and try to feel that I can do anything when I am there.

CR: It is your land.

SN: Yes. Right. And because I'm taking on the ownership, that I'm hoping that other people will feel that ownership through what I'm making.

CR: The films that I think of as being New York State works, of course *Kissed by Lightning*, and also *Niagara*, the five-minute film, is that filmed in the United States or Canada?

SN: In Canada. But, you know, that's taken on the *Maid of the Mist* boat. You get that in Canada. But you can get to the Falls and the other side as well.

CR: So, you're looking at both New York and Canada.

SN: In that video, it's about the border of Niagara Falls, you know? They say I was born in Niagara Falls, and it's a border, so there are elements of Niagara Falls, New York, in there.

CR: That is the most beautiful film. It's incredible what you fit in five minutes.

SN: It's about my daughter who passed away, and my mum. And one week before my mum passed away, we were in a restaurant and she's telling me that she had a dream about her grandmother, and it made her really happy. And so I just thought, *Well, that's quite a beautiful memory of her to me.* You know, that she was happy thinking about her grandmother.

So, that story gets included with the story of my daughter who is, you know, she's a substance abuser. And how she was in jail—it's really a capsule of her life—and how she was in jail, crying, calling for me, and then somebody recognized her voice saying, "Is that you?" And she said it shocked her that somebody could hear her, and recognize her. And then she said that it was kind of funny to her after—she was always crying, and then she starts to laugh because somebody else recognized her. It sort of shocked her into not crying anymore.

It's a very hard video. It was hard to make; but I don't know, sometimes you've just got to make stuff.

CR: Yeah. The film is poetic, and there's so much there. I actually thought that it was your daughter dreaming of your mother.

SN: I left that ambiguous, because I just didn't want it to be so literal and telling the story. So, depending on who I'm talking to, or who knows the story, people can translate it any way they want to. But that's just how the story came about.

CR: I think what's so beautiful about it is the way it weaves the layers of the Falls as this border space, and the sense of all the things that happened at the Falls, over so many centuries, connecting with the speaker. And then it's where the speaker was born, and it's nice to learn that in the film, because you don't know anything else about the speaker.

SN: Yeah.

CR: This sense of loss is so strong in the film. But at the same time, because the Falls are powerful, there's this sense that regrowth can come from the loss. Or that's the feeling that I got from it.

SN: Well, I used the Falls itself, the Falls coming down, is also in the story of the Peacemaker, where wiping away the tears of grief is mentioned. I'm using the Falls as a way of wiping away those tears of grief. That's where you see the finger coming and cleaning the lens.

CR: So the film is connected to "The Essential Sensuality of Ceremony."

SN: Yes.

CR: I understand how hard it is to make art like that. But there is so much power in it. And I'm so sorry about your daughter.

SN: It took me at least ten years to be able to tell people that. And now, I can tell people. Whereas before, I couldn't even say it.

CR: There are things that it takes years, decades, before you can speak of it.

SN: Yes.

CR: There are things where it's just, *this is too heavy*. But *Niagara* is a perfect film, every aspect of it. The fingers wiping away the water is so tactile and touching, that connection with Peacemaker wiping away the tears.

SN: Right.

CR: *The Essential Sensuality of Ceremony* is a beautiful series. I found this article that rudi aker wrote about *The Essential Sensuality of Ceremony*. It's great.

SN: Oh. I'll have to find it.

CR: I can send it to you.

SN: If you could send that, that'd be great.

CR: So the idea of aker's article is that, in *The Essential Sensuality of Ceremony*, the woman photographed in the series is Peacemaker and that this series shows us how serving someone, showing care to someone, is noble . . .

SN: Nice. That sounds really nice.

Notes

Introduction

1. E. Pauline Johnson, *Flint and Feather* (Toronto: Musson Books, 1912), https://pressbooks.library.torontomu.ca/flintandfeather/. In quoting from Johnson's poem "Guard of the Eastern Gate," I note that even as the Mohawk poet writes about Halifax, Nova Scotia, she alludes to the Mohawk as Keepers of the Eastern Door, creating a poem that subtly instates Mohawk power. See *Tekahionwake, Pauline* (2021), written, directed, and produced by Shelley Niro. Seneca scholar Mishuana Goeman explains that Johnson "aimed to educate settlers by articulating a Canadian national landscape that was infused with the deep cultural history of both Natives and the English—a landscape of liberal possibilities." Mishuana Goeman, *Mark Her Words: Native Women Mapping Our Nations* (Minneapolis: University of Minnesota Press, 2013), 51.

2. Niro's multimedia art has long acted as a key interlocutor of the meaning of settler-colonial nation-state boundaries. Jumaane D. Williams, "Air Quality Health Advisory," *The Advocate*, June 8, 2023, https://www.pubadvocate.nyc.gov/blog/2023/06/08/stay-safe-nyc-air-quality-health-advisory/.

3. Dina Gilio-Whitaker, *As Long As Grass Grows: The Indigenous Fight for Environmental Justice, from Colonization to Standing Rock* (Boston: Beacon Press, 2019), 15–23.

4. Michael L. Ross, *The Oil Curse: How Petroleum Wealth Shapes the Development of Nations* (Princeton, NJ: Princeton University Press, 2012), 189–222.

5. Haudenosaunee Confederacy "Who We Are." https://www.haudenosauneeconfederacy.com/who-we-are/ (accessed June 1, 2023).

6. Sue Ellen Herne and Lynne Williamson, "Haudenosaunee Traditional Arts: A Glimpse into Our House," in *North by Northeast: Wabanaki, Awkwesasne Mohawk and Tuscarora Traditional Arts*, ed. Kathleen Mundell (Gardiner, ME: Tilbury House Publishers, 2008), 3.

7. Quoted in *In the Making*, Season 1, Episode 6, "Shelley Niro," directed by Chelsea McMullan, hosted by Sean O'Neill, aired October 26, 2018, Canadian Broadcasting Corporation.

8. Richard White, *The Middle Ground: Indians, Empires, and Republics in the Great Lakes Region*, 1650–1815 (Cambridge: Cambridge University Press, 2010).

9. Richard Hill, "Voices From Here," *The Canadian Encyclopedia*, accessed January 21, 2024, https://www.thecanadianencyclopedia.ca/en/article/voices-from-here-richard-hill.

10. Niro uses digital technology for her contemporary feature-length movies and shorter videos, but in using the term "film" here and throughout this book, I adhere to the convention of naming that yet reflects digital video's origin as a filmic media.

11. Madeline Lennon, *Shelley Niro: Seeing through Memory* (London: Blue Medium Press, 2014), 6–28.

12. Leanne Betasamosake Simpson. "Indigenous Resurgence and Co-Resistance." *Critical Ethnic Studies* 2, no. 2 (2016): 19–34.

13. Jeffrey Ostler, *Surviving Genocide: Native Nations and the United States from the American Revolution to Bleeding Kansas* (New Haven, CT: Yale University Press, 2020), 1–10.

14. Ned Blackhawk, *The Rediscovery of America: Native Peoples and the Unmaking of U.S. History* (New Haven: Yale University Press, 2023), 5.

15. In this book, I use the term coloniality as it is developed by theorists Aníbal Quijano and Walter D. Mignolo; see Walter D. Mignolo and Catherine E. Walsh, *On Decoloniality: Concepts, Analytics, Praxis* (Durham, NC: Duke University Press, 2017).

16. Shelley Niro, in conversation with the author, July 21, 2023.

17. New York City is Lenape land. In admiring Niro's courage in the face of the dangerously poor air quality during the air pollution crisis of June 2023, I am making a metaphorical point.

18. *Kissed by Lightning*, directed by Shelley Niro (2009; Toronto: Shelley Niro Productions, 2009), DVD; *Niagara*, directed by Shelley Niro (2015; Toronto: V tape, 2015), DVD; *It Starts with a Whisper*, directed by Shelley Niro and Anna Gronau (1993; New York: Women Make Movies, 1993), VHS.

19. Responding to multiple recent incidents in which white scholars fabricated public personas as if they were Indigenous, I want to make clear here that I write about Haudenosaunee culture from the perspective of an outsider. I am not Haudenosaunee.

20. Michelle Raheja, *Reservation Reelism: Redfacing, Visual Sovereignty, and Representations of Native Americans in Film* (Lincoln: University of Nebraska Press, 2010), 181, 189.

21. Shelley Niro, in conversation with the author, February 19, 2024.

22. Robert Grumet, *Northeastern Indian Lives: 1632–1816* (Amherst: University of Massachusetts Press, 1996), 299–309. Notes Grumet, "Mohawk Molly Brant was the elder sister of Joseph Brant and common-law wife to William Johnson. . . . Guy Johnson was superintendent of Indian Affairs 1779, and cat-ercorner nephew of Molly Brant against whom she worked."

23. Alan Taylor limns the Mohawk territory as reaching from Hudson Valley to Lake Eerie, from Lake Ontario to the Adirondacks. Haudenosaunee territory had been "broad, contiguous, and overlapping, but under pressure of colonization became fragmented and fissured and discrete, sectioned into tribal reservations." The people thus became "dependent on state annuities," argues Taylor; see Alan Taylor, *The Divided Ground: Indians, Settlers, and the Northern Borderland of the American Revolution* (New York: Knopf, 2006), 4–9.

24. Shelley Niro, personal communication with the author, September 29, 2023.

25. Wanda Nanibush, "The Photography of Shelley Niro," in *Scotiabank Photography Award: Shelley Niro* (Göttingen, Germany: Steidl, 2018), 9.

26. Alyssa Mt. Pleasant, "Land, Liberty, and Loss: Echoes of the American Revolution," *Humanities New York* podcast, September 28, 2022.

27. Eric Hinderaker, *The Two Hendricks: Unraveling a Mohawk Mystery* (Cambridge, MA: Harvard University Press, 2010), 283–84.

28. Patrick Wolfe, *The Settler Complex: Recuperating Binarism in Colonial Studies* (Los Angeles: UCLA Press, 2016), 1–25.

29. Laurence Hauptman, "The Iroquois Confederacy with Prof. Laurence Hauptman," January 4, 2017, in *The Forget-Me-Not Hour*, podcast, MP3 audio, 1:41:43, https://www.blogtalkradio.com/janeewilcox/2017/01/04/the-iroquois-confederacy-with-prof-laurence-hauptman.

30. Hauptman, "The Iroquois Confederacy."

31. Dean R. Snow, Charles T. Gehring, and William A. Starna, eds., *A Journey into Mohawk Country: Early Narratives About a Native People* (Syracuse, NY: Syracuse University Press, 1996), 5.

32. Snow et al., *A Journey*, 9.

33. Snow et al., *A Journey*, 39. Historian Daniel K. Richter adds to our understanding of Haudenosaunee plenitude: "Squash, beans, and corn all grown by the Haudenosaunee act naturally to support each other in fields; women were the keepers of the villages and longhouses, and the tellers of oral traditions." See Daniel K. Richter, *The Ordeal of the Longhouse: The Peoples of the Iroquois League in the Era of European Colonization* (Chapel Hill: University of North Carolina Press, 1992), 24.

34. Richter, *The Ordeal*, 41–43.

35. Richter, *The Ordeal*, 58–59.

36. Arthur C. Parker, "An Analytical History of the Seneca Indians," New York State Archeological Association, Rochester, New York, 1926. https://www.kanehsatakevoices.com/category/blog/ *Kontinónhstats/Mohawk Language Custodian Association/Association pour la preservation de la langue Mohawk*. Accessed March 11th 2024.

37. Deborah Doxtator, "What Happened to the Iroquois Clans? A Study of Clans in Three Nineteenth-Century Rotinonhsyonni Communities" (PhD diss., University of Western Ontario, 1996), 55. Quoted in Theresa McCarthy, "Dẹni:s

nisa'sgao'dę? Haudenosaunee Clans and the Reconstruction of Traditional Haudenosaunee Identity, Citizenship, and Nationhood," *American Indian Culture and Research Journal*, 34, no. 2: 81–101.

38. Eric Hinderaker, *The Two Hendricks: Unraveling a Mohawk Mystery* (Cambridge, MA: Harvard University Press, 2010), 9–10.

39. Maile Arvin, Eve Tuck, and Angie Morrill, "Decolonizing Feminism: Challenging Connections between Settler Colonialism and Heteropatriarchy," *Feminist Formations* 25, no. 1 (Spring 2013): 3.

40. Lennon, *Shelley Niro*, 37–57.

41. Here and throughout this book when I present Mohawk words I do so only in quotes from other sources. I do not speak the Mohawk language. Richter, *The Ordeal*, 8–20. In "The Iroquois Confederacy," Laurence Hauptman notes that "the creation story [highlights] the role of women [in Haudenosaunee culture]. Sky Woman . . . falls through the sky into the water below [but] the water animals save her, planting her on the turtle's back, which becomes Turtle Island. She gets up and begins to dance counter-clockwise, which is the origin of Iroquois horticulture. Sky Woman's daughter has twins, one is helpful and one causes difficulty, [hence] a duality in life, a balance that has to be kept; life shouldn't be too easy or too hard. It requires balance [to] walk in balance. The difficult twin makes things hard while the good twin gives bountiful life."

42. Shelley Niro, in conversation with the author, February 4, 2024.

43. Shelley Niro, in conversation with the author, February 19, 2024.

44. John C. Mohawk, "A View from Turtle Island: Chapters in Iroquois Mythology, History and Culture" (PhD diss., State University of New York at Buffalo, 1994), abstract.

45. Kahente Horn-Miller, "Sky Woman's Great Granddaughters: A Narrative Inquiry Into Kanienkehaka Women's Identity" (PhD diss., Concordia University, Montreal, 2009), 28–31.

46. Michael Doxtater, personal communication with the author, August 8, 2023.

47. Shelley Niro, *Sky Woman with Us*, 7 minutes running time, color. Written, directed, and produced by Shelley Niro, Ontario, Canada, 2002.

48. As Mohawk scholar Paul W. DePasquale notes, Indigenous Canadians disproportionately experience homelessness. See Paul W. DePasquale, ed. *Natives and Settlers Then and Now: Refractions of the Colonial Past in the Present* (Alberta: University of Alberta Press, 2007), xvii; see also Jane Bailey and Sara Shayan, "Missing and Murdered Indigenous Women Crisis: Technological Dimensions," *Canadian Journal of Women and the Law* 28, no. 2 (2016): 321–41.

49. Mohawk composer and musician ElizaBeth Hill has collaborated with Niro not only on *Sky Woman with Us* but on a number of film projects; Hill's beautiful musical compositions enrich and deepen those visual/verbal texts.

50. Shelley Niro, in conversation with the author, February 4, 2024.

51. Shelley Niro, in conversation with the author, February 19, 2024.

52. Raheja, Reservation Reelism, 182.

53. Ferren Gipsin, *Women's Work: From Feminine Art to Feminist Art* (London: Frances Lincoln, 2022); see also Claire Raymond, *Women Photographers and Feminist Aesthetics* (New York: Routledge, 2017), 1–22.

54. Hinderaker, *The Two Hendricks*, 21.

55. Daniel K. Richter, " 'Some of Them . . . Would Always Have a Minister with Them': Mohawk Protestantism, 1683–1719," *American Indian Quarterly* 16, no. 4 (1992): 471–84.

56. Snow et al., *A Journey*, 29–37.

57. Rosalyn Deutsche, *Not-Forgetting: Contemporary Art and the Interrogation of Mastery* (Chicago: University of Chicago Press, 2022), 1.

58. Deutsche, *Not-Forgetting*, 1–2.

59. Shelley Niro, in conversation with the author, January 28, 2024.

60. I refer to the resolution adopted by the General Assembly on September 13, 2007. The English language word "Indigenous" indicates existing in a land from the earliest times, whereas "Native" means born there.

61. Shelley Niro, in conversation with the author, July 21, 2023.

62. Laura E. Smith, "Photography Criticism and Native American Women's Identity: Three Works by Jolene Rickard," *Third Text* 19, no. 1 (2005): 53.

63. Taylor, *The Divided Ground*, 35. Notes Taylor, "Sacred burial mounds and earthen fortifications from a populous era before invasion brought diseases that decimated populations" and were abundant in the area.

64. Wanda Nanibush, "Notions of Land," *Aperture* (Spring 2019), 75.

Chapter 1

1. Richard Hill, *Voices from Here*, Episode 4, filmed on September 5, 2019, on Six Nations of the Grand River Territory, Cinematographer Jonathan Elliott.

2. Douglas M. George-Kanentiio, *Iroquois on Fire: A Voice from the Mohawk Nation* (Lincoln: University of Nebraska Press, 2006), 1. Taiaiake Alfred contends that the Kahnawake Mohawk now occupy territory that was *always* ancestrally part of Mohawk land, the northern limits thereof. See, Taiaiake Alfred, "It's All About the Land" public talk at the Center for the Study of Learning and Performance, Concordia University, Montreal, Quebec, January 25, 2023.

3. Wolfe, *Traces of History*, 29, 188.

4. Margaret Kovach, *Indigenous Methodologies: Characteristics, Conversations, and Contexts* (Toronto: University of Toronto Press, 2021), 26.

5. Margaret Kovach, "Provocations for a Different Art History in a Cross-Disciplinary Context: Comparing Comparativisms," UIC Institute for the Humanities, Chicago and online, February 19, 2024.

6. Johannes Fabian, *Time and the Other: How Anthropology Makes Its Object* (New York: Columbia University Press, 2002), 38–51.

7. To say that they are inherently political does not mean, of course, that photographs and films are inherently progressive. They can also be retrograde purveyors of propaganda. See Walter Benjamin, "Little History of Photography," in *Walter Benjamin: Selected Writings, Volume 2, Part 2: 1931–1934*, trans. Rodney Livingstone and others; ed. Michael W. Jennings, Howard Eiland, and Gary Smith (Cambridge, MA: Belknap Press, 1999), 507–30.

8. Joyce Green, "Rebalancing Strategies: Aboriginal Women and Constitutional Rights in Canada," in *Making Space for Indigenous Feminism*, ed. Joyce Green (Halifax, Nova Scotia: Fernwood, 2017), 186.

9. *Tree*, directed by Shelley Niro (2005; Toronto: Vtape, 2006), DVD.

10. Claire Raymond, *Photography and Resistance: Anticolonialist Photography in the Americas* (London: Palgrave Macmillan, 2022).

11. Shelley Niro, in conversation with the author, January 28, 2024.

12. Quoted in Nadya Kwandibens, "emergence," *tea & bannock, a collective blog by indigenous woman photographers*, April 22, 2016, https://teaandbannock.com/2016/04/22/emergence/.

13. Hulleah Tsinhnahjinnie, "Compensating Imbalances," *Exposure* 29 (1993): 30.

14. Wanda Nanibush, "Outside of Time: Salvage Ethnography, Self-Representation and Performing Culture," in *Time, Temporality, and Violence in International Relations*, eds. Anna Agathangelou and Kyle Killian (London: Routledge, 2016), 115.

15. Hulleah Tsinhnahjinnie, "When Is a Photograph Worth a Thousand Words," 41.

16. Fabian, *Time*, 25–36.

17. As of June 1, 2023, this is the search result from Google.

18. Mark Rifkin, *Beyond Settler Time: Temporal Sovereignty and Indigenous Self-Determination* (Durham, NC: Duke University Press, 2017).

19. Stella Sanford, "Kant, Race, and Natural History," *Philosophy and Social Criticism* 44, no. 9 (2018): 950–77.

20. Hal Foster, "The 'Primitive' Unconscious of Modern Art, or, White Skin Black Masks," in *Recodings: Art, Spectacle, Cultural Politics* (Seattle, WA: Bay Press, 1985), 181–208.

21. Jodi Byrd, *Transit of Empire: Indigenous Critiques of Colonialism* (Minneapolis: University of Minnesota Press, 2011), 51.

22. Philip J. Deloria, "The New World of the Indigenous Museum," *Daedalus* 147, no. 2 (2018): 106–15.

23. Taiaiake Alfred, "It's All About the Land" public talk at the Center for the Study of Learning and Performance, Concordia University, Montreal, Quebec, January 25, 2023.

24. K. Tsianina Lomawaima and Teresa L. McCarty, *To Remain an Indian: Lessons in Democracy from a Century of Native American Education* (New York and London: Columbia University Teacher's College Press, 2006).

25. David Wallace Adams, *Education for Extinction: American Indians and the Boarding School Experience, 1875–1928*, 2nd ed. (Lawrence: University Press of Kansas, 2020).

26. Shelley Niro, in conversation with the author, February 10, 2024.

27. Ian Austen, "'Horrible History': Mass Grave of Indigenous Children Reported in Canada," *New York Times*, May 28, 2021.

28. Joyce Green, ed., *Making Space for Indigenous Feminism* (Halifax, Nova Scotia: Fernwood, 2017), 1–12.

29. Niro is currently at work on a film about Joseph Brant that delves into the complexity of this man who remains a contentious and debated figure within the Mohawk community (Shelley Niro, in conversation with the author, July 21, 2023).

30. Claude Levi Strauss, *Tristes Tropiques*, trans. John Weightman and Doreen Weightman (New York: Penguin Classics, 2012).

31. J. J. Southerland, "L. Frank Baum Advocated Extermination of Native Americans," National Public Radio, October 27, 2010, https://www.npr.org/sections/thetwo-way/2010/10/27/130862391/l-frank-baum-advocated-extermination-of-native-americans.

32. The presence of Niro's three sisters may playfully evoke the Three Sisters (corn, beans, squash) traditional to the Haudenosaunee. Or it may playfully evoke three of Shelley Niro's sisters.

33. Laurence Hauptman, *Conspiracy of Interests: Iroquois Dispossession and the Rise of New York State* (Syracuse: Syracuse University Press, 2001), 3.

34. Shelley Niro, personal communication with the author, October 2, 2017.

35. *The Incredible 25th Year of Mitzi Bearclaw*, directed by Shelley Niro (2019; Los Angeles: Indican Pictures, 2020), online; *Café Daughter*, directed by Shelley Niro, produced by Shelley Niro, Amos Adetuyi and Floyd Kane (2023; Toronto: Blue Circle Entertainment/Freddie Films, 2023), DVD. Michelle Raheja (Seneca) identifies the female lead in *Tree* as Sky Woman, while Niro speaks of this character as "an Earth mother type." Shelley Niro, in conversation with the author, November 17, 2018. See also Raheja, *Reservation Reelism*, 182.

36. Niro has long been a supporter of LGBTQIA+ Indigenous rights. For more on Indigenous LGBTQIA+ histories and resistance, see Qwo-Li Driskill, Chris Finley, Brian J. Gilley, and Scott L. Morgensen, eds., *Queer Indigenous Studies: Interviews in Theory, Politics, and Literature* (Tucson: University of Arizona Press, 2011).

37. Leanne Betasamosake Simpson, *As We Have Always Done: Indigenous Freedom Through Radical Resistance* (Minneapolis: University of Minnesota Press, 2017); see also Jacques Lacan, *Des noms-du-père*, ed. Jacques-Alain Miller (Paris: Éditions du Seuil, 2005); Judith Butler, *Gender Trouble: Feminism and the Subversion of Identity* (New York: Routledge, 1990).

38. Teresa de Lauretis, *Figures of Resistance: Essays in Feminist Theory* (Urbana-Champaign: University of Illinois Press, 2007).

39. Glen Sean Coulthard, *Red Skin, White Masks: Rejecting the Colonial Politics of Recognition* (Minneapolis: University of Minnesota Press 2014), 84.

40. Coulthard, *Red Skin, White Masks*, 84.

41. Coulthard, *Red Skin, White Masks*, 84.

42. Leanne Betasamosake Simpson, "Indigenous Resurgence and Co-Resistance," *Critical Ethnic Studies* 2, no. 2 (Fall 2016): 19–34.

43. Gerald Vizenor, *Manifest Manners: Narratives on Postindian Survivance* (Lincoln: University of Nebraska Press, 1999).

44. Rifkin, *Beyond Settler Time*.

45. Rifkin, *Beyond Settler Time*, vii.

46. Mark Rifkin, "The Silence of Ely S. Parker: The Emancipation Sublime and the Limits of Settler Memory," *Native American and Indigenous Studies* 1, no. 2 (2014): 1–43.

47. Michael Doxtater, email with the author, October 3, 2022.

48. Doxtater, email with the author, October 3, 2022.

49. Gerald Vizenor, ed., *Survivance: Narratives of Native Presence* (Lincoln: University of Nebraska Press, 2008).

50. Vizenor, *Survivance*, 25–28.

51. Shelley Niro, in conversation with the author, June 16th, 2023.

52. Taiaiake Alfred, *Indigenous Pathways of Action and Freedom* (Peterborough, Ontario: Broadview Press, 2005); see also Leanne Betasamosake Simpson, *Dancing on Our Turtle's Back: Stories of Nishnaabeg Re-Creation, Resurgence and a New Emergence* (Winnipeg: Arbeiter Ring, 2011).

53. Patrick Wolfe influentially argues that colonization is not an event, but a structure; see Patrick Wolfe, *Settler Colonialism and the Transformation of Anthropology* (London: Continuum International Publishing Group, 1998), 2. See also Lorenzo Veracini, *Settler Colonialism* (New York: Palgrave Macmillan, 2010).

54. Taylor, *The Divided Ground*, 112.

55. Wolfe argues that settler colonialism is always eliminatory but not always genocidal. In the case of the new nation—that is, the United States' actions against the Six Nations—genocidal ideation is clear; see Patrick Wolfe, "Settler Colonialism and the Elimination of the Native," *Journal of Genocide Research* 8, no. 4 (2006): 387–409.

56. Shelley Niro, in conversation with the author, November 17, 2018, and July 21, 2023.

57. Shelley Niro, in conversation with the author, July 21, 2023.

58. Between 2009 and 2021, "Indigenous women and girls were killed at a rate six times higher than that of their non-Indigenous counterparts," notes Statistique Canada, accessed February 2, 2024, https://www150.statcan.gc.ca/n1/daily-quotidien/231004/dq231004b-eng.htm. According to the United States Bureau of Indian Affairs website, "A 2016 study by the National Institute of Justice (NIJ) found that more than four in five American Indian and Alaska Native women

(84.3 percent) have experienced violence in their lifetime, including 56.1 percent who have experienced sexual violence. In the year leading up to the study, 39.8 percent of American Indian and Alaska Native women had experienced violence, including 14.4 percent who had experienced sexual violence. Overall, more than 1.5 million American Indian and Alaska Native women have experienced violence in their lifetime." Additionally, "According to the National Crime Information Center, in 2016, there were 5,712 reports of missing American Indian and Alaska Native women and girls, though the US Department of Justice's federal missing persons database, but the national information clearinghouse and resource center for missing, unidentified, and unclaimed person cases across the United States, called the National Missing and Unidentified Persons System only logged 116 of those cases"; see Bureau of Indian Affairs, "Missing and Murdered Indigenous People Crisis," accessed July 21, 2023, https://www.bia.gov/service/mmu/missing-and-murdered-Indigenous-people-crisis.

59. Taiaiake Alfred, *Peace, Power, Righteousness: An Indigenous Manifesto* (Oxford and New York: Oxford University Press 1999), vii. Quoted in Penelope Myrtle Kelsey "Condolence Tropes and Haudenosaunee Visuality" *Visualities: Perspectives on Contemporary American Indian Film and Art,* ed. Denise Cummings (East Lansing: Michigan State University Press, 2011), 120.

60. Margaret M. Bruchac, Siobhan Hart, and H. Martin Wobst, eds., *Indigenous Archaeologies: A Reader in Decolonization* (Walnut Creek, CA: Left Coast Press, 2010).

61. Rangihīroa Panoho, "Comparing Comparativisms," College Art Association Conference panel, Chicago and online, February 18, 2024.

62. Byrd, *Transit of Empire.*

Chapter 2

1. As noted in my introduction, Mohawk, the Akwesasne, still live in New York State. The industrial manipulation and massive pollution of the Saint Lawrence River on which this community lives is both tragic and exemplary of the continuing hold of settler-colonialist capitalism. See Liz Scheltens "How US Corporations Poisoned This Indigenous Community," *Vox,* August 16, 2022, https://www.vox.com/2022/8/16/23308638/mohawk-akwesasne-fishing-chemicals-pollution.

2. Shelley Niro, in conversation with the author, July 21, 2023.

3. Taylor, *The Divided Ground,* 34. Obviously, there is scant benefit available to Indigenous Americans to become subjects of a system that was created to defraud them; the law in settler-colonialist nation-states was created specifically to deny Aboriginal rights to land.

4. Audra Simpson, "On Ethnographic Refusal: Indigeneity, 'Voice' and Colonial Citizenship," *Junctures* 9 (2007): 80.

5. Claire Raymond, *The Photographic Uncanny: Photography, Homelessness, and Homesickness* (New York: Palgrave Macmillan, 2020), 221–56.

6. For more on the "Indigenous uncanny," see Faye Ginsburg, "The Indigenous Uncanny: Accounting for Ghosts in Recent Indigenous Australian Experimental Media," *Visual Anthropology Review* 34, no. 1 (2018): 67–76.

7. Hauptman, *Conspiracy*, 1–27, 213–22.

8. Brady J. Crytzer, "Longhouse Lost: The Battle of the Oriskany and the Iroquois Civil War," *Journal of the American Revolution*, July 30, 2020. https://allthingsliberty.com/2020/07/longhouse-lost-the-battle-of-oriskany-and-the-iroquois-civil-war/.

9. Shelley Niro, in conversation with the author, June 16, 2023.

10. United States Department of Environmental Protection, "Just the Facts—Cleaning Up the Hudson River PCBs," last modified February 22, 2016, accessed August 20, 2023, https://www3.epa.gov/hudson/just_facts_08_04.htm.

11. Riverkeeper, "Mohawk River Water Quality Data," accessed June 18, 2023, https://www.riverkeeper.org/water-quality/citizen-data/mohawk-river/.

12. Gilio-Whitaker, *As Long As*, 24–26.

13. Shelley Niro, in conversation with the author, March 12, 2022.

14. Shelley Niro, in conversation with the author, July 21, 2023.

15. Shelley Niro, in conversation with the author, July 21, 2023.

16. Natchee Blu Barnd, *Native Space: Geographic Strategies to Unsettle Settler Colonialism* (Corvallis: Oregon State University Press, 2017), 106.

17. Shelley Niro, *Something Cold and Hard Like Winter* (Waterloo, ON: Robert Langen Art Gallery, 2022), 22–26.

18. Alicia Elliott, "The Balm to the Burn," in *Something Cold and Hard Like Winter*, ed. Shelley Niro (Waterloo, Ontario: Robert Langen Art Gallery, 2022), 18.

19. Knafla and Westra, *Aboriginal Title*, 10.

20. Hauptman, *Conspiracy*, 97.

21. Taylor, *The Divided Ground*, 8.

22. John Demos, ed., *The Unredeemed Captive: A Family Story from Early America* (New York: Knopf, 1994), 4–5.

23. Guy Johnson, quoted in Taylor, *The Divided Ground*, 7.

24. Knafla and Westra, *Aboriginal Title*, 11.

25. Songwriter William Prince (Peguis First Nation), a favorite of Shelley Niro's, writes of these sacred laws in his song *7* (2016); Knafla and Westra, *Aboriginal Title*, 14.

26. Knafla and Westra, *Aboriginal Title*, 28.

27. Knafla and Westra, *Aboriginal Title*, 100–101.

28. Knafla and Westra, *Aboriginal Title*, 101.

29. Knafla and Westra, *Aboriginal Title*, 109.

30. Shelley Niro, personal communication with the author, March 22, 2022.

31. Michael Doxtater, email with the author, October 3, 2022.

32. Richard Hill, ed., "The Myth of the Earth Grasper," in the 43rd Annual Report, BAE, SI, 1925–26, Washington, DC, 1928, recorded and edited by J. N. B. Hewitt, recontextualized by Richard Hill, January 2001.

33. Hill, *Voices from Here*; Hill, "Voices from Here."

34. Hill, *Voices from Here*; Hill, "Voices from Here."

35. Shelley Niro, in conversation with the author, February 19, 2024.

36. Michael Doxtater, email with the author, October 3, 2022.

37. Michael Doxtater, email with the author, October 3, 2022.

38. Traditionally, women tended the crops and the village while men went on hunting and fishing expeditions during spring and summer. Richter, *The Ordeal*, 24.

39. This document does not give the name of the Haudenosaunee speaker whose words were recorded by Mr. Hewitt. However, Six Nations scholar Richard Hill has recontextualized the recording; see Hill, "Myth."

40. Hill, "Myth."

41. Richter, *The Ordeal*, 29.

42. Richter, *The Ordeal*, 29.

43. Richter, *The Ordeal*, 31.

44. Blackhawk, *Rediscovery of America*, 74–75.

45. Michael Doxtater, "The Four Worlds of Onkwehonwe Life, Prophecy and Memory" (lecture presented at Toronto Metropolitan University, Toronto, Canada, September 2022. Shared with the author via email, October 3, 2022).

46. Richter, *The Ordeal*, 32.

47. Richter, *The Ordeal*, 40–41.

48. Richter, *The Ordeal*, 43–44.

49. Audra Simpson, *Mohawk Interruptus: Political Life Across the Borders of Settler States* (Durham, NC: Duke University Press, 2014); see also Hauptman, "The Iroquois Confederacy."

50. Doxtater, *The Four Worlds*.

51. Doxtater, *The Four Worlds*, 23. Mohawk words provided by Michael Doxtater.

52. Doxtater, *The Four Worlds*, 24.

53. Doxtater, *The Four Worlds*, 17–18.

54. Shelley Niro, "La Pieta," 2007, accessed July 1, 2023, https://american-indian.si.edu/collections-search/objects/NMAI_396674; see also personal communication with the author, August 22, 2021.

55. Doxtater, *The Four Worlds*, 32.

56. Hauptman, *Conspiracy*.

57. Doxtater, *The Four Worlds*, 59; Chief Jacob Thomas, *Teachings from the Longhouse*, self-published, 2013.

58. Niro, "La Pieta"; see also personal communication with the author, August 22, 2021.

59. Shelley Niro, "A Good, Long Look," Art Gallery of Southwestern Manitoba, Canada, June 10–July 21, 2021, accessed June 30, 2023, https://agsm.ca/good-long-look.

60. Shelley Niro, Artist's Statement, "La Pieta,"

61. Shelley Niro, artist talk, September 21, 2017, The University of Virginia, Charlottesville.

62. Shelley Niro, "Artist Statement for 'La Pieta,'" 2001–06, digitized photo inkjet prints on canvas, National Museum of the American Indian, Washington, DC. Shelley Niro states: "Image #1, Image #7, *Water*. The first and the seventh images are of water. I use this to symbolize the importance of an element essential for all living things. Without it we would die. The Earth uses it to cleanse and heal itself after periods of chaos and turmoil. Water carries us for nine months in our mother's womb and makes our journey into this world easier. Water promises a life of abundance, growth, safety and hope for the future.

Image #2, *The Mohawk Valley/Infinite View*. This *infinite view* represents what was lost in the Diaspora of Iroquois People when they were forced to leave the Mohawk Valley after the American Revolution. The natural beauty never to be returned to takes my breath away. Again the landscape represents mother, a place always producing, always there, and a place that had to be defended and eventually lost. The maternal homeland still waits for the return of her people.

Image #3, *Trunk*. This image is a close-up of the resources, a single tree. The detail allows the viewer to see what would otherwise be ignored. We can examine each bark chunk, each shadow and crease. The knots act as invitations for us to listen and comment on the physicality of each tree as an individual. They have character and personality and can be cut down at the will of any man.

Image #4, *Young Man's Chest*. This series of images represent the resources that are lost and damaged in times of war. The grand landscape is torn apart. Over time the Earth will heal itself. The loss of young life leaves a definite scar on the world, no matter whose life, whose side of the battle that was fought. Mothers will cry forever.

Image #5, *Gothic Landscape*. I've returned to the landscape, a different type of landscape. This photo was taken in the winter. The leaves and the grass are gone. The bare limbs of the trees hang in anticipation of the spring. As a metaphor for sadness, this forest looks full but is empty at the same time. The bareness waits, never knowing when birds will sing again from its branches.

Image #6, *At the Edge*. This photo was taken at the edge of Caledonia. It was taken before the protests and land claims filled the front pages of the newspaper in the summer of 2005. These hydro towers look like they are sneaking up out of the landscape. They are also representative of the power this place holds, but it's not a spiritual power but one of monetary value. A superficial power putting everyone on hold. Juxtaposed with the Grand River, I find these two connecting elements, catapults my imagination back to a time when our traditional ancestors tried to remain in their contemporary world, negotiating with politicians and businessmen. I feel like we have not moved on since that time.

The Wampum Frame. When I started to think about this series of images, I wanted it to be an abstract slew of pictures, much like visual poetry, I wanted these images to blend together and form not a literal meaning but give an emotional sensation. I wondered how I could make the statement representative of war, motherhood, the destruction of the Earth and the destruction of armies trained to move as a unit and ultimately die or succeed."

63. Shelley Niro, "La Pieta" Artist's Statement.

64. Shelley Niro, personal communication with the author, June 16, 2023.

65. Claire Raymond, "Shelley Niro's Indigenous 'La Pieta'" (paper presented at the College Art Association Annual Conference, Chicago and online, March 2022).

66. Shelley Niro, personal communication with the author, June 30, 2022; see also Richard Hill, "Voices from Here."

67. Simpson, *Mohawk Interruptus*, 143.

68. Shelley Niro, "La Pieta" Artist's Statement.

69. Hill, "Voices from Here."

70. Richter, *The Ordeal*, 24.

Chapter 3

1. Tsosie, "The New Challenge," 68.

2. David Harvey, *A Companion to Marx's Capital* (London: Verso Books, 2010), 289–314.

3. Quoted in Silvia Federici, *Caliban and the Witch* (New York: Autonomedia, 2004).

4. Brian Burkhart, *Indigenizing Philosophy Through the Land: A Trickster Methodology for Decolonizing Environmental Ethics and Indigenous Futures* (East Lansing: Michigan State University Press, 2019), 73.

5. Burkhart, *Indigenizing Philosophy*, 168.

6. Rebecca Tsosie, "The New Challenge to Native Identity: An Essay on 'Indigeneity' and 'Whiteness,'" *Journal of Law and Policy* 18, no. 55 (2005): 55–99.

7. Tsosie, "The New Challenge," 57.

8. Tsosie, "The New Challenge," 59.

9. Tsosie, "The New Challenge," 60–61.

10. National Park Service, "Archeology this Month: Native American Heritage," accessed February 24, 2024, https://www.nps.gov/articles/000/archeology-this-month-native-american-heritage.htm#:~:text=Archeological%20and%20genetic%20evidence%20show,arrived%20by%20land%20and%20sea.

11. Shelley Niro, in conversation with the author, March 8, 2024.

12. Tsosie, "The New Challenge," 63.

13. Tsosie, "The New Challenge," 63.

14. Taylor, *The Divided Ground*, 10.

15. Katharina Pistor, *The Code of Capital: How the Law Creates Wealth and Inequality* (Princeton, NJ: Princeton University Press, 2019).

16. Gilio-Whitaker, *As Long As*, 95–100.

17. Gilio-Whitaker, *As Long As*, 96.

18. Jessica L. Horton, "Indigenous Artists Against the Anthropocene" *Art Journal* (Summer 2017): 49–68.

19. Taylor, *The Divided Ground*, 7; see also Grumet, *Northeastern Indian Lives*, 309.

20. Taylor, *The Divided Ground*, 8.

21. Brian Slattery, "The Metamorphosis of Aboriginal Title," *La Revue Du Barreau Canadien* 85 (2011): 255–86.

22. Charisse Burden-Stelly, "Modern U.S. Racial Capitalism: Some Theoretical Insights," *Monthly Review* 72, no. 3 (2020), https://monthlyreview.org/2020/07/01/modern-u-s-racial-capitalism/.

23. Rebecca Tsosie, "University of Maine Annual Indian Law and History Lecture" (public lecture, University of Maine, Orono, November 18, 2022).

24. Slattery, "Metamorphosis," 285.

25. Slattery, "Metamorphosis," 286.

26. Slattery, "Metamorphosis," 284.

27. J. Sakai, *Settlers: The Mythology of the White Proletariat* (Binghamton, NY: PM Press, 2014).

28. Joseph Brant in 1793, quoted in Taylor, *The Divided Ground*, 132.

29. Taylor, *The Divided Ground*, 10.

30. Wanda Nanibush, "Radical Inclusivity, Relationality, and Indigenous Photography," *Foam Magazine* 64 (August 2023).

31. Taylor, *The Divided Ground*, 10.

32. Taylor, *The Divided Ground*, 11.

33. Louis A. Knafla and Haijo Westra, eds., *Aboriginal Title and Indigenous Peoples: Canada, Australia, and New Zealand* (Vancouver: University of British Colombia Press, 2011), 1. For the past few decades, Haudenosaunee attempts to argue legally for the return of lands have been blocked by the doctrine of timeliness; literally arguing that because the people were pushed off their land they lost the rights to it.

34. Michael Doxtater, in conversation with the author, July 28, 2023.

35. Knafla and Westra, *Aboriginal Title*, 6.

36. Of the Haudenosaunee traditionally, Richter notes that "they possess hardly anything except in common" (Richter, *The Ordeal*, 21), with the admired

goal of the society being "not to accumulate goods but to be in the position to provide them to others" (24).

37. George-Kanentiio, *Iroquois on Fire*, 12–13, 20.

38. Richter, *The Ordeal*, 24.

39. Taylor, *The Divided Ground*, 36.

40. Knafla and Westra, *Aboriginal Title*, 7.

41. Taylor, *The Divided Ground*, 3.

42. Taylor, *The Divided Ground*, 10.

43. Taylor, *The Divided Ground*, 10.

44. Kanentiio, *Iroquois on Fire*, 52. For example, during the mid-twentieth century, the US Indian Land Claims Commission determined that Aboriginal title could not be applied to Indigenous nations pushed off their lands before 1845, extinguishing the right for those peoples and making a mockery of the idea that protects lands held for centuries, if not millennia, before contact.

45. Knafla and Westra, *Aboriginal Title*, 13.

46. Virginia Gewin, "Supreme Court Case Could Reshape Indigenous Water Rights in the Southwest," *Civil Eats*, March 15, 2023, https://civileats. com/2023/03/15/supreme-court-case-could-reshape-Indigenous-water-rights-in-the-southwest/; see also Anna V. Smith, Umar Farooq, and Mark Olalde, "Supreme Court Keeps Navajo Nation Waiting for Water," *ProPublica*, June 26, 2023, https:// www.propublica.org/article/supreme-court-navajo-nation-water-rights-scotus.

47. Knafla and Westra, *Aboriginal Title*, 37, 214.

48. Scheltens, "How US Corporations."

49. Darren Ranco, "Code Red" (lecture at the Maine Historical Society exhibit *Code Red*, Portland, Maine, May 17, 2023).

50. Taylor, *The Divided Ground*, 112.

51. In genocide studies, it is generally held that not only mass destruction but also genocidal intent—expressed verbally—must be present to say genocide has been committed. Regarding the situation of the Haudenosaunee and the United States campaigns against them in the late eighteenth century, both conditions of genocide are inarguably met. See the United Nations Fact Sheet https://www.un.org/ en/genocideprevention/documents/Genocide%20Convention-FactSheet-ENG.pdf Accessed March 27, 2023.

52. Timothy Shaw, "Refugees of Niagara 1779–1780: The Winter of Hunger in Sullivan-Clinton Campaign, Then and Now," accessed June 18, 2023, https:// www.sullivanclinton.com/texts/articles/archives/refugees-niagara/.

53. Shaw, "Refugees of Niagara."

54. Shelley Niro, "Statement for Art Gallery of Hamilton," 2017, accessed June 20, 2023, http://shelleyniro.ca/statement-for-art-gallery-of-hamilton/.

55. Gilad Hirschberger, "Collective Trauma and the Social Construction of Meaning," *Frontiers in Psychology* 9 (2018), https://doi.org/10.3389/fpsyg.2018.01441;

see also Jeffrey Alexander, Ron Eyerman, Bernard Giesen, Neil J. Smelser, and Piotr Sztompka, eds., *Cultural Trauma and Collective Identity: Toward a Theory of Cultural Trauma* (Berkeley: University of California Press, 2004).

56. Shelley Niro, in conversation with the author, July 21, 2023.

57. Niro indicates that the film is a work of mourning for her daughter; Shelley Niro, in communication with the author, November 17, 2018, and July 21, 2023.

58. Richter, *The Ordeal*, 24–25. Squash beans and corn act naturally to support each other in fields; women were the keepers of the villages and longhouses, and the tellers of oral traditions. Also, notes Richter, "The landscape of homeland had to be large to accommodate traditional practices of agriculture and period rebuilding of long houses; women kept the village while men went on hunting and fishing expeditions during spring and summer."

59. Verna St. Denis, "Feminism is For Everyone," in *Making Space for Indigenous Feminism*, ed. Joyce Green (Halifax, Nova Scotia: Fernwood, 2017), 56.

Chapter 4

1. Amber Wardell, "Katie Britt's Phony Fundie Baby Voice: What That Whole Performance Was Supposed to Tell Us," *Medium*, March 10, 2024, https://medium.com/@amber_wardell/katie-britts-phony-fundie-baby-voice-what-that-whole-performance-was-supposed-to-tell-us-c312950a3d54.

2. Michael Doxtater, in conversation with the author, July 28, 2023.

3. Michael Doxtater, in conversation with the author, July 28, 2023.

4. Michael Doxtater, in conversation with the author, July 28, 2023.

5. Michael Doxtater, in conversation with the author, July 28, 2023; see also George-Kanentiio, *Iroquois on Fire*, 20. George-Kanentiio notes that, even *before* the Sullivan-Clinton campaign, millions of acres had been stripped from the Mohawk.

6. Michael Doxtater, in conversation with the author, July 28, 2023.

7. Michael Doxtater, in conversation with the author, July 28, 2023.

8. Michael Doxtater, in conversation with the author, July 28, 2023.

9. Raheja, *Reservation Reelism*, 170.

10. Quoted in Elizabeth Weatherford, "The Journey's Discovery: An Interview with Shelley Niro," in *Native Americans on Film: Conversations, Teaching, and Theory*, eds. M. Elise Marubbio and Eric L. Buffalohead (Lexington: University Press of Kentucky, 2018), 337–57.

11. Jay Hansford C. Vest, "An Odyssey among the Iroquois: A History of Tutelo Relations in New York," *American Indian Quarterly* 29, no. 1/2 (2005): 124–55.

12. Niro and Gronau, *It Starts.*

13. Ostler, *Surviving Genocide*, 71, 76.

14. Raheja, *Reservation Reelism*, 173–74.

15. The aunties are named Emily, Pauline, and Molly, signifying E. Pauline Johnson and Molly Brant (discussed in the introduction), key figures in Mohawk postcontact history. See, Penelope Myrtle Kelsey "Condolence Tropes and Haudenosaunee Visuality," ed. Denise Cummings, *Visualities: Perspectives on Contemporary American Indian Film and Art* (East Lansing: Michigan State University Press, 2011), 122.

16. Raheja, *Reservation Reelism*, 175.

17. Kelsey, *Visualities*, 123–25.

18. Niro and Gronau, *It Starts.*

19. Raheja, *Reservation Reelism*, 176.

20. Shelley Niro, in Lawrence Abbott, "Interviews with Loretta Todd, Shelley Niro, and Patricia Deadman," *Canadian Journal of Native Studies* 28, no. 2 (1998): 359.

21. Raheja, *Reservation Reelism*, 179.

22. The aunties and Shanna do not cross the nation-state border into New York, but at the boundary of Niagara they are facing New York, encountering the border by looking toward New York, the homeland.

23. In addition to its inaugural iteration at the National Museum of the American Indian New York (New York City, New York) Niro's retrospective also traveled to the Art Gallery of Hamilton (Hamilton, Ontario), and The National Gallery of Canada (Ottawa, Ontario).

24. Sam Yellowhorse Kesler, "The Blind Spot in the Great American Protest Song," *NPR Music Features*, February 3, 2021, https://www.npr.org/2021/ 02/03/963185860/the-blind-spot-in-the-great-american-protest-song#:~:text= Although%20the%20song%20is%20often,deaf%22%20for%20such%20a%20 ceremony.

25. Shelley Niro, "Artist's Statement," in *Cultural Contrasts: Inner Voices/ Outer Images* (Stamford, CT: Stamford Nature Center, 1994).

26. *Honey Moccasin*, directed by Shelley Niro (1998; New York: Women Make Movies, 1998), DVD.

27. Timothy C. Winegard, "The Forgotten Front of the Oka Crisis: Operation Feather/Akwesasne," *Journal of Military and Strategic Studies* 11, no. 1–2 (2009), https://jmss.org/article/view/57630.

28. Tabitha de Bruin, "Kanesatake Resistance (Oka Crisis)," in *The Canadian Encyclopedia*, July 11, 2013 (last edited July 9, 2020), https://www.thecanadian encyclopedia.ca/en/article/oka-crisis.

29. Shelley Niro, in conversation with the author, July 21, 2023.

30. Niro and Gronau, *It Starts.*

31. Jeff Corntassel, "Re-Envisioning Resurgence: Indigenous Pathways to Decolonization and Sustainable Self-Determination," *Decolonization: Indigeneity, Education, and Society* 1, no. 1 (2012): 88.

32. Patrick Wolfe, *Traces of History: Elementary Structures of Race* (London: Verso, 2016), 146.

33. Green, *Making Space.*

34. Federici, *Caliban.*

35. Federici, *Caliban*, 62.

36. Federici, *Caliban*, 63.

37. Federici, *Caliban*, 64.

38. Federici, *Caliban*, 65, 66.

39. Federici, *Caliban*, 66.

40. Federici, *Caliban*, 67.

41. Federici, *Caliban*, 70.

42. Federici, *Caliban*, 80.

43. Taylor, *The Divided Ground*, 35.

44. Federici, *Caliban*, 85. I believe that Federici, in using this phrase, is unaware of its earlier coinage, almost a century before, by Seneca archeologist and author Arthur C. Parker. See Arthur C. Parker, "An Analytical History of the Seneca Indians," New York State Archeological Association, Rochester, New York, 1926. https://www.kanehsatakevoices.com/category/blog/ *Kontinónhstats/ Mohawk Language Custodian Association/Association pour la preservation de la langue Mohawk.* Accessed March 11, 2024.

45. Alexander Koch, Chris Brierly, Mark Maslin, and Simon Lewis, "European Colonisation of the Americas Might Have Caused Global Cooling, According to New Research," *World Economic Forum*, February 1, 2019, https://www.weforum. org/agenda/2019/02/european-colonisation-of-the-americas-caused-global-cooling/.

46. Federici, *Caliban*, 86–87.

47. Arvin et al., "Decolonizing Feminism," 9.

48. Claire Raymond, "Roland Barthes, Ana Mendieta, and the Orphaned Image," *The Conversant: Interview Projects, Talk Poetries, Embodied Inquiry* (September 2014): 1–22.

49. Mishuana Goeman and Jennifer Nez Denetdale, "Native Feminisms: Legacies, Interventions, and Indigenous Sovereignties," *Wicazo Sa Review* 24, no. 2 (2009): 9–13. Quoted in Arvin et al., "Decolonizing Feminism," 13.

50. Wolfe, *Traces of History.*

51. Wolfe, *Traces of History*, 2.

52. Wolfe, *Traces of History*, 29.

53. "Who Were the Models for the Buffalo Head Nickel?" *A Very Special Coin Collection blog*, accessed July 4, 2023, http://www.acoincollection.com/ who-were-the-models-for-the-buffalo-nickel/.

54. Tsosie, "New Challenge," 55.

55. Coulthard, *Red Skin, White Masks*, 131.

56. Coulthard, *Red Skin, White Masks*, 131, emphasis in original.

57. Richter, *The Ordeal*, 17.

58. Notes Richter, traditionally villages and fields belonged to Haudenosaunee women. Richter, *The Ordeal*, 18.

59. Mary Eberts, "Being an Indigenous Woman is a High-Risk Lifestyle," in *Making Space for Indigenous Feminism*, ed. Joyce Green (Halifax, Nova Scotia: Fernwood, 2017), 82.

60. Eberts, "Being."

61. Eberts, "Being," 69, emphasis added.

62. Eberts, "Being," 71, emphasis in original.

63. Shelley Niro, in conversation with the author, September 17, 2017.

64. Eberts, "Being," 72. See also US Department of the Interior Indian Affairs, "Missing and Murdered Indigenous People Crisis: Violence Against Native Americans and Alaska Natives Far Exceed National Averages," accessed March 11, 2024, https://www.bia.gov/service/mmu/missing-and-murdered-indigenous-people-crisis.

65. Native Women's Wilderness, "Murdered and Missing Indigenous Women," accessed July 15, 2023, https://www.nativewomenswilderness.org/mmiw.

66. Nanibush, "Photography of Shelley Niro," 10.

67. Shelley Niro, quoted in *Shelley Niro/Scotiabank Photography Award* (Göttingen, Germany: Steidl, 2018).

68. Lennon, *Shelley Niro*, 37–57.

69. Jean-Paul Sartre, Preface to *The Wretched of the Earth*, by Frantz Fanon, trans. Constance Farrington (New York: Grove Wiedenfield, 1991), 9–10.

70. Deloria, "New World," 115; Margaret M. Bruchac, "Of Animacy and Afterlives: Material Memories in Indigenous Collections," in *Invisible Labour in Modern Science*, ed. Jenny Bangham, Xan Chacko, and Judith Kaplan (Lanham, MD: Rowman and Littlefield International, 2022), 71–80.

71. Mel Y. Chen, *Animacies: Biopolitics, Racial Mattering, and Queer Affect* (Durham, NC: Duke University Press, 2012).

Chapter 5

1. Shelley Niro, "For Fearless and Other Indians" (1998/2022), first and second frame.

2. Pistor, *The Code*, 116.

3. Michael Leroy Oberg, *Peacemakers: The Iroquois, the United States, and the Treaty of Canandaigua, 1794* (Oxford: Oxford University Press, 2016), 144.

4. Hauptman, *Conspiracy*, 108.

5. Hauptman, *Conspiracy*, 126.

6. Fanon, *The Wretched*, 98.

7. Manu Vimalassery, Juliana Hu Pegues, and Alyosha Goldstein, "Introduction: On Colonial Unknowing," *Theory and Event* 19, no. 4 (2016), https://muse.jhu.edu/article/633283.

8. Frantz Fanon, *The Wretched of the Earth*, trans. Constance Farrington (New York: Grove Wiedenfield, 1991), 14–15.

9. Fanon, *The Wretched*, 37.

10. Vine, *The United States*.

11. Shelley Niro, "For Fearless and Other Indians" (1998/2022), seventh frame.

12. Donald L. Fixico, *Termination and Relocation: Federal Indian Policy 1945–1960* (Albuquerque: University of New Mexico Press, 1990).

13. Barnd, *Native Space*, 107.

14. Ernesto Laclau, *On Populist Reason* (London: Verso, 2005), 13.

15. Laclau and Mouffe, *Hegemony and Socialist Strategy*, 18.

16. Ernesto Laclau and Chantal Mouffe, *Hegemony and Socialist Strategy: Towards a Radical Democratic Politics* (London: Verso, 2014), 18.

17. Wolfe, *Traces of History*, 188.

18. Wolfe, *Traces of History*, 188.

19. Evan T. Pritchard, *Native New Yorkers: The Legacy of the Algonquin People of New York* (San Francisco: Council Oak Books, 2007).

20. Emma Lazarus, "The New Colossus," National Park Service, originally published November 2, 1883; webpage last updated August 14, 2019, https://www.nps.gov/stli/learn/historyculture/colossus.htm.

21. Simpson, *Mohawk Interruptus*, 60.

22. Simpson, *Mohawk Interruptus*, 60–63.

23. Simpson, *Mohawk Interruptus*, 61.

24. "Conversation with Shelley Niro," *Shelley Niro: 500 Year Itch*, National Museum of the American Indian, New York, June 15, 2023.

25. Smithsonian Institution, "First Major Retrospective of Mohawk Artist Shelley Niro's Work to Go on View at National Museum," press release, May 22, 2023, https://www.si.edu/newsdesk/releases/first-major-retrospective-mohawk-artist-shelley-niros-work-go-view-national-museum.

26. Niro, "Conversation."

27. Riccardo Bellofiore, ed., *Rosa Luxemburg and the Critique of Political Economy* (London: Routledge, 2013).

Chapter 6

1. Settler-culture thought patterns make excuses for compulsive destruction of the Earth that is an inevitable result of the conceptualization of land as a resource—that is, land as an always already part of the capitalist enterprise of creating sellable items, whether that be the land itself as goods to market or the

goods resultant from industrial processes (including industrial agriculture) that destroy the Earth.

2. Haudenosaunee Confederacy, "Confederacy's Creation," accessed June 30, 2023, https://www.haudenosauneeconfederacy.com/confederacys-creation/.

3. As Haudenosaunee scholar Michelle Raheja (Seneca) notes, Niro's "films reconceptualize the figure of the ghost in the service of Native American communities." See Raheja, *Reservation Reelism*, 106.

4. Niro, quoted in Weatherford, "The Journey's Discovery," 355.

5. Shelley Niro, in conversation with the author, July 21, 2023.

6. Weatherford, "The Journey's Discovery," 351.

7. Niro, *Kissed by Lightning*, at 5 minutes, 36 seconds.

8. Niro, *Kissed by Lightning*, at 21 minutes, 23 seconds.

9. Niro, *Kissed by Lightning*, at 35–38 minutes.

10. Kim Tallbear, posting on Joanne Barker's blog, *Tequila Sovereign*, July 1, 2015; quoted in Wolfe, *The Settler Complex*, 8.

11. Wolfe, *The Settler Complex*, 9.

12. Hinderaker, *The Two Hendricks*, 16.

13. Niro, *Kissed by Lightning*, at 40–41 minutes.

14. Niro, *Kissed by Lightning*, at 41 minutes, 20 seconds.

15. Niro, *Kissed by Lightning*, at 47 minutes.

16. Niro, *Kissed by Lightning*, at 47 minutes, 30 seconds.

17. Niro, *Kissed by Lightning*, at 51–52 minutes.

18. Niro, *Kissed by Lightning*, at 57 minutes.

19. Niro, *Kissed by Lightning*, at 57 minutes, 55 seconds.

20. Niro, *Kissed by Lightning*, at 58 minutes.

21. Niro, *Kissed by Lightning*, at 1 hour, 1 minute, 20 seconds.

22. Niro, *Kissed by Lightning*, at 1 hour, 8 minutes.

23. Shelley Niro, in conversation with the author, July 5th, 2024.

24. Hinderaker, *The Two Hendricks*, 16.

25. Hinderaker, *The Two Hendricks*, 18.

26. Hinderaker, *The Two Hendricks*, 21.

27. Niro, "Artist statement." See also Federici, *Caliban*, 62–65.

28. Martin Luther King, *Letter from Birmingham Jail*

29. Michelle Raheja (Seneca) astutely notes that Sky Woman's story "can also be imagined to recur every time a child is born as it moves from space prior to its earthly existence (Sky World) travels through the birth canal . . . and brings its own special gifts in the form of metaphoric seeds to this world." See Raheja, *Reservation Reelism*, 172.

30. Niro, *Kissed by Lightning*, at 1 hour, 11 minutes, 38 seconds.

31. Shelley Niro, in conversation with the author, July 21, 2023.

32. Anne Bolen, "Native New York: Exploring What Makes This State an Indigenous Place," *Magazine of the Smithsonian's National Museum of the*

American Indian 22, no. 1 (2021), https://www.americanindianmagazine.org/story/native-new-york.

33. Shelley Niro, in conversation with the author, February 19, 2024.

34. Hauptman, *Conspiracy*.

35. Eve Tuck and K. Wayne Yang, "Decolonization Is Not a Metaphor," *Decolonization: Indigeneity, Education, and Society* 1, no. 1 (2012): 5.

36. Tuck and Yang, "Decolonization," 7.

37. Tuck and Yang, "Decolonization," 20.

38. Wolfe, "Settler Colonialism"; see also Wolfe, *The Settler Complex*, 10–11.

39. Wolfe, *The Settler Complex*, 11.

40. Tuck and Yang, "Decolonization," 22.

41. Cornelius Castoriadis, *The Imaginary Institution of Society* (Cambridge: Polity Press, 2005).

42. The Oka Crisis exemplifies this situation where, even as the Haudenosaunee attempted simply to defend themselves, they were set upon with military force by the settler nation-state.

43. Harry Swain, *Oka: A Political Crisis and Its Legacy* (Vancouver: Douglas & McIntyre, 2011).

44. Peter G. Peterson Foundation, "The United States Spends More on Defense than the Next 10 Countries Combined," *Peterson Foundation Blog*, April 24, 2023, https://www.pgpf.org/blog/2023/04/the-united-states-spends-more-on-defense-than-the-next-10-countries-combined. I'm aware, of course, that Oka took place in Canada. New York State, however, is in the United States of America.

45. Gina Starblanket, "Contextualizing Indigenous Feminist Resistance," in *Making Space for Indigenous Feminism*, ed. Joyce Green (Halifax, Nova Scotia: Fernwood, 2017), 22–23.

46. Starblanket, "Contextualizing," 25.

47. Vine Deloria, Foreword to *Iroquois on Fire: A Voice from the Mohawk Nation*, by Douglas M. George-Kanentiio (Lincoln: University of Nebraska Press, 2006), vii–x.

48. Hauptman, *Conspiracy*, 1–26, 213–22.

49. Wolfe, *The Settler Complex*; Mignolo, *The Darker Side*.

50. Hauptman, *Conspiracy*, 11.

51. Hauptman, *Conspiracy*, 15, emphasis in original.

52. Hauptman, *Conspiracy*, 18.

53. Hauptman, *Conspiracy*, 22.

54. Quoted in Hauptman, *Conspiracy*, 23.

55. rudi aker, "Tributaries of Care: Shelley Niro's 'The Essential Sensuality of Ceremony,'" *Terms* (Winter 2022): 21–30.

56. aker, "Tributaries of Care," 22.

57. aker, "Tributaries of Care," 23.

58. aker, "Tributaries of Care," 27.

59. aker, "Tributaries of Care," 25.

60. Aileen Moreton-Robinson, "Critical Indigenous Theory: Introduction," *Cultural Studies Review* 15, no. 2 (2009): 11.

61. Simpson, *As We Have*, 140.

62. George-Kanentiio, *Iroquois on Fire*, 24.

Conclusion

1. Byrd, *Transit of Empire*, 19.

2. Eberts, "Being," 93.

3. Taylor, *The Divided Ground*, 192.

4. Alexander Koch, Chris Brierly, Mark Maslin, and Simon Lewis, "Earth System Impacts of the European Arrival and Great Dying in the Americas After 1492," *Quaternary Science Reviews* 207 (2019): 13–36.

5. Richter, *The Ordeal*, 58–59.

6. Demos, *The Unredeemed Captive*, 150–51.

7. Richter, *The Ordeal*, 47.

8. A digitized print of this work is newly on display at the New York State Museum, Albany, New York

9. Amy Lonetree, "Museums as Sites of Decolonization: Truth Telling in National and Tribal Museums," in *Contesting Knowledge: Museums and Indigenous Perspective*, ed. Susan Sleeper-Smith (Lincoln: University of Nebraska Press, 2009), 323.

10. Waziyatawin Angela Wilson, "For Indigenous Eyes Only"; quoted in Lonetree, "Museums," 325.

11. Shelley Niro, personal communication with the author, June 16, 2023.

12. Amy Lonetree, *Decolonizing Museums: Representing Native America in National and Tribal Museums* (Chapel Hill: University of North Carolina Press, 2012).

13. Tuck and Yang, "Decolonization."

14. Lonetree, "Museums," 325.

15. Ostler, *Surviving Genocide*, 44–81; Philip J. Deloria, "Indigenous/American Pasts and Futures," *Journal of American History* 109, no. 2 (2022): 255–70.

16. Gilio-Whitaker, *As Long As*, 136–40.

17. Shelley Niro, in conversation with the author, June 16, 2023.

18. Federici, *Caliban*, 11–21.

19. Taylor, *The Divided Ground*, 113.

20. Taylor, *The Divided Ground*, 97.

21. Taylor, *The Divided Ground*, 199.

22. George-Kanentiio, *Iroquois on Fire*, 134.

23. George-Kanentiio, *Iroquois on Fire*, 134.

24. George-Kanentiio, *Iroquois on Fire*, 135.

25. Brian Isaac Daniels, "Reimagining Tribal Sovereignty through Tribal History: Museums, Libraries, and Archives in the Klamath River Region," in *Contesting Knowledge: Museums and Indigenous Perspectives*, ed. Susan Sleeper-Smith (Lincoln: University of Nebraska Press, 2009), 283.

26. Quoted in Lonetree, "Museums," 326.

Bibliography

Abbott, Lawrence. "Interviews with Loretta Todd, Shelley Niro, and Patricia Deadman." *Canadian Journal of Native Studies* 28, no. 2 (1998): 359.

Adams, David Wallace. *Education for Extinction: American Indians and the Boarding School Experience, 1875–1928.* 2nd ed. Lawrence: University Press of Kansas, 2020.

aker, rudi. "Tributaries of Care: Shelley Niro's 'The Essential Sensuality of Ceremony.'" *Terms* (Winter 2022): 21–30.

Alexander, Jeffrey, R. Eyerman, B. Giesen, N. Smelser, and P. Sztompka, eds. *Cultural Trauma and Collective Identity: Toward a Theory of Cultural Trauma.* Berkeley: University of California Press, 2004.

Alfred, Taiaiake. *Heeding the Voices of Our Ancestors. Kahnawake Mohawk Politics and the Rise of Native Nationalism.* Edited by Don Mills. Oxford: Oxford University Press, 1995.

Alfred, Taiaiake. *Indigenous Pathways of Action and Freedom.* Peterborough, ON: Broadview Press, 2005.

Alfred, Taiaiake."It's All About the Land" public talk at the Center for the Study of Learning and Performance, Concordia University, Montreal, Quebec, January 25, 2023.

Alfred, Taiaiake. *Peace, Power, Righteousness: An Indigenous Manifesto.* Oxford and New York: Oxford University Press, 1999.

Arvin, Maile, Eve Tuck, and Angie Morrill. "Decolonizing Feminism: Challenging Connections between Settler Colonialism and Heteropatriarchy." *Feminist Formations* 25, no. 1 (Spring 2013): 8–34.

Austen, Ian. "'Horrible History': Mass Grave of Indigenous Children Reported in Canada." *New York Times*, May 28, 2021.

Bailey, Jane, and Sara Shayan. "Missing and Murdered Indigenous Women Crisis: Technological Dimensions." *Canadian Journal of Women and the Law* 28, no. 2 (2016): 321–41.

Barnd, Natchee Blu. *Native Space: Geographic Strategies to Unsettle Settler Colonialism.* Corvallis: Oregon State University Press, 2017.

Bellofiore, Riccardo, ed. *Rosa Luxemburg and the Critique of Political Economy.* London: Routledge, 2013.

Benjamin, Walter. "Little History of Photography." In *Walter Benjamin: Selected Writings Volume 2, Part 2: 1931–1934.* Translated by Rodney Livingstone, et al. Edited by Michael W. Jennings, Howard Eiland, and Gary Smith, 507–30. Cambridge, MA: Belknap Press, 1999.

Blackhawk, Ned. *The Rediscovery of America: Native Peoples and the Unmaking of U.S. History.* New Haven, CT: Yale University Press, 2023.

Bolen, Anne. "Native New York: Exploring What Makes This State an Indigenous Place." *Magazine of the Smithsonian's National Museum of the American Indian* 22, no. 1 (2021). https://www.americanindianmagazine.org/story/native-new-york.

Bruchac, Margaret M. "Of Animacy and Afterlives: Material Memories in Indigenous Collections." In *Invisible Labour in Modern Science,* edited by Jenny Bangham, Xan Chacko, and Judith Kaplan, 71–80. Lanham, MD: Rowman and Littlefield International, 2022.

Bruchac, Margaret M., Siobhan Hart, and H. Martin Wobst, eds. *Indigenous Archaeologies: A Reader in Decolonization.* Walnut Creek, CA: Left Coast Press, 2010.

Burden-Stelly, Charisse. "Modern U.S. Racial Capitalism: Some Theoretical Insights." *Monthly Review* 72, no. 3 (2020). https://monthlyreview.org/2020/07/01/modern-u-s-racial-capitalism/.

Bureau of Indian Affairs. "Missing and Murdered Indigenous People Crisis." Accessed July 21, 2023. https://www.bia.gov/service/mmu/missing-and-murdered-Indigenous-people-crisis.

Burkhart, Brian. *Indigenizing Philosophy Through the Land: A Trickster Methodology for Decolonizing Environmental Ethics and Indigenous Futures.* East Lansing: Michigan State University Press, 2019.

Butler, Judith. *Gender Trouble: Feminism and the Subversion of Identity.* New York: Routledge, 1990.

Byrd, Jodi. *Transit of Empire: Indigenous Critiques of Colonialism.* Minneapolis: University of Minnesota Press, 2011.

Castoriadis, Cornelius. *The Imaginary Institution of Society.* Cambridge: Polity Press, 2005.

Chen, Mel Y. *Animacies: Biopolitics, Racial Mattering, and Queer Affect.* Durham, NC: Duke University Press, 2012.

Corntassel, Jeff. "Re-Envisioning Resurgence: Indigenous Pathways to Decolonization and Sustainable Self-Determination." *Decolonization: Indigeneity, Education, and Society* 1, no. 1 (2012): 86–101.

Coulthard, Glen Sean. *Red Skin, White Masks: Rejecting the Colonial Politics of Recognition.* Minneapolis: University of Minnesota Press, 2014.

Crytzer, Brady J. "Longhouse Lost: The Battle of the Oriskany and the Iroquois Civil War." *Journal of the American Revolution.* July 30, 2020. https://

allthingsliberty.com/2020/07/longhouse-lost-the-battle-of-oriskany-and-the-iroquois-civil-war/.

Daniels, Brian Isaac. "Reimagining Tribal Sovereignty through Tribal History: Museums, Libraries, and Archives in the Klamath River Region." In *Contesting Knowledge: Museums and Indigenous Perspectives*, edited by Susan Sleeper-Smith, 283–303. Lincoln: University of Nebraska Press, 2009.

de Bruin, Tabitha. "Kanesatake Resistance (Oka Crisis)." In *The Canadian Encyclopedia* (online) July 11, 2013, https://www.thecanadianencyclopedia.ca/en/article/oka-crisis.

de Lauretis, Teresa. *Figures of Resistance: Essays in Feminist Theory*. Urbana-Champaign: University of Illinois Press, 2007.

Deloria, Philip J. "Indigenous/American Pasts and Futures." *Journal of American History* 109, no. 2 (2022): 255–70.

Deloria, Philip J. "The New World of the Indigenous Museum." *Daedalus* 147, no. 2 (2018): 106–15.

Deloria, Vine. Foreword to *Iroquois on Fire: A Voice from the Mohawk Nation*, vii–x. By Douglas M. George-Kanentiio. Lincoln: University of Nebraska Press, 2006.

DePasquale, Paul W., ed. *Natives and Settlers Then and Now: Refractions of the Colonial Past in the Present*. Alberta: University of Alberta Press, 2007.

Demos, John, ed. *The Unredeemed Captive: A Family Story from Early America*. New York: Knopf, 1994.

Deutsche, Rosalyn. *Not-Forgetting: Contemporary Art and the Interrogation of Mastery*. Chicago: University of Chicago Press, 2022.

Doxtator, Deborah. "What Happened to the Iroquois Clans? A Study of Clans in Three Nineteenth-Century Rotinonhsyonni Communities." PhD diss., University of Western Ontario, 1996.

Doxtater, Michael. "The Four Worlds of Onkwehonwe Life, Prophecy and Memory." Lecture presented at Toronto Metropolitan University, Toronto, Canada, September 2022.

Driskill, Qwo-Li, Chris Finley, Brian J. Gilley, and Scott L. Morgensen, eds. *Queer Indigenous Studies: Interviews in Theory, Politics, and Literature*. Tucson: University of Arizona Press, 2011.

Eberts, Mary. "Being an Indigenous Woman is a High Risk Lifestyle." In *Making Space for Indigenous Feminism*, edited by Joyce Green, 69–93. Halifax, Nova Scotia: Fernwood, 2017.

Elliott, Alicia. "The Balm to the Burn." In *Something Hard and Cold Like Winter*, edited by Shelley Niro, 12–21. Waterloo, Ontario: Robert Langen Art Gallery, 2022.

Fabian, Johannes. *Time and the Other: How Anthropology Makes Its Object*. New York: Columbia University Press, 2002.

Fanon, Frantz. *The Wretched of the Earth*. Translated by Constance Farrington. New York: Grove Wiedenfield, 1991.

Federici, Silvia. *Caliban and the Witch*. New York: Autonomedia, 2004.

Fixico, Donald L. *Termination and Relocation: Federal Indian Policy 1945–1960*. Albuquerque: University of New Mexico Press, 1990.

Foster, Hal. "The 'Primitive' Unconscious of Modern Art, or, White Skin, Black Masks." In *Recodings: Art, Spectacle, Cultural Politics*, 181–208. Seattle, WA: Bay Press, 1985.

George-Kanentiio, Douglas M. *Iroquois on Fire: A Voice from the Mohawk Nation*. Lincoln: University of Nebraska Press, 2006.

Gewin, Virginia. "Supreme Court Case Could Reshape Indigenous Water Rights in the Southwest." *Civil Eats*. March 15, 2023. https://civileats.com/2023/03/15/supreme-court-case-could-reshape-Indigenous-water-rights-in-the-southwest/.

Gilio-Whitaker, Dina. *As Long As Grass Grows: The Indigenous Fight for Environmental Justice, from Colonization to Standing Rock*. Boston: Beacon Press, 2019.

Ginsburg, Faye. "The Indigenous Uncanny: Accounting for Ghosts in Recent Indigenous Australian Experimental Media." *Visual Anthropology Review* 34, no. 1 (2018): 67–76.

Gipsin, Ferren. *Women's Work: From Feminine Art to Feminist Art*. London: Frances Lincoln, 2022.

Goeman, Mishuana. *Mark Her Words: Native Women Mapping Our Nations*. Minneapolis: University of Minnesota Press, 2013.

Goeman, Mishuana, and Jennifer Nez Denetdale. "Native Feminisms: Legacies, Interventions, and Indigenous Sovereignties." *Wicazo Sa Review* 24, no. 2 (2009): 9–13.

Green, Joyce, ed. *Making Space for Indigenous Feminism*. Halifax, Nova Scotia: Fernwood, 2017.

Green, Joyce. "Rebalancing Strategies: Aboriginal Women and Constitutional Rights in Canada." In *Making Space for Indigenous Feminism*, edited by Joyce Green, 166–91. Halifax, Nova Scotia: Fernwood, 2017.

Grumet, Robert. *Northeastern Indian Lives: 1632–1816*. Amherst: University of Massachusetts Press, 1996.

Harvey, David. *A Companion to Marx's Capital*. London: Verso Books, 2010.

Haudenosaunee Confederacy. "Confederacy's Creation." Accessed June 30, 2023. https://www.haudenosauneeconfederacy.com/confederacys-creation/.

Haudenosaunee Confederacy. "Who We Are." Accessed June 1, 2023. https://www.haudenosauneeconfederacy.com/who-we-are/.

Hauptman, Laurence. *Conspiracy of Interests: Iroquois Dispossession and the Rise of New York State*. Syracuse, NY: Syracuse University Press, 2001.

Hauptman, Laurence. "The Iroquois Confederacy with Prof. Laurence Hauptman." *The Forget-Me-Not Hour*. January 4, 2017. Podcast, MP3 audio, 1:41:43. https://www.blogtalkradio.com/janeewilcox/2017/01/04/the-iroquois-confederacy-with-prof-laurence-hauptman.

Herne, Sue Ellen, and Lynne Williamson. "Haudenosaunee Traditional Arts: A Glimpse into Our House." In *North by Northeast: Wabanaki, Awkwesasne Mohawk and Tuscarora Traditional Arts*, edited by Kathleen Mundell, 1–12. Gardiner, ME: Tilbury House Publishers, 2008.

Hill, Richard, ed. "The Myth of the Earth Grasper." In the 43rd Annual Report, BAE, SI, 1925–26, Washington, DC, 1928, recorded and edited by J. N. B. Hewitt; recontextualized by Richard Hill, January 2001.

Hill, Richard. "Voices From Here." *The Canadian Encyclopedia*. Accessed January 21, 2024. https://www.thecanadianencyclopedia.ca/en/article/voices-from-here-richard-hill.

Hinderaker, Eric. *The Two Hendricks: Unraveling a Mohawk Mystery*. Cambridge, MA: Harvard University Press, 2010.

Hirschberger, Gilad. "Collective Trauma and the Social Construction of Meaning." *Frontiers in Psychology* 9 (2018). https://doi.org/10.3389/fpsyg.2018.01441.

Horn-Miller, Kahente. "Sky Woman's Great Granddaughters: A Narrative Inquiry Into Kanienkehaka Women's Identity." PhD diss., Concordia University, Montreal, 2009.

Horton, Jessica L. "Indigenous Artists Against the Anthropocene." *Art Journal* (Summer 2017): 49–68.

Kelsey, Penelope Myrtle. "Condolence Tropes and Haudenosaunee Visuality." *Visualities: Perspectives on Contemporary American Indian Film and Art*, edited by Denise Cummings, 119–30. East Lansing: Michigan State University Press, 2011.

Kesler, Sam Yellowhorse. "The Blind Spot in the Great American Protest Song." *NPR Music Features*. February 3, 2021. https://www.npr.org/2021/02/03/963185860/the-blind-spot-in-the-great-american-protest-song#:~:text=Although%20the%20song%20is%20often,deaf%22%20for%20such%20a%20ceremony.

King, Martin Luther Jr. *Letter from Birmingham Jail*. New York: Penguin Classics, 2018.

Knafla, Louis A., and Haijo Westra, eds. *Aboriginal Title and Indigenous Peoples: Canada, Australia, and New Zealand*. Vancouver: University of British Colombia Press, 2011.

Koch, Alexander, Chris Brierly, Mark Maslin, and Simon Lewis. "Earth System Impacts of the European Arrival and Great Dying in the Americas After 1492." *Quaternary Science Reviews* 207 (2019): 13–36.

Koch, Alexander, Chris Brierly, Mark Maslin, and Simon Lewis. "European Colonisation of the Americas Might Have Caused Global Cooling, According to New Research." *World Economic Forum*, February 1, 2019. https://www.weforum.org/agenda/2019/02/european-colonisation-of-the-americas-caused-global-cooling/.

Kovach, Margaret. *Indigenous Methodologies: Characteristics, Conversations, and Contexts*. Toronto: University of Toronto Press, 2021.

Kovach, Margaret. "Provocations for a Different Art History in a Cross-Disciplinary Context: Comparing Comparativisms." UIC Institute for the Humanities, Chicago and online, February 19, 2024.

Kwandibens, Nadya. "Emergence." *Tea & Bannock, a Collective Blog by Indigenous Woman Photographers*. April 22, 2016. https://teaandbannock.com/2016/04/22/emergence/.

Lacan, Jacques. *Des noms-du-père*. Edited by Jacques-Alain Miller. Paris: Éditions du Seuil, 2005.

Laclau, Ernesto. *On Populist Reason*. London: Verso, 2005.

Laclau, Ernesto, and Chantal Mouffe. *Hegemony and Socialist Strategy: Towards a Radical Democratic Politics*. London: Verso, 2014.

Lazarus, Emma. "The New Colossus." National Park Service. Originally published November 2, 1883; webpage last updated August 14, 2019. https://www.nps.gov/stli/learn/historyculture/colossus.htm.

Lennon, Madeline. *Shelley Niro: Seeing Through Memory*. London: Blue Medium Press, 2014.

Lonetree, Amy. *Decolonizing Museums: Representing Native America in National and Tribal Museums*. Chapel Hill: University of North Carolina Press, 2012.

Lonetree, Amy. "Museums as Sites of Decolonization: Truth Telling in National and Tribal Museums." In *Contesting Knowledge: Museums and Indigenous Perspective*, edited by Susan Sleeper-Smith, 322–38. Lincoln: University of Nebraska Press, 2009.

McCarthy, Theresa. "Dẹni:s nisa'sgao'dẹ? Haudenosaunee Clans and the Reconstruction of Traditional Haudenosaunee Identity, Citizenship, and Nationhood." *American Indian Culture and Research Journal*, 34, no. 2 (2010): 81–101.

Mignolo, Walter D. *The Darker Side of Western Modernity: Global Futures, Decolonial Options*. Durham, NC: Duke University Press, 2011.

Mignolo, Walter D., and Catherine E. Walsh. *On Decoloniality: Concepts, Analytics, Praxis*. Durham, NC: Duke University Press, 2017.

Mohawk, John C. "A View from Turtle Island: Chapters in Iroquois Mythology, History and Culture." PhD diss., State University of New York at Buffalo, 1994.

Moreton-Robinson, Aileen. "Critical Indigenous Theory: Introduction." *Cultural Studies Review* 15, no. 2 (2009): 11–12.

Mt. Pleasant, Alyssa. "Land, Liberty, and Loss: Echoes of the American Revolution." *Humanities New York*. September 28, 2022. Podcast, MP3 audio.

Nanibush, Wanda. "Notions of Land." *Aperture* (Spring 2019): 72–77.

Nanibush, Wanda. "Outside of Time: Salvage Ethnography, Self-Representation and Performing Culture." In *Time, Temporality, and Violence in International Relations*, edited by Anna Agathangelou and Kyle Killian. London: Routledge, 2016.

Nanibush, Wanda. "Radical Inclusivity, Relationality, and Indigenous Photography." *Foam Magazine* 64 (August 2023).

Nanibush, Wanda. "The Photography of Shelley Niro." In *Scotiabank Photography Award: Shelley Niro*, 9–11. Göttingen, Germany: Steidl, 2018.

Native Women's Wilderness. "Murdered and Missing Indigenous Women." Accessed July 15, 2023. https://www.nativewomenswilderness.org/mmiw.

Niro, Shelley. "A Good, Long Look." Art Gallery of Southwestern Manitoba, Canada, June 10–July 21, 2021. Accessed June 30, 2023. https://agsm.ca/good-long-look.

Niro, Shelley. "Artist's Statement." *Cultural Contrasts: Inner Voices/Outer Images.* Stamford, CT: Stamford Nature Center, 1994.

Niro, Shelley, dir. *Café Daughter.* 2023; Sudbury, Ontario, 2023. DVD.

Niro, Shelley. "Conversation with Shelley Niro." *Shelley Niro: 500 Year Itch.* New York: National Museum of the American Indian. June 15, 2023.

Niro, Shelley, dir. *Honey Moccasin.* 1998; New York: Women Make Movies, 1998. DVD.

Niro, Shelley, dir. *Kissed by Lightning.* 2009; Toronto: Shelley Niro Productions, 2009. DVD.

Niro, Shelley, dir. *Niagara.* 2015; Toronto: V tape, 2015. DVD.

Niro, Shelley. *Something Hard and Cold Like Winter.* Waterloo, Ontario: Robert Langen Art Gallery, 2022.

Niro, Shelley. "Statement for Art Gallery of Hamilton," 2017. Accessed June 20, 2023. http://shelleyniro.ca/statement-for-art-gallery-of-hamilton/.

Niro, Shelley, dir. *The Incredible 25th Year of Mitzi Bearclaw.* Los Angeles: Indican Pictures, 2020.

Niro, Shelley, dir. *Tree.* Toronto: Vtape, 2006. DVD.

Niro, Shelley, and Anna Gronau, dirs. *It Starts with a Whisper.* New York: Women Make Movies, 1993. VHS.

Oberg, Michael Leroy. *Peacemakers: The Iroquois, the United States, and the Treaty of Canandaigua, 1794.* Oxford: Oxford University Press, 2016.

Ostler, Jeffrey. *Surviving Genocide: Native Nations and the United States from the American Revolution to Bleeding Kansas.* New Haven, CT: Yale University Press, 2020.

Peter G. Peterson Foundation. "The United States Spends More on Defense than the Next 10 Countries Combined." *Peterson Foundation Blog.* April 24, 2023. https://www.pgpf.org/blog/2023/04/the-united-states-spends-more-on-defense-than-the-next-10-countries-combined.

Pistor, Katharina. *The Code of Capital: How the Law Creates Wealth and Inequality.* Princeton, NJ: Princeton University Press, 2019.

Pritchard, Evan T. *Native New Yorkers: The Legacy of the Algonquin People of New York.* San Francisco: Council Oak Books, 2007.

Raheja, Michelle. *Reservation Reelism: Redfacing, Visual Sovereignty, and Representations of Native Americans in Film.* Lincoln: University of Nebraska Press, 2010.

Ranco, Darren. "Code Red." Lecture presented at the Maine Historical Society exhibit *Code Red*, Portland, Maine, May 17, 2023.

Raymond, Claire. *Photography and Resistance: Anticolonialist Photography in the Americas*. London: Palgrave Macmillan, 2022.

Raymond, Claire. "Roland Barthes, Ana Mendieta, and the Orphaned Image." *The Conversant: Interview Projects, Talk Poetries, Embodied Inquiry* (September 2014): 1–22.

Raymond, Claire. "Shelley Niro's Indigenous 'La Pieta.'" Paper presented at the College Art Association Annual Conference, Chicago and online, March 2022.

Raymond, Claire. *The Photographic Uncanny: Photography, Homelessness, and Homesickness*. New York: Palgrave Macmillan, 2020.

Raymond, Claire. *Women Photographers and Feminist Aesthetics*. New York: Routledge, 2017.

Richter, Daniel K. *The Ordeal of the Longhouse: The Peoples of the Iroquois League in the Era of European Colonization*. Chapel Hill: University of North Carolina Press, 1992.

Richter, Daniel K. "'Some of Them . . . Would Always Have a Minister with Them': Mohawk Protestantism, 1683–1719." *American Indian Quarterly* 16, no. 4 (1992): 471–84.

Rifkin, Mark. "The Silence of Ely S. Parker: The Emancipation Sublime and the Limits of Settler Memory." *Native American and Indigenous Studies* 1, no. 2 (2014): 1–43.

Rifkin, Mark. *Beyond Settler Time: Temporal Sovereignty and Indigenous Self-Determination*. Durham, NC: Duke University Press, 2017.

Riverkeeper. "Mohawk River Water Quality Data." Accessed June 18, 2023. https://www.riverkeeper.org/water-quality/citizen-data/mohawk-river/.

Ross, Michael L. *The Oil Curse: How Petroleum Wealth Shapes the Development of Nations*. Princeton, NJ: Princeton University Press, 2012.

Sakai, J. *Settlers: The Mythology of the White Proletariat*. Binghamton, NY: PM Press, 2014.

Sanford, Stella. "Kant, Race, and Natural History." *Philosophy and Social Criticism* 44, no. 9 (2018): 950–77.

Sartre, Jean Paul. Preface to *The Wretched of the Earth*, by Frantz Fanon, translated by Constance Farrington, 7–35. New York: Grove Wiedenfeld, 1991.

Scheltens, Liz. "How US Corporations Poisoned This Indigenous community." *Vox*. August 16, 2022. https://www.vox.com/2022/8/16/23308638/mohawk-akwesasne-fishing-chemicals-pollution.

Shaw, Timothy. "Refugees of Niagara 1779–1780: The Winter of Hunger in Sullivan-Clinton Campaign, Then and Now." Accessed June 18, 2023. https://www.sullivanclinton.com/texts/articles/archives/refugees-niagara/.

Simpson, Audra. "On Ethnographic Refusal: Indigeneity, 'Voice' and Colonial Citizenship." *Junctures* 9 (2007): 67–80.

Simpson, Audra. *Mohawk Interruptus: Political Life Across the Borders of Settler States.* Durham, NC: Duke University Press, 2014.

Simpson, Leanne Betasamosake. *Dancing on Our Turtle's Back: Stories of Nishnaabeg Re-Creation, Resurgence and a New Emergence.* Winnipeg: Arbeiter Ring, 2011.

Simpson, Leanne Betasamosake. "Indigenous Resurgence and Co-Resistance." *Critical Ethnic Studies* 2, no. 2 (Fall 2016): 19–34.

Simpson, Leanne Betasamosake. *As We Have Always Done: Indigenous Freedom Through Radical Resistance.* Minneapolis: University of Minnesota Press, 2017.

Slattery, Brian. "The Metamorphosis of Aboriginal Title." *La Revue Du Barreau Canadien* 85 (2011): 255–86.

Smith, Anna V., Umar Farooq, and Mark Olalde. "Supreme Court Keeps Navajo Nation Waiting for Water." *ProPublica.* June 26, 2023. https://www.propublica. org/article/supreme-court-navajo-nation-water-rights-scotus.

Smith, Laura E. "Photography Criticism and Native American Women's Identity: Three Works by Jolene Rickard." *Third Text* 19, no. 1 (2005): 53–66.

Smithsonian Institution. "First Major Retrospective of Mohawk Artist Shelley Niro's Work to Go on View at National Museum." Press release, May 22, 2023. https://www.si.edu/newsdesk/releases/first-major-retrospective-mohawk-artist-shelley-niros-work-go-view-national-museum.

Snow, Dean R., Charles T. Gehring, and William A. Starna, eds. *A Journey into Mohawk Country: Early Narratives About a Native People.* Syracuse, NY: Syracuse University Press, 1996.

Southerland, J. J. "L. Frank Baum Advocated Extermination of Native Americans." National Public Radio. October 27, 2010. https://www.npr.org/sections/thetwo-way/2010/10/27/130862391/l-frank-baum-advocated-extermination-of-native-americans.

St. Denis, Verna. "Feminism is For Everyone." In *Making Space for Indigenous Feminism*, edited by Joyce Green, 42–62. Halifax, Nova Scotia: Fernwood, 2017.

Starblanket, Gina. "Contextualizing Indigenous Feminist Resistance." In *Making Space for Indigenous Feminism*, edited by Joyce Green, 21–41. Halifax, Nova Scotia: Fernwood, 2017.

Strauss, Claude Levi. *Tristes Tropiques.* Translated by John Weightman and Doreen Weightman. New York: Penguin Classics, 2012.

Swain, Harry. *Oka: A Political Crisis and Its Legacy.* Vancouver: Douglas & McIntyre, 2011.

Taylor, Alan. *The Divided Ground: Indians, Settlers, and the Northern Borderland of the American Revolution.* New York: Knopf, 2006.

Thomas, Jacob. *Teachings from the Longhouse.* Self-published, 2013.

Tsinhnahjinnie, Hulleah. "Compensating Imbalances." *Exposure* 29 (1993): 30.

Tsinhnahjinnie, Hulleah. "When Is a Photograph Worth a Thousand Words?" In *Photography's Other Histories*. Edited by Christopher Pinney and Nicholas Peterson. Durham, NC: Duke University Press, 2003.

Tsosie, Rebecca. "The New Challenge to Native Identity: An Essay on 'Indigeneity' and 'Whiteness.'" *Journal of Law and Policy* 18, no. 55 (2005): 55–99.

Tsosie, Rebecca. "University of Maine Annual Indian Law and History Lecture." Public lecture at the University of Maine, Orono, November 18, 2022.

Tuck, Eve, and K. Wayne Yang. "Decolonization Is Not a Metaphor." *Decolonization: Indigeneity, Education, and Society* 1, no. 1 (2012): 1–40.

United States Department of Environmental Protection. "Just the Facts—Cleaning Up the Hudson River PCBs." Last modified February 22, 2016. Accessed August 20, 2023. https://www3.epa.gov/hudson/just_facts_08_04.htm.

United States Department of the Interior Indian Affairs. "Missing and Murdered Indigenous People Crisis: Violence Against Native Americans and Alaska Natives Far Exceed National Averages." Accessed March 11, 2024. https://www.bia.gov/service/mmu/missing-and-murdered-indigenous-people-crisis.

Veracini, Lorenzo. *Settler Colonialism*. New York: Palgrave Macmillan, 2010.

Vest, Jay Hansford C. "An Odyssey Among the Iroquois: A History of Tutelo Relations in New York." *American Indian Quarterly* 29, no. 1/2 (2005): 124–55.

Vimalassery, Manu, Juliana Hu Pegues, and Alyosha Goldstein. "Introduction: On Colonial Unknowing." *Theory and Event* 19, no. 4 (2016). https://muse.jhu.edu/article/633283.

Vine, David. *The United States of War: A Global History of America's Endless Conflicts from Columbus to the Islamic State*. Berkeley: University of California Press, 2020.

Vizenor, Gerald. *Manifest Manners: Narratives on Postindian Survivance*. Lincoln: University of Nebraska Press, 1999.

Vizenor, Gerald, ed. *Survivance: Narratives of Native Presence*. Lincoln: University of Nebraska Press, 2008.

Wardell, Amber. "Katie Britt's Phony Fundie Baby Voice: What That Whole Performance Was Supposed to Tell Us." *Medium*. March 10, 2024. https://medium.com/@amber_wardell/katie-britts-phony-fundie-baby-voice-what-that-whole-performance-was-supposed-to-tell-us-c312950a3d54.

Weatherford, Elizabeth. "The Journey's Discovery: An Interview with Shelley Niro." In *Native Americans on Film: Conversations, Teaching, and Theory*, edited by M. Elise Marubbio and Eric L. Buffalohead, 337–57. Lexington: University Press of Kentucky Press, 2018.

White, Richard. *The Middle Ground: Indians, Empires, and Republics in the Great Lakes Region, 1650–1815*. Cambridge: Cambridge University Press, 2010.

Williams, Jumaane D. "Air Quality Health Advisory." *The Advocate*. June 8, 2023. https://www.pubadvocate.nyc.gov/blog/2023/06/08/stay-safe-nyc-air-quality-health-advisory/.

Winegard, Timothy C. "The Forgotten Front of the Oka Crisis: Operation Feather/ Akwesasne." *Journal of Military and Strategic Studies* 11, no. 1–2 (2009). https://jmss.org/article/view/57630.

Wolfe, Patrick. "Settler Colonialism and the Elimination of the Native." *Journal of Genocide Research* 8, no. 4 (2006): 387–409.

Wolfe, Patrick. *Settler Colonialism and the Transformation of Anthropology.* London: Continuum International Publishing Group, 1998.

Wolfe, Patrick. *The Settler Complex: Recuperating Binarism in Colonial Studies.* Los Angeles: UCLA Press, 2016.

Wolfe, Patrick. *Traces of History: Elementary Structures of Race.* London: Verso, 2016.

Index

Page numbers in *italics* denote illustrative material.